Robert Burns and the Sentimental Era

Carol McGuirk

Robert Burns
and the Sentimental Era

The University of Georgia Press
Athens

© 1985 by the University of Georgia Press
Athens, Georgia 30602

Designed by Sandra Strother Hudson
Set in Mergenthaler Caslon 540 with Caslon 471 italic display

The paper in this book meets the guidelines for
permanence and durability of the Committee on
Production Guidelines for Book Longevity of the
Council on Library Resources.

Printed in the United States of America

89 88 87 86 85   5 4 3 2 1

Library of Congress Cataloging in Publication Data

McGuirk, Carol.
Robert Burns and the sentimental era.
Bibliography: p.
Includes index.
1. Burns, Robert, 1759–1796—Criticism
and interpretation. 2. Sentimentalism in literature.
I. Title.
PR4342.S44M38 1985   821'.6   84-12378
ISBN 0-8203-0739-4 (alk. paper)

Illustrations in this book are used with the
permission of the Rare Book and Manuscript Library
and the Avery Architectural and Fine Arts Library of
Columbia University. The portrait of Burns on the
title page was the frontispiece to his *Poems, Chiefly in
the Scottish Dialect* (Edinburgh, 1787) and was
engraved by John Buego. The illustration for part 1
is from an 1800 edition of Henry Mackenzie's *The
Man of Feeling*; for part 2, from James S. Storer's
Views in Edinburgh (1820); for part 3, from an early
nineteenth-century edition of *The Works of Robert
Burns* edited by James Currie.

*This publication has been supported by the
National Endowment for the Humanities,
a federal agency which supports the study of such fields
as history, philosophy, literature, and languages.*

In spite of the disturbing pressures
of personal partiality, of national partiality,
let us try to reach a real estimate of the
poetry of Burns.

Matthew Arnold, "The Study of Poetry"

Contents

Acknowledgments

For criticism and encouragement during the early stages of research and writing, I am much indebted to John H. Middendorf; also to Leo Braudy, Otis Fellows, Frederick M. Keener, and Carl R. Woodring. For instrumental critical and editorial advice on later drafts, I am grateful for the generous help of Harold Bloom, Jane Larkin Crain, Lea Kenig, Ellen Pollak, and Helen Vendler. It is to a brief conversation with Donald A. Low at Stirling University that I owe the notion of looking into John Aikin's relationship to Burns; and it is to Dr. G. Scott Wilson, and to Mr. Fisher of Glasgow's Mitchell Library, that I owe my introduction to Scotland's library resources. My thanks also to Hazel Wright of the Mitchell Library for sterling assistance at a later stage. For their energetic commitment to providing a forum for interdisciplinary work-in-progress in eighteenth-century Scottish studies, I should like to thank Henry Fulton, Mary Anne Schofield, and Richard Sher in particular, and the American Society for Eighteenth-Century Studies in general. My editors at the University of Georgia Press, Karen Orchard and Debra Winter, have made the final stages of my work on this book a reward and a pleasure.

My thanks to *Studies in English Literature, 1500–1900*, for permitting me to use in a different form parts of my article "Sentimental Encounter in Sterne, Mackenzie and Burns" (20, no. 3 [Summer 1980]: 505–15). For kind permission to quote from manuscript material in their collections, my thanks also to the Mitchell Library and to the Trustees of the National Library of Scotland. Columbia University has generously granted permission for me to reproduce engravings from books in its collection as illustrations in this book: to Kenneth Lohf, to the extraordinary staff at the Rare Books Reading Room, and to Marty Messik of Butler Library's office of reproduction services, my heartfelt thanks.

For her unfailing intellectual support and unflagging friendship, I want to thank Julia Prewitt Brown, who has provided insightful critical commentary on every draft. Finally, for extensions of colleagality and friendship too various to be specified, but too deeply appreciated to go unnoted, I offer special thanks to Robin Kronstadt Blum, Charles Cantalupo, Lorenzo Carcaterra and Susan Toepfer, Pat Crain, Jean Creighton, Marianne DeKoven, Jerry Aline Flieger, Celeste Goodridge, Miriam Hansen, Katie McGuirk, Kathleen Middleton, Laurie Prencipe, John Reichert, Sarah Roche-Mahdi, Marianna Torgovnick, Larry and Elizabeth Vélez, and Colin Wagner.

Introduction

Robert Burns was one of the great poets of the eighteenth century and the only great poet ever to emerge from the British peasant class. Yet the first lines of an autobiographical song he wrote in 1787 suggest the prevailing attitude of contemporary critics:

> There was a lad was born in Kyle,
> But what na day o' what na style,
> I doubt it's hardly worth the while
> To be sae nice wi' Robin.[1]

Modern critics tend to assume that Burns is "hardly worth the while" of critical study. His poetry is too simple and unambiguous to need close textual analysis and too linked to a separate Scottish tradition to justify inclusion in general discussions of late eighteenth-century poetry.

In "Robert Burns's Declining Fame," Raymond Bentman outlines the situation:

> Wherever one looks in the scholarship and criticism of the past twenty-five years, Burns is given little or no attention. Works which discuss the eighteenth century . . . works which concentrate on the poetry of "sensibility" . . . and works which concentrate on the transition . . . to early nineteenth-century ideas and styles mention Burns either incidentally or not at all. . . . Anthologies have begun to exclude him. . . . The few studies which run counter to this trend, and which attempt to document Burns's position in the British tradition, fall on barren ground. No one refutes them and no one accepts them.[2]

A similar complaint was voiced as early as 1939 by DeLancey Ferguson in the preface to his critical biography *Pride and Passion*. His previous writings on Burns, he wrote, though often critical of the established mythology, had been greeted only by "an almost passionate apathy."[3]

I think that there are two reasons for this critical apathy. One is the widespread presumption that Burns was the product of a separate Scottish vernacular tradition, writing well only when writing unselfconsciously in the Scottish dialect. Scholars unacquainted with vernacular Scots hesitate to discuss as part of the British tradition a poet claimed so jealously for a regional Scottish tradition. The complicated matter of the vernacular Scots tradition will be discussed at more length below. There is a related issue to be defined and debated first: the academic inclination to relegate all dialect poetry to secondary status.

VLADIMIR NABOKOV, speaking not of Burns but of James Joyce and *Finnegan's Wake*, once declared his indifference to "all regional literature written in dialect—even if it be the dialect of genius."[4] He argued elsewhere that "the nationality of a worthwhile writer [should be] of secondary importance. . . . The writer's art is his real passport. His identity should be immediately recognized by a special pattern or unique coloration. His habitat may confirm the correctness of the determination but should not lead to it" (p. 63).

This is in principle surely correct. The world of a writer ought to incorporate more than a sense of his geographical locus. If the Scottishness of Burns—his local habitat—is of supreme importance, there is no reason to include him in general discussions of eighteenth-century British and European poetry. Unfortunately, there is also no particular reason to read him unless one is a Scotsman interested in one's cultural roots. This is a typical assumption of modern criticism that I think should be challenged: in my view, the use of dialect neither determines nor excessively restricts the range of Burns's poetic vision.

To continue exposition of the opposing viewpoint, however, the clearest expression of Burns's essentially regional significance occurs in Matthew Arnold's "The Study of Poetry." Arnold admired the dexterity of Burns's diction and the touches of pathos in his poems, but he excluded Burns from the highest rank of poets. Arnold judged that Burns, for all his genius, lacked "high seriousness," and he implicitly linked that deficiency to Burns's narrowness of subject and style:

The real Burns is of course in his Scotch poems. Let us boldly say that of much of this poetry, a poetry dealing perpetually with Scotch drink, Scotch religion, and Scotch manners, a Scotchman's estimate is apt to be personal. A Scotchman is used to this world . . . he has a tenderness for it; he meets its poet half way. In this tender mood he reads pieces like the *Holy Fair* or *Halloween*. But this world of Scotch drink, Scotch religion, and Scotch manners is against a poet, not for him, when it is not a partial countryman who reads him; for in itself it is not a beautiful world. . . . [It] is often a harsh, a sordid, a repulsive world.[5]

Arnold's relegation of Burns's poems to a "Scotch" world leads logically enough to the exclusion of Burns from the tradition of poetry in English, reserving for Burns the separate (and I think unequal) place he now occupies by critical consensus.

This critical consensus is aligned with the assumptions of classical literary theory. Samuel Johnson, discussing Abraham Cowley, defined the "grandeur of generality" as the goal of the highest type of poetry.[6] Following Longinus and other classical theorists, Johnson insisted that particularity, locality, should not dominate a poem. Great writing is what pleases many and pleases long: Johnson judged as an artistic limitation any undue preoccupation with the "peculiarities of studies or professions, which can operate but upon small numbers; or . . . the accidents of transient fashions or temporary opinions."[7] In Johnson's view, as in Nabokov's and Arnold's, any poet too narrowly descriptive of local customs and manners is necessarily a minor figure.

I believe that if Burns is to be reconstituted as a major poet it will not be by stressing his excellence in the use of dialect, but by showing how his work (including his poetry in dialect) does at its best achieve the classical standard of universality. Burns's dialect is, in Nabokov's words, a "special pattern and unique coloration," but it is not the boundary of his poetic identity. Burns combines dialect with neoclassical English, local with cosmopolitan references, in virtually all his writings to ensure effects that transcend narrow "particularity." Burns's continuing popularity among general readers is one proof of this. Despite academic neglect, his poems and songs are still widely quoted, still alive. Dialect and all, Burns in fact meets one of the best-established criteria for classic literary stature. In Longinus's words: "you should consider that to be truly beautiful and sublime which pleases all people at all times."[8]

"Ca' the yowes to the knowes" is one example of a song by Burns that goes beyond regional concerns to achieve Burns's characteristic effect of emotional transcendence. The song is notable for its synthesis of local (descriptive) and general (emotional) elements. It uses vernacular words (containing more dialect than an earlier and less successful set of stanzas to the same traditional tune); but the dialect usage here enhances rather than restricts the mood of evocative tenderness. The locus of this song is not so much the physical as the emotional world:

Ca' the yowes to the knowes,
  Ca' them whare the heather grows,
Ca' them whare the burnie rowes,
    My bonie Dearie.

1.

Hark, the mavis' evening sang
Sounding Clouden's woods amang;
Then a faulding let us gang,
    My bonie Dearie.
  Ca' the etc.

2.

We'll gae down by Clouden side,
Through the hazels spreading wide
O'er the waves, that sweetly glide
    To the moon sae clearly.
  Ca' the etc.

3.

Yonder Clouden's silent towers,
Where at moonshine midnight hours
O'er the dewy bending flowers
    Fairies dance sae cheary.
  Ca' the etc.

4.

Ghaist nor bogle shalt thou fear;
Thou'rt to Love and Heaven sae dear,
Nocht of Ill may come thee near,
    My bonie Dearie.
  Ca' the etc.

5.
Fair and lovely as thou art,
Thou hast stown my very heart;
I can die—but canna part,
    My bonie Dearie.
Ca' the etc.

(2:738–39)

Burns's dialect usage in this song is tactful. The words are spelled or pronounced in a manner slightly different from the English, but they are nonetheless easily understood from that perspective: "yowes" for "ewes," "ghaists" for "ghosts," "stown" for "stolen," "gang" for "go," and so forth. Vernacular words in this song become the basis for a self-conscious pastoral diction—a synthesized language more than a dialect. This invented language is the vehicle for conveying Burns's invented world of idealized and powerful feelings. "Ca' the yowes" is not primarily a descriptive song. Local details spice the first three stanzas but protective emotions dominate the conclusion. Like virtually all of Burns's best writings, the song uses descriptive elements like dialect to heighten the reality of the emotional state it chiefly embodies.

All this may sound like simple common sense, but it goes against several widely held critical assumptions about Burns's work. The majority of those critics who study Burns accept, in my view, too many limitations on his emotional range and his achievement as an artist. Too many are content to glorify the "Scottishness": this, ironically enough, encourages critics who are not themselves Scottish enthusiasts to presuppose a regional range for his achievement and to ignore Burns. Hardly less damaging to Burns's reputation than the indifference of eighteenth-century specialists or his exclusion from anthologies are the warnings that accompany some of the collections that do include his works: "The interests of Burns's poetry will be best served if there are no false expectations. Burns had very little visionary imagination of the kind that creates whole mythical or fictive worlds, like Hardy or Faulkner, Blake or Yeats, or even like the Pope of 'The Rape of the Lock' and 'The Dunciad.' His poetic world is his real one, that of southwest Scotland."[9] Yet surely the "Scotland" of songs like "Ca' the yowes" is as much an invented world as those of

Hardy, Faulkner, Blake, or Yeats—or any other artist. (Just as surely, those writers blended real elements with imagination to embody their fictive worlds.) It is a sign of Burns's success that his world seems "real" and "natural." And it is a feature of Burns's classic stature that this world is broadly human and accessible to readers.

The view of Burns as lacking in imaginative power is not confined to recent criticism. The modern judgment expressed above is not far removed from that of James Currie, Burns's first editor and biographer, in his long-discredited yet evidently still influential assessment:

> If fiction be, as some suppose, the soul of poetry, no one had ever less pretentions to the name of poet than Burns. . . . the subjects on which he has written are seldom, if ever, imaginary; his poems, as well as his letters, may be considered as . . . the transcript of his own musings on the real incidents of his humble life. . . . His writings may therefore be regarded as affording a great part of the data on which our account of his personal character has been founded; and most of the observations we have applied to the man, are applicable, with little variation, to the poet.[10]

The insistence on Burns as a poet somehow incapable of fiction seems linked to an assumption that his countrymen, or perhaps members of his social class (Currie's definitive use of "humble" is interesting in this regard), were incapable of imaginative projection, or out of sympathy with it. Yet the notion that Burns is always autobiographical, however much it inflates his personality, greatly deflates his art. Besides, the logic is circular: the man is his works, and they in their turn directly define the man. The task of the critic becomes not the analysis of texts, but the documentation of various personality traits (or typically "Scottish" qualities) in the poet's writings:

> Indeed, the deep spring of his finest poetry was not literary at all—not even the vernacular tradition—but what he called his "social disposition"; a heart "compleatly tinder," . . . and "a strong appetite for sociability."[11]
>
> . . . most of his poems are made out of a highly inconsistent man's battle with the world. Even on the occasions when he did create a *persona*, its function was to body forth some mood or trait or experience of his own, or of the people round about him.[12]

Burns's friend Maria Riddell noted in 1796 that "poetry . . . was actually not his *forte*,"[13] and the direction of critical attention has been shifting ever since away from Burns's writings. From 1786, when Burns was first published, Burns's artless effects have been too often judged a simple consequence of his lack of art: "The humble bard, whose work now demands our attention, cannot claim a place among . . . polished *versifiers*. His simple strains, artless and unadorned, seem to flow without effort, from the native feelings of the heart."[14]

The collective force of such assumptions is by now very powerful. My intention is not, in fact, to question the basic assumption per se— that Burns the man was central to Burns the poet. This is just as true of Burns as it is of every other poet. I do hope to show how in Burns's case these critical formulas have tended to limit critical receptivity to the accomplished grace that is just as characteristic of Burns as the marvelous realism of his poetic voice—a voice so compelling that it is accepted by most of Burns's major critics as literally "real."

Discussion of "My bonie laddie's young but he's growin yet," another song by Burns, may begin to challenge this general deflation of Burns as a conscious artist by showing his shaping of folk elements to evoke a powerful feeling. In this case, the feeling is a mood of tender melancholy. (As in many of Burns's songs, the speaker is female—in obvious violation of the theory that he is always autobiographical):

> O Lady Mary Ann looks o'er the castle-wa',
> She saw three bonie boys playin at the ba',
> The youngest he was the flower amang them a',
> My bonie laddie's young but he's growin yet.—
>
> O Father, O Father, an ye think it fit,
> We'll send him a year to the College yet,
> We'll sew a green ribban round about his hat,
> And that will let them ken he's to marry yet.—
>
> Lady Mary Ann was a flower in the dew,
> Sweet was its smell and bonie was its hue,
> And the langer it blossom'd, the sweeter it grew,
> For the lily in the bud will be bonier yet.—
>
> Young Charlie Cochran was the sprout of an aik,
> Bonie, and bloomin and straught was its make,
> The sun took delight to shine for its sake,
> And it will be the brag o' the forest yet.—

The Simmer is gane when the leaves they were green,
And the days are awa that we hae seen,
But far better days I trust will come again,
For my bonie laddie's young but he's growin yet.—

(2:642)

One source for this song was the ballad "The Trees They Do Grow High." Burns converted the folk material from narrative to lyric form—his version conveys a feeling more than telling a story. Two stanzas from the ballad were preserved in the manuscript collection of the antiquary David Herd—a collection to which Burns probably had access. This is a sample of Burns's raw material:

She looked o'er the castle-wa',
She saw three lords play at the ba':
"O the youngest is the flower of a',
But my love is lang o' growing."[15]

The fragment suggests by contrast Burns's achievement in enlarging the emotional perspective of folk material. His version expands from the discrete, almost discontinuous, folk narrative to his desired effect of integrated feeling. Burns's "Scotland," as evoked in songs like "My bonie laddie's young," is felt and imagined—expanded, and therefore partly fictive. Although this enlarged emotional perspective is particularly striking in Burns's songs, I think that throughout his writings Burns aims at higher levels of poetic synthesis than is generally assumed, even by many of the scholars specializing in study of his writings.

THE FIRST PRINCIPLE of contemporary Burns studies—the notion that his best work is the product of a Scottish vernacular tradition—cannot be separated from the related assumption that Burns did not understand English or the English tradition. "Scottish" spontaneity was the beneficent Jekyll, "English" ambition the all-devouring Hyde, of his creative personality. The argument has been made by critics as distinguished as David Daiches, John Speirs, and D. Nichol Smith. John C. Weston states the general position: "Burns's best poems are of a tradition entirely different from the English one, and thus cannot be classified by standards other than their own" (p. xxiii). Any interest in Burns as a part of the eighteenth-century British and

European mainstream is likely to be quelled at the outset by such statements as this: "His many sentimental and moralizing poems in the English mode, based on the style and in the mood of Pope, Thomson, Shenstone . . . and Gray, are inferior because the tradition is alien to him" (p. xxv). James Kinsley, editor of the definitive edition of Burns's poems and songs, is another of the critics implying the bad effect of the English tradition on Burns: "[He] took much—indeed, too much—from [the English Augustan] tradition in diction, imagery and poetic form, and seldom happily."[16]

Burns's supposed failure to master English models often is linked to the argument that all Scotsmen have difficulty acquiring a flexible use of English. David Buchan, writing generally of this problem, outlines the cultural dilemma of Scotsmen in the eighteenth century:

> In eighteenth-century Scotland the effects of literacy are intrinsically bound up with the effects of the anglicization of Scottish life; literacy meant not just learning to read and write but learning to read and write *in another language.* For Scotsmen, the fragmentation of consciousness that attends the arrival of literacy became polarized in the two languages: English became primarily visual and cerebral, and Scots became primarily aural and emotional. . . . English was, and is, likely to freeze . . . the creative flow of a native Scots speaker.[17]

Buchan's account, while persuasive, is colored by the same trace of cultural nostalgia for the Scots that has also colored discussion of Burns's relationship to his dual tradition, blinding critics to the possibility of any "good" influence from the English.

The matter is complicated, because Burns did write many bombastic poems in which the influence of James Thomson's or William Shenstone's elevated English diction is all too evident. But most other mid and late eighteenth-century poets also wrote quantities of bad verse straining at effects of sublimity. Thomas Gray, to name only one, frequently aimed too high. Patricia Spacks, writing of Gray in *The Poetry of Vision*, cites F. Doherty's analysis of Gray's language, noting a division between good "vivid" Gray and bad "rhetorical" Gray: "[Doherty,] examining Gray's language in some detail . . . concluded that the poet's productions are of two kinds: those dominated by his 'public,' highly rhetorical 'voice,' and those in which his 'real voice' is discernable. The latter category includes most of the poems which seem relatively acceptable . . . to the modern reader."[18]

That Thomas Gray is often overly rhetorical has never been taken as proof that he did not understand English. Perhaps what critics accept as a national dichotomy—Burns's division between realistic Scots and elevated English models—is a general problem for poets of his time. Operating under the current assumptions, however—which consider Burns as a Scotsman first and only secondarily as a poet—investigation of such possibilities is barred by preconceptions and obstacles.

The assumption that Burns was incapable of understanding English, when added to the other assumption already discussed—that Burns was an oddly literal poet, deficient in imagination—probably accounts for the often condescending tone of Burns criticism. Yet, as later chapters will show, Burns's blending of English with Scots in his best vernacular poetry shows a sensitivity to the possibilities of both languages that is nothing short of masterful. Burns's diction, like his poetic world, seems "natural" but is designed and invented: a mixture of local dialect, archaic Middle Scots, dialect words of regions other than his own, sentimental idioms, and "high" English rhetoric. Burns uses all these elements to create in his best work an apparently seamless fabric of what are nonetheless totally disparate elements. Raymond Bentman, author of the essay on Burns's declining fame quoted earlier, was one of the first critics to do a philological analysis of Burns's "mixed" poetic language:

> Burns wrote some poems in pure English . . . but he wrote no poems in pure vernacular Scottish. The "Scottish" poems are written in a literary language, which was mostly, although not entirely English, in grammar and syntax, and, in varying proportions, both Scottish and English in vocabulary. . . . These mixed poems, which I call the "vernacular" poems, vary [in the proportion of Scottish and English elements]. . . . Throughout the vernacular poems Burns . . . employs the relative pronouns "wha," "whase," and "wham" . . . none of which exist in spoken Scottish. . . . He changes "Green grows the rashes" to "Green grow the rashes" which is grammatical English but ungrammatical Scottish.[19]

Yet Bentman's conclusion implies the same negative view of English influence that characterizes other Burns criticism:

> Among the hundred and sixty-odd words which Burns uses more than fifty times, a considerable majority are English and most of the others

differ from English in spelling but not in meaning. . . . The indication, however, is not that Burns found few Scottish words useful but that he found so many useful that he did not have to depend on them repeatedly, as he seems to have with such English words as "sweet," "fair," "heart," "soul," "nature," and "love." Burns apparently found Scottish words to have a suggestiveness, a poetic ambiguity, a fluidity, which he seems to have found in late eighteenth-century English in only self-consciously "poetic" and rather tired words. (p. 246)

The repeated English words that Bentman notes were the catchwords of the sentimental era: their frequency points to the sentimental message that is at the center of so many of Burns's poems and songs. But if "love" and "heart" were "tired" words when Shenstone used them, they are vibrant in such works by Burns as "Mary Morison":

> O Mary, canst thou wreck his peace,
>   Wha for thy sake wad gladly die!
> Or canst thou break that heart of his,
>   Whase only faute is loving thee!
> If love for love thou wilt na gie,
>   At least be pity to me shown;
> A thought ungentle canna be
>   The thought o' Mary Morison.
>
>   (1:43)

Especially in his songs, Burns's blending of vernacular Scottish enlivens the sentimental, while the generalizing, self-consciously "poetic" English component broadens the significance of the vernacular. Burns's synthesis of the two creates an inimitable effect of meaningful simplicity, an effect by no means characteristic of all poets in the Scottish folk tradition. Once attuned to Burns's enterprise of bridging local and cosmopolitan traditions (his vernacular predecessor Allan Ramsay had pursued the same ideal, though with less consistent success), one can begin to appreciate the degree of self-conscious artistry that Burns brought to his poetry. He incorporated English with Scots to introduce ideal dimensions into the realistic folk models—indeed, to suggest the ideal possibilities of the "real." As Sir Walter Scott noted, "Burns had the *tact* to make his poetry tell by connecting it with the stream of public thought and sentiment of his age."[20]

Finally, Burns's use of English was not only permitted but encouraged by the Scottish tradition itself. The vernacular movement was never isolated; rather, it was—from the fifteenth century—notable for its flexibility in adapting English and European literary influence. Vernacular writers, who signed and published their writings, should be distinguished from folk poets, whose tradition was collective, anonymous and oral. Burns used folk material, but he was a vernacular writer—an individual maker of his works. If Robert Henryson could find inspiration in Chaucer, and Allan Ramsay (as I have argued elsewhere)[21] in the London Augustans of his day, why deny Burns that part of his literary heritage that encouraged receptivity to the literary world outside Scotland?

The only major eighteenth-century vernacular poet who was not notably eclectic was Burns's own favorite, Robert Fergusson (1750–74). This poet did in fact exhibit the divided personality often ascribed to Burns: he wrote excellent dialect poetry and stilted English verse. But there are important differences between Fergusson and Burns. The most significant is that Fergusson used a purer dialect, confining his vocabulary and grammar largely to the northeastern dialect and spurning the archaic Middle Scots words and sentimental interpolations so characteristic of Burns. His attitude toward the literary fads of contemporary London was consistently (often hilariously) sarcastic. But this highly talented and caustic purist was the only major eighteenth-century vernacular poet to fail with the literary public. The one collection published before Fergusson's early death sold less than five hundred copies, a poor showing for midcentury Edinburgh. Indeed, it seems to have been precisely the eclecticism and flexibility of Ramsay and Burns that made their use of dialect acceptable to a Scottish literary public somewhat touchy about imputations of provincialism. Ramsay's best-seller was *The Tea Table Miscellany*—as the title indicates, a heavily anglicized song collection. Burns's most popular works were his early poems, the essential urbanity of which I will demonstrate in the first four chapters of this book. In short, the separateness so often claimed for the Scottish vernacular tradition would surprise the vernacular poets themselves, most of whom worked strenuously to integrate their own world with the larger one beyond Scotland.

BURNS lived from 1759 to 1796, a lifespan coinciding with the rise and fall of the cult of sensibility or sentimental movement. References in Burns's letters and poems show that he was well read in sentimental fiction and poetry and that his enthusiasm for writers like

Laurence Sterne, Henry Mackenzie, and William Shenstone was especially keen during the years he was composing his early, masterful *Poems, Chiefly in the Scottish Dialect* (Kilmarnock, 1786). Yet because of the critical tendency to see sentimental influence only in Burns's weakest poetry, discussion of the sentimental has been confined mostly to expressions of regret at its presence. While the shibboleth of Burns criticism continues to be his native (and naive) earthiness, sentimentalism is bound to be viewed as a destructive and alien mode. Indeed, misconceptions about the "sentimental" are almost as rife as misconceptions about Burns.

Unlike such currently respectable terms as "romantic" and "metaphysical," which were coined by critics as terms of insult, "sentimental" began as a fashionable term and only later acquired its negative connotation. Among the aims of this book is the historical reconstitution of the term—the establishment of what the word "sentimental" meant to the first generation of writers who used it. Later chapters will refine what is offered here as a rough definition. Being sentimental required a pursuit of intense responsiveness that always created some pathology of feeling in a text. In other words, the response to events in the text called for by the sentimental writer always exceeds (he would say transcends) what any reasonable response to those events would be; or the text solicits intense reader reactions to dire events that probably would have been averted by protagonists committed to the normal social world of survival and compromise. (While Richardson's *Clarissa* [1748] is rather early to be classified as sentimental, the difference between Clarissa's unyielding spirituality and her friend Anna Howe's practicality is exactly the difference between sentimental and "normal" viewpoints.)

Assiduous cultivation of the reader's sympathy does not, however, mean that sentimental writing is always emotionally false. Many writers of the age of sensibility used a sentimental perspective with self-conscious irony (as Sterne did) or for producing insight into psychological extremes (as Goethe did in *Werther*). Burns's sentimentalism typically produces charming, gently comic effects, as in "To a Mouse." The sentimental compulsion to record—and to generate—intense responses and feelings did lead always to the manipulation of the reader. But when the writer happens to be adept at manipulation—James Boswell, for instance, describing Samuel Johnson's death in his *Life of Johnson*—classic literature results. So while not assuming that sentimental influences were always a positive force in Burns's poetry, I am far from assuming they were necessarily disastrous.

To SUMMARIZE BRIEFLY how I differ from other critics in my approach to Burns: the worst obstacle to a just assessment of Burns is the assumption of literary critics generally that, as a dialect poet, Burns is necessarily a figure of limited significance. Even among Burns's critics there are three widespread assumptions that have contributed to the decline of his reputation. None of these assumptions is wholly false. Yet however true as statements about particular poems, they should be discarded as central critical premises on the ground that they have failed to do justice to the full range of Burns's poetic achievement.

The first critical misapprehension is the notion that Burns, incapable of creating a persona, writes always about himself. This is problematic chiefly because it has encouraged a low assessment of Burns's artistry and imagination. (It has also led to the undervaluing of Burns's later songs, few of which fit into an autobiographical mold.) The second concerns the separateness of the Scottish vernacular tradition. While no one would deny that vernacular writers of the eighteenth century were politically estranged from the English power structure and inclined to a strong statement of their national identity, even a cursory reading of the major Scottish vernacular poets shows strong influence from the English and European literary mainstream. Most vernacular writers looked to London for clues on how to achieve urbane effects. The final mistaken assumption is the notion that sentimental influences were inherently inimical to Burns's earthy Scottish realism, an assumption that misjudges both Burns and the sentimental movement itself. Burns did write a number of bad sentimental poems, but in a majority of his works he gracefully incorporated sentimental elements. (Incidentally, another problem with the idea of the sentimental as an "alien" mode is the strong link between eighteenth-century Scotland and the sentimental movement. From Francis Hutcheson and Adam Smith to Henry Mackenzie, author of *The Man of Feeling* and the earliest influential review of Burns's poems, Scotland's literati were strongly associated with the sentimental cult.)

Having given all my objections, however, I must also acknowledge my debt to excellent previous scholarship on Burns. My own thesis would have little solidity if it were not for the foundation supplied by such critics and scholars as J. Delancey Ferguson, James Kinsley, Thomas Crawford, Donald A. Low, David Daiches, James C. Dick, Raymond Bentman, John C. Weston, Mary Ellen Brown, and Christina Keith. The last major critical study of Burns (barring revisions of earlier works) appeared in 1960. Crawford's *Burns: A Study of the Poems and Songs* offers close readings of virtually everything Burns ever wrote. The problem of literary influence that will engage me in this book is practically the only issue concerning Burns to which Crawford seems indifferent: "There is no longer any need to demonstrate Burns's indebtedness to the Scots (or the English) literary tradition" (p. xii). I hasten to acknowledge, however, the importance to my work of his continuously insightful critical judgments, particularly on Burns's early writings.

A number of other comparatively recent studies have also helped to document sentimental influences on Burns. Kinsley's definitive edition of *The Poems and Songs of Robert Burns* (1968) appended a series of character sketches of Burns made by his contemporaries that suggested the biographical emphasis of the middle section of my study. "The Reading of Robert Burns," published in 1970 in the *Bulletin of the New York Public Library,* is a compilation by John Robotham (using the notes from Ferguson's edition of *The Letters of Robert Burns* and other sources) of all authors and texts ever quoted or alluded to by Burns. This was invaluable in providing a quick way of verifying that Burns was in fact acquainted with works he appeared to be adapting in his poems. Donald Low's *Robert Burns: The Critical Heritage* (1974) includes the important early critical responses to Burns. A companion volume also edited by Low, *Critical Essays on Robert Burns* (1975), is a first-rate collection, among which "Robert Burns, Writer of Songs," by Cedric Thorpe-Davie, was of special significance to my work at that stage. These scholarly studies, with a number of others listed in the selective bibliography, made this book possible. In fact, the convenient collection of early reviews in *The Critical Heritage* probably made it inevitable by some hand, so clearly does it show sentimental forces at work in the initial critical reception of Robert Burns.

In his introduction to *Critical Essays on Robert Burns,* Low wrote:

Much still has to be done to explore [Burns's] creative borrowings, and his affinities with other authors. Maria Riddell noted in a "Character Sketch" of Burns in 1796 that there was a resemblance between the

I

The Early Poems

*"Ah, hang your reasoning!" said the Epicurean.
"I hate reasoning. I do everything
by my feelings."*
William Blake, *An Island in the Moon*

1

Sentimental Encounter

In 1814, Gilbert Burns wrote of his brother's poems that "every attentive reader of Burns's Works, must have observed, that he frequently presents a caricature of his feelings, and even of his failings—a kind of mock-heroic account of himself and his opinions."[1] Coming from the poet's almost pathologically cautious younger brother, this is a surprisingly bold insight, one that helps to establish the link between Burns's early writings and the sentimental movement.

In 1759, the year Robert Burns was born, Laurence Sterne published the first two volumes of *Tristram Shandy*, which might well be described in Gilbert Burns's phrase as Tristram's "mock-heroic account of himself and his opinions." Nine years later, Sterne further explored the "feelings and failings" of one character in *Tristram Shandy* when he made him protagonist of *A Sentimental Journey*, the novel that entrenched a recent coinage: the adjective "sentimental."

One way of beginning to understand eighteenth-century sentimentalism is to remember that its first explicit spokesman, Parson Yorick, owed his name to the most famous stage prop in history—the jester's skull in *Hamlet*. To Yorick, and to his descendants from Harley the Man of Feeling to young Werther, the world was a stage, a backdrop for a series of histrionic gestures aimed at an audience of readers. The sentimental hero viewed everything as Hamlet viewed Yorick's skull: as an object that suggested a subject. The plots of sentimental novels seem disjointed by conventional standards (*The Man of Feeling*, a "fragment," "begins" at chapter 11) because their chief interest is not in the actions of the hero, but in the soliloquies he delivers to the stage props in his vicinity.

A Sentimental Journey moves from pathos to bathos according to whether the prop seized upon is suggestive (the caged starling) or incongruous (the Dead Ass). In the absence of a mad Maria, Yorick makes do with whatever comes to hand:

> . . . was I in a desert, I would find out wherewith in it to call forth my affections—If I could not do better, I would fasten them upon some sweet myrtle, or seek some melancholy cypress to connect myself to—I would court their shade, and greet them kindly for their protection—I would cut my name upon them, and swear they were the loveliest trees throughout the desert: if their leaves wither'd, I would teach myself to mourn, and when they rejoiced, I would rejoice along with them.[2]

Sterne shows in this passage that he is aware of Yorick's parasitic nature. The sentimental process, as Yorick defines it, is to look around, select an object, "fasten" the attention on it, and finally identify it as somehow the property of the sentimental spokesman ("I would cut my name upon them"). Yorick's need to cut his name on his environment compels him to work up responses even to the prosaic things in his field of vision. When he cannot "do better," he focuses on the carriage he is traveling in. And he is so worn out by the intensity of his one-sided relationships with insensate things like his *Desobligeant* that he cannot respond with ordinary kindness when characters like the mendicant monk solicit his benevolence. Throughout the challenges of his journey—the supplicants and victims who beseige him—Yorick prefers dramatic interpretation to real assistance. He is not able even to break the bars of the starling's cage.

Samuel Johnson, on the whole hostile to the sentimental, called the basis of all stability "subordination," that civilizing process by which people discipline their actions, and as far as possible their wishes, to conform to the rules of society.[3] But society does not rule the sentimental hero. Yorick and Harley are so distracted by their fixation on eccentric objects that they never acquire the tact necessary to sustain more conventional relationships. (Harley's social innocence is demonstrated by his inability to transact business, advance his interests with his family, or propose to his Miss Walton.) But although the sentimental hero is outside society, subordination is still necessary to his stability; it just becomes subordination of all the objects in his world to his dominating sensibility. And the objects he admits into his world are the rejected—lunatics, beggars, convicts—of the society he rejects. Men of the world follow a survival principle; men of feeling look after the lost causes.

The benevolist chooses abandoned or humiliated objects to chastise a callous society and also to proclaim his personal transcendence of society's materialism. Yorick's social alienation is burlesqued: when he uses the Dead Ass to admonish the polity ("'Shame on the world!' said I to myself" [p. 141]), the distance between his prosaic vehicle and the impassioned tenor of his message is too great to be bridged without irony. Mackenzie is seldom ironic, but Harley achieves authentic social criticism in some of his encounters. The sentimental viewpoint is exploited in different ways among sentimental novelists—sentimentalism could take on satiric and philosophic as well as humanitarian guises. But one trait that remains constant in sentimental character is the hero's egotism in pursuing the humble; for the lower the object he encounters and reclaims, the more status he achieves in perceiving its significance. His acuteness notices these humble or pathetic things, his good-heartedness accepts them, and his virtuosity triumphs in communicating their significance to readers. (Novelists who acknowledge the compulsive element in sentimental heroism—Sterne and Goethe, for instance—seem better to post-Freudian readers than authors like Mackenzie, whose "psychology" of sensibility goes no deeper than contemporary cant.)

Writers before Sterne and Mackenzie had sympathized with social outcasts, of course: Richardson's *Clarissa* and Pope's "Elegy to the Memory of an Unfortunate Lady" have been called sentimental because of their vindication of heroine-victims. But these earlier writers displayed their heroines as the subjects rather than the objects of compassion; Richardson and Pope subordinated their own presence so that a central icon of feminine distress could dominate. Sentimental novels following Sterne, however, made the presence of an interpreting sensibility seem more important than the wretchedness described. Yorick's emotions during his scene with Maria seem more powerful than her own. The cult of feeling from Yorick on is characterized by a preference in the sentimental spokesman for props that cannot upstage him. In perceiving the claims of humble things, the benevolist simultaneously demonstrates his benevolence and his supremacy.

The customary perspective of the sentimental hero, then, is a downward view of pathetic objects. This process of condescension is essential to sentimental rhetoric, and the conclusions of sentimental novels often extend to readers the pleasure of adopting that perspective when the hero himself becomes a pathetic object, or corpse. *The*

Man of Feeling offers its most charged view of Harley in the scene where his friends (and the readers they stand for) gaze down at his inanimate "form." Neuter references stress Harley's new status as meaningful artifact:

> I entered the room where his body lay; I approached *it* with reverence. . . . I saw that *form*, which, but a little before, was animated with a soul which did honour to humanity, stretched without sense or feeling before me. . . . I turned, with the last farewel upon my lips, when I observed old Edwards standing behind me. I looked him full in the face; but *his eye was fixed on another object:* he pressed between me and the bed, and *stood gazing* on the breathless remains of his benefactor.[4]

All the ingredients of sentimental scrutiny combine in this passage: the "objectification" of a subject, the pensive downward glance of the sentimental interpreter, and the reverence for the relics of existence that exempts the hero from any commitment to the process of existence. As *The Man of Feeling* concludes, Harley's friend again looks down, this time at Harley's grave, and defends his preoccupation with this shrine: "I sometimes visit his grave; I sit in the hollow of the tree. It is worth a thousand homilies! every nobler feeling rises within me! every beat of my heart awakens a virtue!—but it will make you hate the world—No: there is such an air of gentleness around, that I can hate nothing; but, as to the world—I pity the men of it" (pp. 132–33).

"Pity," not unmixed with contempt, for "men of the world" was a literary pose adopted by Burns as a young man in consequence of his sentimental reading. In his early twenties, Burns wrote to his former schoolmaster John Murdoch:

> My favorite authors are of the sentim[l] kind, such as Shenstone, particularly his Elegies, Thomson, Man of feeling, a book I prize next to the Bible, Man of the World, Sterne, especially his Sentimental journey, Macpherson's Ossian, &c. these are the glorious models after which I endeavour to form my conduct, and 'tis incongruous, 'tis absurd to suppose that the man whose mind glows with sentiments lighted up at their sacred flame—the man whose heart distends with benevolence to all the human race . . . —can he descend to mind the paultry conccerns [sic] about which the terrae-filial race fret, and fume, and vex themselves?[5]

Passages like this, which not only praise sentimental writers but adopt their heroic hostility to social bustle, occur in many of Burns's letters to early patrons and preceptors. And during the years Burns was wearing out successive copies of *The Man of Feeling* by carrying it next to his heart, he was writing poems that drew on sentimental techniques—notably such early poems of direct address as "To a Mouse," "To a Louse," and "To a Mountain Daisy."

These poems use a selectively vernacular diction and the "standard Habbie" verse form Ramsay had popularized early in the eighteenth century. But his adherence to a "Scottish" verse form should not prevent us from noticing that Burns's poems of direct address use the sentimental structure of benevolent condescension observed above in Mackenzie and Sterne. Here is the same process by which a sensitive interpreter stoops to ponder some humble object—mouse, louse, daisy—that has captured his eye by chance; and here is the same use of that object to set the speaker apart from the mainstream of normal sociability. Burns's peasant persona is just like Yorick or Harley in that everything he encounters is grist to his sentimental mill. Even in the desert of peasant poverty, he finds things to "fasten" on and claim as subjects of discourse, objects of compassion.

When Matthew Arnold wondered at the paradoxical amiability of poems that seldom stray from scrutiny of a "harsh" "Scotch" world,[6] he was responding to Burns's sentimental procedure of selecting especially low things to surround with a saving aura of emotional significance. The effectiveness of Burns's poems of direct address seems to illustrate the radical statement of David Hume in his influential essay "Of the Standard of Taste" (1757): "Beauty is no quality in things themselves: it exists merely in the mind which contemplates them."[7] When Burns addresses himself to the louse, he is not—as some of his vernacular predecessors were—celebrating "lowness" as "lowness," but upholding the notion of such sentimental heroes as Yorick and Harley that a keen sensibility can perceive meaning in any object. Burns's persona is unconventional only in giving the encountered object a measure of independence from his contemplating mind: it receives a realistic description along with a sentimental amplification.

In "To a Mouse," for instance, the opening stanza describes the mouse as it emphasizes its vulnerability:

> Wee, sleeket, cowran, tim'rous *beastie*,
> O, what a panic's in thy breastie!
> Thou need na start awa sae hasty,
>   Wi' bickering brattle!

> I wad be laith to rin an' chase thee,
>   Wi' murd'ring *pattle!*
>   (1:127)

In the second stanza Burns begins to draw the mouse into a human context when he attributes its fear of him to conscious censure rather than to instinct:

> I'm truly sorry Man's dominion
> Has broken Nature's social union,
> An' justifies that ill opinion,
>   Which makes thee startle,
> At me, thy poor, earth-born companion,
>   An' *fellow-mortal!*

The meter emphasizes the farmer's sentimental wonder that a mouse should "startle" "At *me,* thy *poor,* earth-born companion, / An' *fellow-mortal.*" Burns avoids the voyeuristic overtones of sentimental scrutiny by seeing the mouse as a peer—a victim, perhaps, but a fellow victim. Mice and men have mortality in common, and Burns's speaker suggests that both are equally prey to anxiety:

> Thou saw the fields laid bare an' wast,
> An' weary *Winter* comin fast,
> An' cozie here, beneath the blast,
>   Thou thought to dwell,
> Till crash! the cruel *coulter* past
>   Out thro' thy cell.
>
> That wee-bit heap o' leaves an' stibble,
> Has cost thee monie a weary nibble!
> Now thou's turn'd out, for a' thy trouble,
>   But house or hald,
> To thole the Winter's *sleety dribble,*
>   An' *cranreuch* cauld!

Burns's description of the way a field mouse prepares for winter is realistic enough to convince the reader that the emotions he projects simultaneously into her (that nest-building seemed "weary," for instance) are just as "real."

When the owner of the Dead Ass in *A Sentimental Journey* laments that the Ass has succumbed not to overwork but to depression over the misfortunes of its owner, that "the weight of myself and my afflictions together, have been too much for him" (p. 140), Sterne's character seems more deranged than benevolent. Burns establishes his mouse as a normal mouse before turning it to sentimental purposes. The narrator describes mice plausibly for six stanzas before generalizing about what their fate might stand for:

> But Mousie, thou art no thy-lane,
> In proving *foresight* may be vain:
> The best laid schemes o' *Mice* an' *Men*,
> 　　Gang aft agley,
> An' lea'e us nought but grief an' pain,
> 　　For promis'd joy!

This is so conclusive that it is always surprising to see a stanza following it. The conclusion of "To a Mouse" reverts to mainstream sentimentality. The benevolent speaker, in the tradition of Yorick, Maria, and the handkerchief, ultimately uses the meditation to call attention to himself:

> Still, thou are blest, compar'd wi' *me!*
> The *present* only toucheth thee:
> But Och! I *backward* cast my e'e,
> 　　On prospects drear!
> And *forward*, tho' I canna *see*,
> 　　I *guess* an' *fear!*

Burns's conclusion contradicts the spirit of the poem. If the "present only" touches the field mouse, how can she have been said to have "schemes"? When Burns shifts in line 43 to an explicitly italicized "me," he shifts from compassion to self-pity. The poem begins by emphasizing the common liability of mice and men to blows of fate that wreck their plans. When Burns switches from this view of the mouse to the declaration that she is "blest, compar'd wi' *me*," he has undercut earlier images of her "weary" construction of a nest, her distress at its destruction, and her bleak prospect of a homeless winter. He has violated his illusion and made it too clear that the subject of meditation has been only a mouse's nest, not an ideal of security. Burns worked best from sentimental models when he resisted the temptation to compete with the contemplated object.

When Burns's farmer spares the field mouse, he is acting as if there is only one field mouse in the world—his field mouse. He takes up its cause as if its vermin status is irrelevant to his transcendent response to its suffering. Mouse self-interest and farmer self-interest do not run along similar lines: mice eat what farmers raise. Thus there is no real basis for Burns's sympathy for the mouse, only the subjective basis provided by his perception of their common vulnerability to fate. In extending sympathy to his mouse, Burns's speaker reveals that he has left the folk tradition of common sense and entered the sentimental tradition of rare sensibility. In an interesting passage from his "Answer to the 'Guidwife of Wauchope House,'" who had written Burns a vernacular epistle praising his patriotic use of Scottish subjects, Burns imagines himself as a young ploughman who cannot prune a Scotch thistle growing in his barley:

> The rough bur-thistle spreading wide
>   Amang the bearded bear,
> I turn'd my weeding heuk aside,
>   An' spar'd the symbol dear.
>   (1:326)

This preference for symbolic thistles over edible barley is clearly sentimental.

Samuel Johnson once declared that sheep-shearing could "not be made poetical,"[8] but Burns as virtuoso of sensibility could do the trick with a louse. "To a Louse: On Seeing One on a Lady's Bonnet at Church" is a more consistent poem than "To a Mouse." It mixes description of the progress of the strutting "ferlie" up "Jenny's" new bonnet with wry warnings against vanity that would probably seem sententious outside this eccentric context:

> O *Jenny* dinna toss your head,
> An' set your beauties a' abroad!
> Ye little ken what cursed speed
>   The blastie's makin!
> Thea *winks* and *finger-ends*, I dread,
>   Are notice takin!
>
> O wad some Pow'r the giftie gie us
> *To see oursels as others see us!*

It wad frae monie a blunder free us
    An' foolish notion:
What airs in dress an' gait wad lea'e us,
    And ev'n Devotion!

                   (1:194)

Burns uses an odd context—and the oddity of his selectively vernacular vocabulary—to bring a truism to life: seeing *"oursels as others see us"* would quickly eliminate delusions of grandeur.

Coleridge wrote of Burns: "Genius produces the strongest impressions of novelty while it rescues the most admitted truths from the impotence caused by the very circumstance of their universal admission."9 This is the effect of "To a Louse." People do not have to read the Bible to know in their bones that pride goeth before a fall, but "To a Louse" restates this admonition in such unusual terms that Burns's moral takes on the story's concreteness along with its "novelty." Still, it is the competitive benevolence of the cult of feeling that underlies this poem's pious parable. Otherwise, Burns's speaker might well be subjecting himself to the sermon of the minister (the poem takes place during a church service) rather than using the louse to construct a rival sermon on vanity.

Of the poems of direct address in Burns's earliest collection, the Kilmarnock edition of 1786, only "To a Mountain Daisy" fails to charm. Burns's eagerness to take on the wretchedness of a crushed flower seems ultimately more strange than novel, and the description Burns needs to authenticate his message is too often interrupted by digression. When the sentimental amplification comes in stanza 6, it rings false. Burns tries to make the daisy a symbol for too many things and the poem becomes hysterical.

The opening stanza mixes description of the daisy with the establishment of its relationship to the narrator:

Wee, modest, crimson-tipped flow'r,
Thou's met me in an evil hour;
For I maun crush amang the stoure
    Thy slender stem:
To spare thee now is past my pow'r,
    Thou bonie gem.

                   (1:228)

Stanzas 2 through 4, though abandoning description of the daisy to attack "flaunting" garden flowers, do offer an image that seems to be the bridge between Gray's flower born "to blush unseen / And waste its sweetness on the desert air" ("Elegy," lines 55–56) and Wordsworth's "violet by a mossy stone" ("She Dwelt Among Untrodden Ways"):

> But thou, beneath the random bield
> > O' clod or stane,
> Adorns the histie *stibble-field*,
> > Unseen, alane.

It is in stanza 5 that the poem becomes shrill:

> There, in thy scanty mantle clad,
> Thy snawie bosom sun-ward spread,
> Thou lifts thy unassuming head
> > In humble guise;
> But now the *share* uptears thy bed,
> > And low thou lies!
>
> Such is the fate of artless Maid. . . .
> Such is the fate of simple Bard. . . .
> Such fate to *suffering Worth* is giv'n. . . .
> > > > > (1:229)

Burns tries to turn the uprooting of a weed into a combination of "The Vanity of Human Wishes" and the Sermon on the Mount, but the moralizing does not sound authentic. More detailed description (like the shaking of the frightened mouse or the "*gawze* and *lace*" over which the louse progresses) might have made the daisy and the incident that prompted the poem seem real enough in themselves to bear Burns's eventual insistence on their symbolic significance, but the descriptive details provided only work against each other. The flower's "unassuming head," for one thing, sounds incongruous after description of its flamboyant "sun-ward spread" bosom. Whenever Burns slights description, he appears—uncomically—to adopt Yorick's godlike assumption that emotional responses can be created by simple fiat.

Poems like "To a Mouse" and "To a Louse," although constructed around a conventional sentimental pose, could only have been written by Robert Burns; but the concluding stanzas of "To a Mountain

Daisy" might have been done by almost any eighteenth-century poet in an emotional mood. Gray's "Elegy" influenced "To a Mountain Daisy," and an unusually fervent poem by Pope that Burns admired was one of the sources for his final stanza:

> Ev'n thou who mourn'st the *Daisy*'s fate,
> *That fate is thine*—no distant date;
> Stern Ruin's *plough-share* drives, elate,
>   Full on thy bloom,
> Till crush'd beneath the *furrow*'s weight,
>   Shall be thy doom!

Burns's conclusion resembles lines near the end of Pope's "Elegy to the Memory of an Unfortunate Lady":

> Poets themselves must fall, like those they sung;
> Deaf the prais'd ear, and mute the tuneful tongue.
> Ev'n he, whose soul now melts in mournful lays,
> Shall shortly want the gen'rous tear he pays. [10]

Between 1717 and 1786 the threshold of responsiveness in poets had lowered so much that Pope's vehement reaction to the suicide of a young woman could be adapted by Burns in a poem about a severed stem.

A passage in Shaftesbury's *Characteristics* suggests one distant source for Burns's piling of significance onto the daisy—for the way the flower's fate becomes his own: "Whatever is void of mind, is void and darkness to the mind's eye. This languishes and grows dim whenever detained on foreign subjects, but thrives and attains its natural vigour when employed in contemplation of what is like itself." [11] This intriguing passage provides one context for the egotism that underlies all the alert benevolence of "feeling." Even Uncle Toby, prime example of gentleness that thinks twice about swatting a fly, whistles "Lillabullero" whenever the conversation strays too far from fortifications: his interest "grows dim" when "detained on foreign subjects." Likewise, in "To a Mountain Daisy" Burns has been so intent on finding what he likes (and what is like him) in the image of the flower that he has failed to acknowledge through description that it is something meaningful in its own right.

Trenchant Sterne called such impositions of individual-penchant-as-universal-regulator a "hobby horse." In "To a Mountain Daisy,"

Burns has revealed that his search for pathetic images is a hobby horse—that his is not a disinterested compassion. His expressions of pity for a wild flower thus seem more self-serving than moving. In "To a Mouse" and "To a Louse," he is more successful, for he describes his objects more and insists on their significance less. (There is also a difference in tone among the poems. "To a Louse" and "To a Mouse" affect a genial Uncle Toby style of benevolence, while "To a Mountain Daisy" is more reminiscent of Mackenzie's Harley at his most lachrymose.)

David Sillar, a friend of Burns's during the 1780s, preserved this incident from Burns's sentimental phase: "It was . . . his custom to read at table. In one of my visits to Lochlie, in time of a sowen supper, he was so intent on reading, I think 'Tristram Shandy,' that his spoon falling out of his hand, made him exclaim, in a tone scarcely imitable, 'Alas, poor Yorick!' "[12] Sillar's story suggests not only Burns's absorption at this time in postures of feeling, but also the poverty of the environment in which he enacted those sentimental fantasies. The life of a Scottish tenant farmer, which Burns once summed up as combining all the "chearless gloom of a hermit with the unceasing moil of a galley-slave" (*Letters*, 1:108), is transformed in Burns's poems of direct address. In poems like "To a Mouse" and "To a Louse," techniques evolved by ironist Sterne and benevolist Mackenzie for milking significance from a stage-prop world are used to circumscribe Burns's bare peasant world with an aura of warmth and idealism. The cult of feeling, which turned ruins into the notion of the picturesque, trained Burns to find a creative vitality in his poverty.

2

"Love and Liberty"

$$\mathbf{I}$$n his prologue to Addison's *Cato* (written in 1713, two years after the publication of Shaftesbury's *Characteristics*), Pope said that the identification of viewers with the suffering hero was the object of tragedy:

> To wake the soul by tender strokes of art,
> To raise the genius, and to mend the heart;
> To make mankind, in conscious virtue bold,
> Live o'er each scene, and be what they behold.[1]

Like the sentimental scrutiny of inanimate objects, this earlier view of emotional projection into a tragic hero imposes a voyeuristic role on the reader or audience. The actions of the drama are not merely to be observed, but to be experienced with an eager sympathy verging on competitive envy of the hero on view. Pope says of our relationship to Cato: "Who sees him act, but envies every deed? / Who hears him groan, and does not wish to bleed?" (p. 96). This is sentiment worthy of Parson Yorick. But not all eighteenth-century readers responded to Cato this way. Johnson (in any case a foe of empathic interpretations of drama) analyzed the audience's relationship to Cato in terms far different from Pope's: "Cato is a being above our solicitude; a man of whom the gods take care, and whom we leave to their care with heedless confidence."[2]

In his enthusiasm for Cato as both hero and victim, Pope anticipated a major preoccupation of the sentimental movement: its cult of pain and failure. In Pope's time, however, the suffering of the hero Cato was still subordinated in emphasis to the excellence of the political principles for which he suffered. Later in the eighteenth century, suffering came to be the index rather than the probable by-product of nobility. Cato chose his fate; such later sentimental heroes as Boswell's Johnson, Sterne's Tristram, Cowper's Castaway, and Goldsmith's Vicar had their more or less thrust upon them (in most cases by circumstance; in Johnson's case by Boswell himself). These later sentimental exemplars (I speak of Johnson here as he exists in Boswell) owe their heroic stature largely to the vicissitudes that have shaped them. (*The Vicar of Wakefield* imitates the Book of Job's "plot" of progressive catastrophe to show that Dr. Primrose is defined and elevated by his unmerited suffering: he is not, like Cato, a hero who has willed his fate.)

Pope praised *Cato* two generations before Burns began to write, and the relationship between writers, their fictional heroes, and their readers had greatly changed between 1713 and 1786. Burns, however, seems to have memorized the more emotional works by Pope: the prologue to *Cato*, "Eloisa to Abelard," and "Elegy to the Memory of an Unfortunate Lady" (as well as *An Essay on Man*, in some ways benevolist).[3] Burns's early writings sometimes seem more reminiscent of Pope in their approach to the description of heroism and suffering than of the later, more fatalistic, sentimental writers.

"Love and Liberty," for instance, drew its title and central theme from a couplet in "Eloisa to Abelard":[4] "O happy state! when souls each other draw, / When love is liberty, and nature, law" (p. 327).[5] As with Pope's sympathy for Eloisa, Burns's defense of beggars in "Love and Liberty" suggests that he was challenged and stimulated by the distance of his subject from the conventional world of his audience. As in Pope, the defense of characters in emotional rebellion from social norms has political and ethical dimensions. Like Eloisa, Burns's beggars refuse to feel as society decrees that they should; like her, they embrace instead a stubborn, and not especially idealistic, individuality. Like Eloisa, the beggars curse "all laws but those which love has made."[6] The conflict between passion and decorum that characterizes Eloisa's monologue is evident as well in the songs of the beggars.

One central difference exists: Eloisa, like Cato, was of noble birth. To Pope, as to Aristotle, lineage enhanced the significance of a character's fate. By contrast, Burns's beggars—noisily employed in getting drunk at the Mauchline inn of Poosie Nansie—can only be called high in the limited physiological sense of the term. Yet the beggars' arrogance is not just a burlesque version of the independent nobility

of character that Pope praised as heroic. Burns uses these obstreper-
ous characters to express a libertarian creed. No less than Cato or
Eloisa, Burns's beggars are moral spokesmen. Their "low" social status shows their genesis during the sentimental era, with its cult of
responsiveness to outcasts. But the fierceness with which the beggars
articulate their creed and attack the norm seems achieved through
Burns's emulation of Pope.

In an annotation of the moral epistles, Joseph Warton said of Pope:
"[his] use . . . of language certainly consists in raising clear, complete
and circumstantial images and in turning readers into spectators."[7]
This is Burns's technique in "Love and Liberty" as well. Though
"low," the beggars are not presented in sentimental terms as victims,
as objects of sympathy. They are "circumstantial images": striking,
persuasive, concrete viewpoints. The only condescending sentimental pose in the poem is struck in a footnote explaining "Poosie Nansie": "The Hostess of a noted Caravansary in M——, well known to
and much frequented by the lowest orders of Travellers and Pil-
grims."[8] Within the body of the cantata, however, no such external
perspective is applied: each beggar speaks (like Eloisa) for himself,
addressing a receptive audience of peers. Since we readers are also
"listening," we are implicated in the cantata's impetuous defense of
love and liberty: we are implicitly peers, like the poem's audience. To
quote again Pope's account of the effect of *Cato*, we "become" what
we "behold": part of a society of outcasts whose low status by conventional norms is a matter of free choice. As with the hero Cato, the
beggars' separation from the world of normality and compromise is
viewed as a distinction to be proud of, not a handicap to be overcome.
Their fate is their free choice: their "nature" (like Cato's) is their
"law." And we readers "live o'er" the beggars' songs, like the audience at a performance of *Cato*, to learn a new role for ourselves—
extreme, attractive, and impossible.

Eloisa had wished to recapture a prelapsarian state of pure passion.
Burns replies in "Love and Liberty" that there is one situation where
love can flourish without repression—among people who have so little left to lose and such minimal expectations that the demands of
"DECORUM" can be laughed off as "cant." Courts are for "cowards,"
churches for the aggrandizement of pharisaic priests, and liberty a
"glorious feast" for people who know they have appetites.

Some seventy years before Burns defended the pleasures of beggary, Shaftesbury said that people's basic instincts, unless they had cultivated depravity, were toward the good—a philosophy congruent with Pope's sympathy for Eloisa's passion and for the suicidal heroine of "Elegy to the Memory of an Unfortunate Lady." In Pope's view, the unfortunate lady did not just capitulate to sinful pride when she killed herself (Johnson's indignant view of her conduct). On the contrary, she superimposed a private ideal of heroic constancy over a conventional ideal of feminine submissiveness and then obeyed herself instead of convention. Pope seems to have seen her suicide as a "moral" one, like Cato's.

In "Love and Liberty," Burns extends Shaftesbury's theory of instinctive merit and enlarges Pope's definition of the hero-as-outcast when he shows characters like the beggars, who do cultivate depravity, defining what constitutes merit and makes for an exemplary life. The beggars speak from a variety of private perspectives, but all of them insist that virtue lies in convivial feelings, not in conventional actions. The song of the soldier's doxy is especially interesting:

> I once was a Maid, tho' I cannot tell when,
> And still my delight is in proper young men:
> Some one of a troop of DRAGOONS was my dadie,
> No wonder I'm fond of a SODGER LADDIE.
>   Sing lal de dal etc.
>
> The first of my LOVES was a swaggering blade,
> To rattle the thundering drum was his trade;
> His leg was so tight and his cheek was so ruddy,
> Transported I was with my SODGER LADDIE.
>
> But the godly old Chaplain left him in the lurch,
> The sword I forsook for the sake of the church;
> He ventur'd the SOUL, and I risked the BODY,
> 'Twas then I prov'd false to my SODGER LADDIE.
>
> Full soon I grew sick of my sanctified *Sot*,
> The Regiment AT LARGE for a HUSBAND I got;
> From the gilded SPONTOON to the FIFE I was ready;
> I asked no more but a SODGER LADDIE.
>
> But the PEACE it reduc'd me to beg in despair,
> Till I met my old boy in a CUNNINGHAM fair;
> His RAGS REGIMENTAL they flutter'd so gaudy,
> My heart it rejoic'd at a SODGER LADDIE

And now I have lived—I know not how long,
And still I can join in a cup and a song;
But whilst with both hands I can hold the glass steady,
Here's to thee, MY HERO, MY SODGER LADDIE.

(1:198)

Burns's polemical use of these beggars is unmistakable in the song. The only thing the "martial chuck" regrets is her "marriage" to the chaplain, for which she betrayed her otherwise constant devotion to the military. She dismisses her chaplain as a "sanctified *Sot*," although she glories in her own drunkenness; the insult seems to lie in the adjective "sanctified." Another instance of her reversal of convention is her attitude toward the declaration of peace. What causes the rest of society to rejoice only reduces the soldier's doxy to "beg in despair."

To the doxy, fulfillment is a matter of supplying appetite, not of adhering to social requirements like conjugal fidelity. Burns's Bard extends the doxy's support of instinctive behavior when he says that avoiding depression is a matter of supplying necessity and desensitizing oneself to more abstract problems. Feelings, he implies, are good only when applied to well-defined objects like food, drink, and sex. Once people begin to cultivate feelings about society or fate, emotion becomes anxiety and is no longer fun:

He was a care-defying blade,
    As ever BACCHUS listed!
Tho' Fortune sair upon him laid,
    His heart she ever miss'd it.
He had no WISH but—to be glad,
    Nor WANT but—when he thristed;
He hated nought but—to be sad,
    An' thus the Muse suggested
        His sang that night.

(1:205)

Any objections to the illegality of the beggar's liaisons are countered by the Bard when he attacks the legitimacy of marriage. Marriage may generally be the ritual middleman between desire and fulfillment—in polite society, between the potency and the existence falls the Shadow—but shadowy rituals strike the Bard as luxuries, like traveling coaches for people who already have legs:

Does the train-attended CARRIAGE
   Thro' the country lighter rove?
Does the sober bed of MARRIAGE
   Witness brighter scenes of love?
....

Life is all a VARIORUM,
   We regard not how it goes;
Let them cant about DECORUM,
   Who have character to lose.
....

   A fig for those by LAW protected,
   LIBERTY's a glorious feast!
   COURTS for Cowards were erected,
      CHURCHES built to please the Priest.
                                    (1:208–9)

The final line of "Eloisa to Abelard" ("He best can paint 'em who shall feel 'em most"),[9] which is itself modeled on the conclusion to Addison's *Campaign* ("And those who paint 'em truest praise 'em most"),[10] made a strong impression on Burns. Among his bagatelles there are two imitations of the lines. In the conclusion to his poem written on the window of an inn at Stirling (a thoughtful patron had given Burns a diamond-tipped pen), he said of the Hanoverians: "Who know them best despise them most,"[11] and elsewhere Burns returned a compliment thus: "Praise from thy lips 'tis mine with joy to boast, / They best can give it who deserve it most" (*Letters*, 1:72). In "Love and Liberty," Burns follows Pope's statement that to "feel" most is to "paint" best. Burns "feels" these characters—presenting them vividly and not judging their rash or unconventional statements. Indeed, their violence and candor, as with Eloisa, becomes the index of their interest as characters and determines their heroic stature. Like Eloisa, the beggars give expression to rebellious instincts that conventional wisdom (prudence) teaches most people to repress. An essential difference, besides that already noted between Eloisa's nobility and the low social status of the beggars, is that Burns's outcasts speak in a setting of convivial cheer rather than solitary frenzy, so that their tone is more defiant than desperate.

Though "Love and Liberty" has been called a comedy, it is more accurate to think of it as polemic. Burns's effort is not so much to amuse as to shock. His beggars offer uniformly direct and impudent answers of expedience to age-old questions of ethics. What is our nature as humans? All men are created foolish, replies Merry Andrew: one might as well profess the inescapable. "Is it in heaven a crime to love too well?" Not really, answers the tinker:

> I've ta'en the gold and been enroll'd
> In many a noble squadron;
> But vain they search'd when off I march'd
> To go and clout the CAUDRON.
>
> (1:204)

Thus, although Burns describes beggars he once observed at a Mauchline tavern, his cantata goes beyond a simple recreation of that experience. "Love and Liberty" is designed to deliver an unmistakable message about the heroic stature of all who follow their own instincts: all for whom love is liberty and nature, law. The merry carelessness of the beggars is shown in each song to be no accident, but the result of a conscious—though instinctively based—code of conduct. (Merry Andrew aligns himself with deliberate foolishness; the callet with the military; the bard with his bottle as the source of poetic inspiration.) Like Uncle Toby's, their hobby horses are odd but organizing factors in their social relationships. To return to the Augustan comparison, as Addison used Cato (with Pope's approval) to inculcate an uncompromising patriotism, Burns used real beggars to inculcate an uncompromising law of rule-by-instinct. In both cases, a general principle underlies characterization, defining certain qualities as heroic.

I HAVE STRESSED analogies between Pope and Burns at some length because they have never been sufficiently studied by critics of "Love and Liberty." Like all Burns's best work, however, "Love and Liberty" synthesizes a variety of literary and cultural influences. I do think that the influence on the cantata of folk songs about beggars is less central than has sometimes been assumed. Burns set his verses to Scots tunes in "Love and Liberty," and in that important sense his cantata draws on folk sources. And songs about beggars were indeed popular throughout eighteenth-century Britain; several of these contributed stock characters or phrases to Burns's cantata. Discussion of several of these songs, however, will show why they are better called "popular British" than "Scottish folk" material.[12]

Probably the first to suggest a purely folk context for interpretations of the cantata was Thomas Stewart, its first publisher, who silently changed the title to "The Jolly Beggars," thus directing attention to similarities with several pieces in Ramsay's popular *Tea Table Miscellany,* especially "The Happy Beggars" and "Merry Beggars." Following Stewart's cue, several critics have suggested that the vitality of the poem is the result of its close alignment with the Scots folk tradition. It should be pointed out, however—as Crawford does in *Society and the Lyric*—that the songs in question were among the English contributions to *The Tea Table Miscellany.* The women cadgers of "The Happy Beggars," for instance, like John Gay's wenches in *The Beggar's Opera,* speak a diluted Augustanese. They present themselves as models of feminine simplicity in such ironic terms that no reader could ever visualize real beggars in hearing their songs:

> We scorn all ladies' washes,
>   With which they spoil each feature,
> No patch or paint our beauties want,
>   We live in simple nature.
> ....
> No cholic, spleen or vapours,
>   At morn, or evening tease us;
> We drink no tea, or ratafia;
>   When sick, a dram can ease us.[13]

To use Pope's description of watching *Cato,* we cannot become what we behold when we encounter these beggars. They are already parodies of what we are: the vocabulary of sophistication (ladies' washes, ratafia) belies the beggar status applied to the speakers by the song.

"Merry Beggars" seems closer to social criticism and further from parody than the songs of the women; yet there, too, a comic touch concludes most quatrains, to lighten the effect:

> Make room for a soldier in buff,
>   Who valiantly strutted about,
> Til he fancy'd the peace breaking off,
>   And then he most wisely sold out.[14]

The "soldier in buff" is nothing like Burns's "son of Mars" in "Love and Liberty," who—progressively mutilated in combat and private brawling (like all characters in the cantata, he has one major hobby)—still concludes his history with "I could meet a troop of HELL at the sound of a drum" (1:197). In other stanzas, however, defiance which does sound Burnsian replaces the easy irony of the soldier:

> I still am a merry gut-scraper,
>   My heart never yet felt a qualm;
> Tho' poor, I can frolic and vapour
>   And sing any tune but a psalm.
> ....
> Whoe'er would be merry and free,
>   Let him list, and from us may he learn:
> In palaces who shall you see
>   Half so happy as we in a barn?[15]

The injunction to the reader ("Let him list, and from us may he learn") is more clumsy than Burns's implicit use of beggars as teaching aids in "Love and Liberty." Yet Burns also includes a fiddler among his cast of characters, referring to him as a merry gut-scraper (Burns emphasizes the somewhat punitive sexual overtones of the epithet). And the chorus of "Merry Beggars" anticipates Burns's celebration of hayloft romance in the final section of "Love and Liberty":

> With the ready brick and fable
>   Round we wander all the day;
> And at night, in barn or stable,
>   Hug our doxies on the hay.
>   (1:208)[16]

So it is beyond doubt that echoes of *The Tea Table Miscellany* were in Burns's mind as he worked on "Love and Liberty." Indeed, there is one song in Ramsay's collection that parallels one important section of "Love and Liberty" more closely than "Merry Beggars." This is song 66, which certainly influenced the "Merry Andrew" song in the cantata. As mentioned before, Burns's Merry Andrew views everything as an issue in foolishness. A professional idiot, he is critical of the work of amateurs:

> Sir Wisdom's a fool when he's fou;
>   Sir Knave is a fool in a Session,

> He's there but a prentice, I trow,
> But I am a fool by profession.
>
> (1:199)

Song 66 does with the word "trifle" what Burns's character does with "fool":

> A parson's a trifle at sea,
> A widow's a trifle in sorrow,
> A peace is a trifle to-day,
> To break it a trifle tomorrow.
> ....
> But with people's malice to trifle,
> And to set us all on a foot;
> The author of this is a trifle,
> And his song is a trifle to boot.
>
> (2:70–71)[17]

The Merry Andrew song does not occur in the two extant manuscript copies of "Love and Liberty," though Burns's authorship of it is not in question. Kinsley (3:1151–52) agrees with Weston ("The Text of Burns's 'The Jolly Beggars' ")[18] that this song was part of an early draft of the cantata. That Burns edited this imitative section out of "Love and Liberty" as he revised supports my view that although the popular tradition of beggar songs was available to Burns, he chose to subordinate that material in "Love and Liberty." The songs from *Tea Table Miscellany* are amusing and bear incidental resemblances to Burns, but one would never call them "puissant and splendid" productions, which was Matthew Arnold's praise of "Love and Liberty."[19]

Burns did rely on stock figures from the popular beggar songs to fill out his assortment of characters. But the value Pope placed on a rhetoric of uncompromising individuality in early works like "Eloisa to Abelard" was ascendant in Burns's mind as he wrote his libertarian manifesto. Burns used a Scottish cast to make his point, but his sympathy for and close study of the early writings of Pope showed him how to suffuse the beggars' defiance with classic literary intensity.

THE ETHICAL AND RELIGIOUS IMPLICATIONS of Burns's espousal of freedom and free love have often excited comment. Hugh Blair was shocked: "The Whole of What is called the Cantata, the Songs of the Beggars and their Doxies, with the Grace at the end of them, are altogether unfit in my opinion for publication. They are by much too licentious" (Low, *The Critical Heritage*, p. 82). Francis Jeffrey, a better critic than Blair, but like Blair a man of rather narrow sympathies, attacked the morals of poems like "Love and Liberty" in his review of Cromek's *Reliques of Robert Burns* (1809): "the cardinal deformity indeed of all [Burns's] productions, was his contempt, or affectation of contempt, for prudence, decency and regularity; and his admiration of thoughtlessness, oddity, and vehement sensibility:—his belief, in short, in *the dispensing power* of genius and social feeling, in all matters of morality and common sense" (Low, *The Critical Heritage*, p. 182). Jeffrey's disapproval of Burns's "admiration of thoughtlessness" is rather like Johnson's criticism of Pope's sympathy for the unfortunate lady. The suicide that Pope saw as a heroic act of self-expression, Johnson saw as a damning act of self-will. How could society hold together if rebels like the lady were to be valued above law-abiding people like her family? Likewise, Jeffrey viewed Burns's defense of characters who rejected courts, churches, and marriage vows—attacking the whole idea that rituals can (and must) confer legitimacy on actions—as an attack on civilization.

Burns, like Pope, probably intended only the open-minded exploration of emotional extremes. For instance, a late letter of Burns to his editor George Thomson attempts to justify his steady output of amorous lyrics addressed to women other than his wife: "Conjugal love is a Passion which I deeply feel, & highly venerate; but somehow it does not make such a figure in Poesy as that other species of the Passion—'Where Love is liberty & Nature law'" (*Letters*, 2:271). But perhaps Johnson and Jeffrey were correct in interpreting such a reliance on emotional extremes to stimulate the "figures of Poesy" as a dangerous habit of thought. Where Jeffrey went wrong was in ascribing Burns's sympathy for illicit emotions and unrepentant rebels to his lack of "chivalry," to his peasant incomprehension of why and how the upper classes rein in their instincts. The target in satiric poems like "Love and Liberty" is not chivalry but Calvinism; the society specifically undermined is the communion of saints, the "Auld Licht" (conservative) Calvinists who still dotted the landscape of southwestern Scotland during Burns's youth, although an increasing number of moderate preachers was beginning to make inroads. Indeed, the "Scottish" dimension of this poem is not so much literary as theological.

The conservative Calvinists held that regularity of life was a sign of divine election (of guaranteed salvation) and that misfortune could be interpreted as a sign of God's disfavor. In "Love and Liberty," Burns's attack on such rigidity itself takes a rigid form: the blessed and the damned have only exchanged roles. The beggars say that regularity of conduct means a lack of grace (spirit, good nature) in people. Poverty and hardship, because they sensitize people to appreciate good things when they happen, are opportunities for displaying grace—not burdens inflicted by a disapproving divinity. This is simultaneously an attack on the tenets of conservative Calvinism and a polemical reversal of them. The doxy is a heroine because she is honest about her feelings. Her sanctified "husband" is pushed out of the inner circle of tolerance and convivial approval not for anything that he does, but for being what he is. His category is wrong: he is the "church," not the "sword." Categorical damnation is the basic principle of conservative Calvinism. In the original system, God decides who is "justified" and who is reprobated: who receives grace and who does not. In "Love and Liberty," Burns implies that our feelings themselves irrevocably determine our ability to partake in "the glorious feast."

Out of a variety of sources—the Pope exemplars of heroic passion, the sentimental use of humble things as teaching aids, the British vogue for beggar songs, and the New Testament polemics against materialism—Burns synthesized a cantata that also stands as his sentimental version, perhaps inversion, of Calvinism. Love and liberty replace sanctity as the mark of salvation; but, as in Calvinism, without this mark salvation is impossible. Abounding grace is replaced by abundant spirits, but not to feel means damnation.

3

Sentimental "Election" in the Vernacular Epistles and "The Vision"

The polemical reversal of Calvinism that characterizes "Love and Liberty" also appears in Burns's vernacular epistles, composed between 1784 and 1787, around the same time as the cantata. It is certain that when Burns lifted his eyes from humble or passive objects and looked at people, his compassion became far more selective. And his poems became less conventionally sentimental while simultaneously more committed to the notion that feelings are supremely important. In "Epistle to Davie," for instance, Burns says that the sole index of blessedness is a good heart:

> It's no in titles nor in rank;
> It's no in wealth like *Lon'on Bank*,
>> To purchase peace and rest;
> It's no in makin muckle, *mair:*
> It's no in books; it's no in Lear,
>> To make us truly blest:
> If Happiness hae not her seat
>> And center in the breast,
> We may be *wise*, or *rich*, or *great*,
>> But never can be *blest:*
> Nae treasures, nor pleasures
>> Could make us happy lang;
> The *heart* ay's the part ay,
>> That makes us right or wrang.
>> (1:67)

As in "Love and Liberty," this is election through sensibility. The "heart" or "breast" replaces the soul as the faculty through which

27

grace is expressed, and nothing people do determines their merit, which is set by nature, not nurture. Written in 1785, the "Epistle to J. L——k" (John Lapraik) offers an outright attack on education:

> What's a' your jargon o' your Schools,
> Your Latin names for horns an' stools;
> If honest Nature made you *fools*,
>   What sairs your Grammars?
> Ye'd better taen up *spades* and *shools*,
>   Or *knappin-hammers*.
> ....
> Gie me ae spark o' Nature's fire,
> That's a' the learning I desire;
> Then tho' I drudge thro' dub an' mire
>   At pleugh or cart,
> My Muse, tho' hamely in attire,
>   May touch the heart.
> ....
> Awa ye selfish, warly race,
> Wha think that havins, sense an' grace,
> Ev'n love an' friendship should give place
>   To *catch-the-plack!*
> I dinna like to see your face,
>   Nor hear your crack.
>
> But ye whom social pleasure charms,
> Whose hearts the *tide of kindness* warms,
> Who hold your *being* on the terms,
>   "Each aid the others,"
> Come to my bowl, come to my arms,
>   My friends, my brothers!
>   (1:87–89)

The "warly" race (worldly folk) are the vernacular equivalent of sentimental Mackenzie's pitied "men of the world"; Burns also rejects them in "Green grow the Rashes." Worldly people center their lives around getting things, such as money, status, and an education. But people sparked with "Nature's fire" (grace) concentrate instead on feeling things, such as friendship, pity, and pleasure. Again, the verdict on those who do not follow Burns's ideal of feeling is categorical. In the epistle to Lapraik, damnation has fallen not only on hypocrites and misers, but on college graduates, deflated in the line which shows education as a process of turning "stirks" (bullocks) into "Asses." Like Calvinism, which brands as ineffectual the good works of people who are not of the elect, Burns's system assumes that nothing can come of trying to refine the intellect: "Nature" already has either fired us with creativity or branded us as fools.

In his second epistle to Lapraik, Burns uses explicitly theological images to condemn the worldly and elevate "poor, thoughtless devils":

> Were this the *charter* of our state,
> "On pain o' *hell* be rich an' great,"
> *Damnation* then would be our fate,
> 　　　Beyond remead;
> But, thanks to *Heav'n*, that's no the gate
> 　　　We learn our *creed.*
>
> For thus the royal *Mandate* ran,
> When first the human race began,
> "The social, friendly, honest man,
> 　　　Whate'er he be,
> 'Tis *he* fulfills *great Nature's plan,*
> 　　　And none but *he.*"
>
> O *Mandate,* glorious and divine!
> The followers o' the ragged Nine,
> Poor, thoughtless devils! yet may shine
> 　　　In glorious light,
> While sordid sons o' Mammon's line
> 　　　Are dark as night!
> 　　　　　　　　　　　　(1:92)

The denunciation of wealth here uses the same metaphors as a fire-and-brimstone sermon. Not only the legitimacy of being poor, but the ultimate salvation of "none but" the "social, friendly, honest man" is emphasized. Burns combines Calvinist predestination with his own notion of "Nature's plan" (perhaps adapted from Pope's *Essay on Man*), and the result is that dogmatic defense of secular spontaneity which is so characteristic of Burns's early poetry. Though tolerance is one of the qualities Burns champions in these early vernacular epistles, the form his defense takes is itself intolerant. Excluded from his offer of brotherhood are the rich, the famous, the "great," the critical, the hypocritical, and the prudent. Hypocrites deserve categorical denunciation: the others, of course, do not necessarily deserve Burns's blanket condemnation. Burns is as prone to damn all who do not conform to his own ideas as Holy Willie himself, the butt of Burns's most spirited attack on Auld Licht vindictiveness.

"Holy Willie's Prayer" eavesdrops on the evening devotions of an especially virulent Auld Licht partisan. Burns adapts Allan Ramsay's use of the comic monologue; as in such Ramsay poems as "The Last Speech of the Wretched Miser" or "Lucky Spence's Last Advice," Burns offers an apparently unedited transcription of remarks that no wholesome person could possibly support. Willie thanks God for the Divine grace that sets him so unmistakably apart from the unregenerate in the community; he records, with brief apology, last night's lapse with Meg. He then concentrates on the real business of his prayer, which is to request God's vengeance on the New Licht congregation of Ayr and on several of his personal enemies, including Burns's good friends Gavin Hamilton and Bob Aiken. Because an absurdity— Willie's greed for righteousness—is seen as the driving force behind his vindictiveness, Willie is made to seem more comical than evil. But in Burns's view, native selfishness like Willie's had been encouraged to blossom into hypocrisy, intolerance, and smugness by the failure of strict Calvinism to stress good works. When dealing with a lone conservative, Burns could play the corruption of conscience for laughs, but in other poems that conjure up a coterie of the righteous, his exasperation flares into diatribe:

> But I gae mad at their grimaces,
> Their sighan, cantan, grace-prood faces,
> Their three-mile prayers, an' hauf-mile graces,
>   Their raxan conscience,
> Whase greed, revenge an' pride disgraces
>   Waur nor their nonsense.
> ....
> O Pope, had I thy satire's darts
> To gie the rascals their deserts,
> I'd rip their rotten, hollow hearts,
>   An' tell aloud
> Their jugglin' hocus pocus arts
>   To cheat the crowd.
>
> God knows, I'm no the thing I shou'd be,
> Nor am I even the thing I cou'd be,

> But twenty times, I rather wou'd be
>   An atheist clean,
> Than under gospel colors hid be,
>   Just for a screen.
>
>   (1:124–25)

The earnestness of Burns's disagreement with Auld Licht tenets can scarcely be overestimated. A pious (and in Burns's view hypocritical) righteousness was one theme that would always send him into his own version of emotional righteousness. In a letter to Gavin Hamilton, who had been keeping company with William Auld, the conservative Mauchline minister who had once presided over Burns's public penance as a fornicator, Burns insists that Auld Licht rigidity is opposed to everything valued by sensible and kindly people;

> As I understand you are now in habits of intimacy with that Boanerges of Gospel power, Father Auld, be earnest with him that he will wrestle in prayer for you, that you may see the vanity of vanities in trusting to, or even practising, the carnal moral works of charity, humanity, generosity and forgiveness, things which you practised so flagrantly, that it was evident you delighted in them, neglecting, or perhaps profanely despising the wholesome doctrine of faith without works, the only anchor of salvation. (*Letters*, 1:142)

Burns's delight in using the images favored by the "Auld Licht" to express his own subversive values is evident in this letter. Strictly speaking, however, Burns's opposing doctrine of "charity, humanity, generosity and forgiveness" was also a system of salvation through grace, of faith without works. In "Address to the Unco Guid," perhaps his most famous assault on righteousness, his defense of wayward conduct is based on his acceptance of fatality. Passionate people are fated to occasional excess as conclusively as frigid women are fated to consistent virtue. And the final stanza concludes with the image of a judging God, though not a god of the reasoning head:

> Who made the heart, 'tis *He* alone
>   Decidedly can try us,
> He knows each chord its various tone,
>   Each spring its various bias:
> Then at the balance let's be mute,
>   We never can adjust it;

What's *done* we partly may compute,
But know not what's *resisted*.

(1:54)

In the "Epistle to a Young Friend" (1786), Burns moves away from countering Auld Licht categories of good and evil with his own; he progresses from polemics to an acknowledgment of the complexity of all actions. People are not herded into two groups, the totally right and the totally wrong, for "self" is not viewed statically. The implicit message of "Address to the Unco Guid"—that motives and actions are mysterious—is extended in "Epistle to a Young Friend":

I'll no say, men are villains a';
The real, harden'd wicked,
Wha hae nae check but *human law*,
Are to a few restricked:
But Och, mankind are unco weak,
An' little to be trusted;
If *Self* the wavering balance shake,
It's rarely right adjusted!

(1:248)

There is an echo of Shaftesbury in Burns's notion that an innate moral sense is sufficient to govern all but a "few" "harden'd" criminals. In any case, in this epistle a life pattern of misfortune, indiscretion, and high spirits is not considered either damning (as in narrow pietism) or saving (as in such other early works as "Love and Liberty"). And "honest poverty" stands for something. Not for everything, as in the beggars' songs, and not for nothing, as in the materialism of the "warly" race—but something:

Yet they wha fa' in Fortune's strife,
Their fate we should na censure,
For still th' *important end* of life,
They equally may answer:
A man may hae an *honest heart*,
Tho' Poortith hourly stare him;
A man may tak a neebor's part,
Yet hae nae *cash* to spare him.

(1:249)

In this most rationalizing of Burns's vernacular epistles, the subjunctive appears more often than is customary in Burns. Personality is not a fixed quantity but a wavering balance between slavery to convention and slavery to excessive Self. "Epistle to a Young Friend" is one case where Johnson seems a parallel rather than the antithesis of Burns:

> The great CREATOR to revere,
>   Must sure become the *Creature;*
> But still the preaching cant forbear,
>   An e'en the rigid feature:
> Yet ne'er with Wits prophane to range,
>   Be complaisance extended;
> An *atheist-laugh*'s a poor exchange
>   For *Deity offended!*
>
> When ranting round in Pleasure's ring,
>   Religion may be blinded;
> Or if she give a *random-fling,*
>   It may be little minded;
> But when on Life we're tempest-driven,
>   A Conscience but a canker—
> A correspondence fix'd wi' Heav'n,
>   Is sure a noble *anchor!*
>
>   (1:250)

The dislike of cant, the view that "random" transgression is less wrongful than a habit of self-exculpation, and the acknowledgment of the difficulty of keeping oneself within the boundaries fixed by society and ethical theorists all sound like Johnson. This judicious Johnsonian tolerance (perhaps stimulated by the extreme youth of the addressee) seems different from the defensive tolerance of other vernacular epistles, where people are valued or condemned according to categories prejudged by Burns.

To his own community in southwest Scotland, the most striking feature of Burns's work—and the basis for his notoriety—seems to have been precisely this defense of occasional misconduct. Depending on their own religious bias—conservative Auld Licht or moderate New Licht—people were either delighted or appalled.[1] In 1786, when Jean Armour's father discovered that she had become pregnant by Burns, he refused to accept their marriage agreement (which would have legitimized the baby), preferring public penance for his daughter to an alliance with the irreligious local bard. (To do Armour's dislike of Burns justice, I should add that Burns's father had died a bankrupt in 1784, that Burns and his family were still far from prosperous, and that Burns was already under the financial obligation of providing for his illegitimate daughter by Elizabeth Paton.) In any case, following the publication and sensational success of *Poems, Chiefly in the Scottish Dialect* (Kilmarnock, 1786), a multitude of vernacular poets sprang up like mushrooms after a heavy rain around the Auld Licht–New Licht controversy to which Burns's poetry had given new energy—this even though many of the most pointed satires, such as "Holy Willie's Prayer," had not been included in the volume.

Typical of the scandalized conservative reaction was *Animadversions on Some Poets and Poetasters of the Present Age Especially R——t B——s and J——n L——K* (1788). This slender volume was mostly the work of James Maxwell, whose arguments for a strict line in religion consisted chiefly of threatening the lax with an uncomfortable afterlife. (Reading these Auld Licht effusions, one sees the origin of such Burns dicta as "The *fear o' Hell*'s a hangman's whip, / To haud the wretch in order" [1:250].) Of Burns and his fellow vernacular poet John Lapraik, Maxwell says with ghoulish satisfaction: "Tho' now the Lord's supper they make like a fair, / The time will soon come when they'll howl in despair."[2] Such transparent, almost innocent spite is pure Holy Willie. The conclusion of the attack on Burns also dwells with ill-concealed complacency on the image of Burns meeting his fate in the netherworld:

> . . . he 'gainst whom thou dar'st rebel,
> Can soon imprison thee in hell.
> There must thou gnaw thy burning chains,
> Where Satan, thy grand master, reigns:
> Then see what satires thou can'st make,
> Amidst that black infernal lake.
>
> (p. 10)

On a higher plane is the anti-Burns invective of Ebenezer Picken in his *Poems and Epistles, Mostly in Scottish Dialect* (1788). Burns's "Address to the Deil," in which the Adversary is hailed by such nicknames as "Auld Hangie," "Clootes," "Nick," and "Auld Hornie," suggested Picken's poem "The Deil's Answer to His Vera Wordy Frien' R—— B——." This poem is competently versified, though irony thuds in too heavily at the end:

> Auld Hornie, Clootes an' me thegither,
> Hae ownt an' said without a swither,
> That thou deserves the name o' brither,
>   An' e'en sae be't:
> For earth ne'er smil't on sic anither
>   Sin' Judas die't.[3]

On Burns's side of the controversy were John Lapraik (1727–1807) and David Sillar (1760–1830), each recipients of vernacular epistles from Burns. Like Burns, both Lapraik and Sillar upheld an ideal of good fellowship over censorious piety and of natural genius over the refinements of art. Sillar brought up the issue of education in the preface to his *Poems* (1789), where he refused to make the conventional apologies even Burns had thought necessary for lack of formal poetic training: "Natural genius alone is sufficient to constitute a poet; for, the imperfections in the works of many poetical writers, which are ascribed to want of education, may, he believes, with more justice, be ascribed to want of genius. He leaves every person to judge of his by his writings."[4] Though one is well-disposed toward Sillar, whom Burns praised as "Ace o' Hearts"[5] and who at least did not try to cash in on the vogue Burns had created for the title *Poems, Chiefly in the Scottish Dialect*, he was no natural genius. His "Reply to Burns's Calf, by an Unco Calf" is representative:

> I'm sorry sirs, I hae't tae say,
> Our passions are sae strong,
> As make us tine the beaten way,
> And run sae aften wrong.
>
> Then for the future let's be mute,
> Reverin' those above us,
> We' such as we, let's not dispute
> And syne our frien's will love us.
>   (p. 179)

Though sometimes affecting a servile tone that Burns would never have adopted, and though a proselytizing nondrinker, Sillar generally follows Burns in advocating tolerance for the occasional lapses of good fellows. (The first line of the second stanza is taken from Burns's "Then at the balance let's be mute," which begins the concluding quatrain of "Address to the Unco Guid.")

Lapraik, the bard of Muirkirk, did not meet Burns—who initiated the friendship by sending Lapraik a vernacular epistle—until several exchanges of verse had taken place between them. The interest and encouragement of Burns, a much younger man, led Lapraik to publish his first verse collection in 1788. "The Poet's Apology for Rhyming" is typical of Lapraik's output of good-hearted doggerel:

> I'm not so vain as to pretend
>   To teach men to behave;
> Yet still am of a *nobler mind*,
>   Than ever be their *slave*.
>
> I love a friend that's frank and free,
>   Who tells to me his mind:
> I hate to hing upon a *hank*,
>   With *hums* and *has* confin'd.[6]

These passages from Sillar and Lapraik show the futility of ascribing the richness of Burns's vernacular epistles wholly to the existence of a tradition of vernacular correspondence and to the local controversy in Mauchline and southwest Scotland between the New Licht and Auld Licht. These influences alone produced poets like Sillar and Lapraik, but Burns—stimulated to write by this local power struggle, and cheered by the existence of other rural poets to whom he could address his letters—drew also for support of his defense of love and liberty on his extensive reading in the ongoing eighteenth-century debate about individual rights. The forceful application of principles he had gleaned from his reading—plus a liberal dose of self-justification—combined with his confident use of traditional Scots verse forms to make his liberal polemics outstanding.

Burns had one of those minds that absorbs influences as blotting paper absorbs ink, and along with vernacular traditions, British and European liberal traditions were strong and usually salutary in his early poems. Indeed, Burns's mastery of mainstream intellectual issues was perceived by at least one of his fellow vernacular writers, who—though wrongly ascribing to formal schooling an education Burns had

scraped together for himself—was penetrating enough to see through
Mackenzie's description of Burns as "heav'n-taught":

> For by the scraps o' French an' Latin,
> That's flung athort your buik fu' thick in,
> It's easy seen you've aft been flitting
>   Frae school to school;
> An' nae thanks to your head an' wittin',
>   Tho' you're nae fool.
>   ....
> The prints—newspapers an' reviews,
> Frae time to time may aft you rouse,
> An' say you're *Heaven-taught*—your views
>   are clear an' fair,
> And a' your ain, gi'en by THE MUSE
>   *O'er the banks o' Ayr;*
>
> But waesuck, that'll no gae down
> Wi' ilka chiel about this town
> That struts in black, an' eke a gown;
>   Na, Na, they canna
> Believe that poets fa' aroun',
>   Like flakes o' manna![7]

James Macauley's warning that a rustic posture was incompatible with
the broad allusiveness of Burns's work—that a claim to naiveté would
never "go down" with educated readers—overestimated by a wide
margin the common sense of the contemporary sentimental public
who, for reasons that will be discussed in later chapters, wanted to
view Burns as an unspoiled, untutored genius. Modern critics, in
compensating for that still popular misconception, have perhaps confined themselves too narrowly to analysis of local and traditionally
Scots influences on his work. The truth is that, although the ratio is
never constant, there is always some interplay in Burns's poetry between local and cosmopolitan elements.

THE MOST ECLECTIC of Burns's early works is "The Vision." The
duans into which the poem is divided had been "Ossian's" way of
dividing a long poem. Coila, the lowland Muse who appears to Burns,
is modeled on Scota, who appears in *Helenore* (1768), a vernacular
poem by Alexander Ross. The verse form is Ramsay's standard Hab-

bie; many of Burns's images recall Thomson's *Seasons,* and the mood
of the poem suggests Mackenzie's tearful sentimentality. Finally, if
much of Burns's early poetry builds up a case for election-by-sen-
sibility, this is the poem in which Burns himself is explicitly "justified," when his supervisor, the Lowland Muse, crowns him with
native holly.

Burns is a specialist in fine opening stanzas, and "The Vision" has
two of his most vivid:

> The sun had clos'd the *winter-day,*
> The Curlers quat their roaring play,
> And hunger'd Maukin taen her way
>   To kail-yards green,
> While faithless snaws ilk step betray
>   Whare she has been.
>
> The Thresher's weary *flingin-tree,*
> The lee-lang day had tir'd me;
> And when the Day had clos'd his e'e,
>   Far i' the West,
> Ben i' the *Spence,* right pensivelie,
>   I gaed to rest.
>
>   (1:103)

The final lines of stanza 2 begin the transition from scenery painting
to transcendent vision. ("Right pensivelie, / I gaed to rest" has the
ring of Chatterton's diction; Southey, later noting such uses of vernacular diction to establish an archaic as well as a folk atmosphere,
would call all Scottish vernacular verse "a sort of Rowleyism.")[8]

Worried about poverty, Burns's farmer-poet begins to form a resolution to abandon poetry for practicality. But the farmer is interrupted
by the appearance at his parlor door of a "tight, outlandish Hizzie":

> Green, slender, leaf-clad *Holly-boughs*
> Were twisted, gracefu', round her brows,
> I took her for some SCOTTISH MUSE,
>   By that same token;
> And come to stop those reckless vows,
>   Would soon been broken.
>
> A "hare-brain'd, sentimental trace"
> Was strongly marked in her face;

> A wildly-witty, rustic grace
>   Shone full upon her;
> Her *eye*, ev'n turn'd on empty space,
>   Beam'd keen with *Honor*.
>   (1:104)

This Muse who appears out of nowhere to legitimize Burns has all the characteristics he has been promoting in the vernacular epistles just discussed: the "hare-brain'd sentimental trace" that he has championed against stolid prudence, the "wildly-witty" "grace" that he has valued over studied efforts to achieve, and the "honor" that he has said results from a value for feelings.

The remainder of duan 1 describes the diorama of lowland scenery and history that whirls around in Coila's mantle. This is an attempt at such epic digressions as Homer's description of the shield of Ajax or Vergil's description of the gates at Carthage; but the spate of footnotes interrupting the poem to explain the references show, in their digression from digression, that Burns was aware of the weakness of this part of his poem.

In duan 2, Coila addresses Burns, reversing the usual procedure in his early poems, where he delivers the soliloquies himself. She explains that there are ranks of Scottish spirits. The highest ranks preside over the lives of patriots and poets, and the lower ones teach tillage to farmers and song to rustic bards. Coila identifies herself as this sort of "lower" spirit. (The passage evidently draws, though not comically, on Pope's system of presiding spirits in *The Rape of the Lock*.) Introductions over, Coila informs Burns (as Pope's sylph had told Belinda) that he has always been an object of special solicitude for her. From his "natal hour" she has "mark'd" his "embryo-tuneful flame." (Among stiff competition, that last is probably the strangest image in the poem.) Her mission is to assure Burns's farmer that being a bard is his only destiny. His receptive nature has determined his fate:

> "I saw thee seek the sounding shore,
> Delighted with the dashing roar;
> Or when the *North* his fleecy store
>   Drove thro' the sky,
> I saw grim Nature's visage hoar,
>   Struck thy young eye.

"Or when the deep-green-mantl'd Earth,
Warm-cherish'd ev'ry floweret's birth,
And joy and music pouring forth,
            In ev'ry grove,
I saw thee eye the gen'ral mirth
            With boundless love.

"When ripen'd fields, and azure skies,
Call'd forth the *Reaper's* rustling noise,
I saw thee leave their ev'ning joys,
            And lonely stalk,
To vent thy bosom's swelling rise,
            In pensive walk.

                                        (1:111–12)

This is *The Seasons* in brief. Burns has become so engrossed by his effort to secure a Thomsonian cadence for his vision (with echoes of other poets from Milton to Warton) that there seems little of his own voice in duan 2. Like the concluding stanzas of "To a Mountain Daisy," this section of "The Vision" might have been designed by some committee for the preservation of eighteenth-century clichés. And as with "To a Mountain Daisy," Burns's syrupy English is not so much the cause as a symptom of what has gone wrong.

Typically, Burns is at his best in his early work when he is aggressively defensive: justifying his feelings, praising his friends, attacking his enemies, and showing the world that everything—including odd subjects like mice and beggars—means something to a sensitive poet. That "The Vision" is preoccupied with justifying Burns would seem, at first glance, to suggest that its "plot" offers fine defensive potential. But a second look reveals that the defense in this case is carried on, not by a Burns persona, but by a transcendent Muse who issues sentimental dicta while his speaker looks on. For once, Burns allows himself to be the object of condescension in his poem. He is Maria to the Muse's Yorick; Belinda to Coila's sylph. This persona is depressed from the outset as well as passive during the narrative; such a situation always seemed to bring out the imitator (as opposed to the synthesizer) in Burns.

Edward Young's *Conjectures on Original Composition* (1759) offers a succinct account of the dangers of "illustrious examples" that suggests why Burns's imitation of other poets created such a problem for "The

Vision": "Illustrious examples engross, prejudice and intimidate. They *engross* our attention, and so prevent a due inspection of ourselves; they *prejudice* our judgment in favour of their abilities, and so lessen the sense of our own; and they *intimidate* us with the splendour of their renown, and thus under diffidence bury our strength."⁹ A less sympathetic context for Burns's failure is offered by Jeffrey in the review of Cromek's *Reliques* discussed above: "[Any conscious assumption of a grand design led Burns to a] frequent mistake of mere exaggeration and violence for force and sublimity. . . . He has generally had recourse to a mere accumulation of hyperbolical expressions, which encumber the diction instead of exalting it, and show the determination to be impressive without the power of executing it" (Low, *The Critical Heritage*, p. 84). "Diffidence" caused by Burns's admiration of the "splendour" of predecessors like Thomson has indeed "buried" his customary strengths under a "mere accumulation of hyperbolical expressions" in parts of duan 2.

But although no one would ever call "The Vision" Burns's best poem, it yields rich evidence concerning the ideas underlying Burns's early writings. The most famous stanza of "The Vision" contains Burns's strongest statement about the predestined fallibility of good-natured people, and about the relationship of this fallibility to poetic genius:

> "I saw thy pulse's maddening play,
> Wild-send thee Pleasure's devious way,
> Misled by Fancy's *meteor-ray*,
>   By Passion driven;
> But yet the *light* that led astray,
>   Was *light* from Heaven.
>
>   (1:112)

Impulses are grace—"light from Heaven." Divine in origin, they are, like grace, ineluctable. A madness in the pulse leads to transgression but also to poetry. The gift of genius involves excess. All this is oddly parallel to Blake's notion of creativity, at least in such early writings as *The Marriage of Heaven and Hell* (ca. 1790–93). Different as the two poets were in other respects, both thought that artists were governed by energies that inevitably set them against the norm. Like Burns, Blake comes close to saying that a blameless life precludes art: "The Weak Man may be Virtuous Enough, but will Never be an Artist."

And for Blake as for Burns, "virtue" has lost its classical meaning of inner strength, becoming merely a socially acceptable level of timidity and weakness: "Those who restrain desire, do so because theirs is weak enough to be restrained."[10]

The problem with "The Vision" is that Burns exploits this notion of fated transgression not only to justify but to glorify himself, presenting such things as his financial problems as part of the cosmic template for the poetic character. As in "To a Mountain Daisy," the self-pity of the enterprise interferes with the readers' bestowal of sympathy. Jeffrey took issue with such tendencies in Burns's work because he said they violated logic as well as taste:

> A man may say of his friend, that he is a noble-hearted fellow,—too generous to be just, and with too much spirit to be always prudent and regular. But he cannot be allowed to say this even of himself; and still less to represent himself as a hare brained sentimental soul, constantly carried away by fine fancies and visions of love and philanthropy, and born to confound and despise the cold-blooded sons of prudence and sobriety. This apology evidently destroys itself, for it shows that conduct to be the result of deliberate system, which it affects at the same time as the fruit of mere thoughtlessness and casual impulse. (Low, *The Critical Heritage*, pp. 182–183)

There is some evidence that Jeffrey is referring here to "The Vision," in his description of Burns as "carried away by . . . visions" and as a "hare brained sentimental soul," and any dislike of Burns's motives in that poem is understandable. But if Burns's purity of motive is questionable in "The Vision," this is not because of Burns's deficient formal education (Jeffrey's theory) but because of Burns's excessive deference to such sentimental heroes as Harley and Yorick, who also despised all "cold-blooded sons of prudence and sobriety." The illogic for which Jeffrey criticizes Burns is inherent in the sentimental value system. If that system is flawed, at least the flaws are not of Burns's devising. The real difficulty in this poem is that Burns parrots rather than synthesizes the paradoxical, circular sentimental doctrine of heroism-through-feelings.

The qualities Coila praises in Burns—fervent responsiveness to nature and boundless love that, while connecting the poet in benevolence to society, simultaneously raises him above it—were cultivated by practically the entire polite world of Burns's day. In "The Vision," as in "To a Mountain Daisy," these conventional sentimental values are at once stated too abstractly and laid on too heavily. We lose a sense of Burns's farmer-speaker as a particular person. The Lowland Muse distinguishes him from other sentimental personae only in species, not in genus:

> "Thou canst not learn, nor can I show,
> To paint with *Thomson's* landscape-glow;
> Or wake the bosom-melting throe,
>   With *Shenstone's* art;
> Or pour, with *Gray*, the moving flow,
>   Warm on the heart.
>
> "Yet all beneath th'unrivall'd Rose,
> The lowly Daisy sweetly blows;
> Tho' large the forest's Monarch throws
>   His army shade,
> Yet green the juicy Hawthorn grows,
>   Adown the glade.
>
>   (1:112–13)

In better poems than "The Vision," Burns works according to his description above. He admires the achievements of the Thomsons, the Shenstones, the Grays; yet he remains aware of the rustic grace his skilled use of vernacular can uniquely promote. The hawthorn shares the category "tree" with the oak, while remaining a different sort of tree. Critics of Burns sometimes confound his vernacular species with genus: they assume he is different in kind from other poets of his time. This leads to interpretations of poems like "The Vision" which condemn his failure to master an "alien" diction. Yet the weakness of "The Vision," as of "To a Mountain Daisy," lies not so much in its abuses of sentimental diction as in its inconsistencies of sentimental posture. In stanzas such as the two quoted above, Burns is obviously trying hard to be an oak (a Thomson, a Gray) at the same time he is assuring his readers that he is happy enough as a hawthorn.

BURNS'S CONCEPTION of the poetical character—his idealization of impulse and his view of transgression as misdirected light from Heaven—encumbers overly rhetorical poems such as "The Vision" but also broadens the dimensions of his finest early work, such as the vernacular epistles. A sentimental value for individual feelings as the basis for all meaning underlies the libertarian system articulated so confidently in such early works as "Love and Liberty" and the satires. The elevation of humble objects and gentle benevolists that Burns encountered in his sentimental reading seems to have imbued him with a sense of destiny. Even a tenant farmer—as obscure as Harley, as quixotic as Yorick, as prospectless as Uncle Toby—could participate in this literary movement. The most apparently folk-oriented of Burns's early writings ("Love and Liberty," to name one example) are congruent with the sentimental reverence for individual response. Sentimental principles sometimes led Burns into excessive postures, but they also helped to support his conviction that he was a true poet. (Both points are demonstrated by "The Vision.") The following chapter will discuss some psychological and political aspects of the cult of feeling, analyzing poems and novels with which Burns was well acquainted, to show how his sentimental reading helped to shape Burns's sense of creative merit.

4

Laws of Sentimental Polity

Sarah Fielding's *Remarks on Clarissa* (1749) offers an intriguing description of Richardson's plot and its tragic inevitability: "poor *Clarissa;* whose misfortune it was to be placed amongst a Set of Wretches, who were every one following the Bent of their own peculiar Madness, without any consideration for the innocent Victim who was to fall a Sacrifice to their ungovernable Passions."[1] The passage provokes two reactions: surprise that Fielding has not also noted that "poor Clarissa" follows the bent of her personality with the same dedication as the villains in the novel; and wonder that a plot structure that would occur throughout eighteenth-century fiction after *Clarissa* was seen so early and understood so well.

By 1759 writers as differently disposed as Sterne and Johnson were publishing fiction in which central characters tried to impose their "own peculiar Madness" on a usually recalcitrant outside world. *Tristram Shandy* is a satire, and *Rasselas* is a cautionary fable; the individual law asserted by characters in these works is in both cases progressively undercut. Unlike the stern virtue of Addison's Cato, the individual codes of these characters are not intended to be adopted by society for the improvement of public morals. On the contrary, a reader—observing rather than sharing Uncle Toby's innocent mania for war, or the cranky disposition of the hermit in *Rasselas*—sees not the authority of their individual systems, but the way that their eccentricities isolate and define them. Everybody in *Tristram Shandy* follows "the Bent of [his] own Peculiar Madness" with compulsive consistency, but there are just too many different systems on the premises, and even conversation becomes impossible at Shandy Hall. In *Rasselas*, the hero encounters a succession of characters who are as convinced of the truth of their private codes as is Dr. Slop of the efficiency of his excommunication of Obadiah. Yet in *Rasselas*, fate intervenes to expose the inadequacies of these private codes, and a reader is warned away from imposing personal strictures on reality. The stoical philosopher in *Rasselas* lectures cogently on fortitude, but abandons himself to grief when his daughter dies. Johnson portrays any private attempt to enforce a systematic code—any secular theory claiming to organize all meaning for all time—as itself an irrational fantasy of power, fated to collapse in the face of a complicated and largely unsympathetic universe.

In the years following the publication of *Tristram Shandy* and *Rasselas*, however, a radical change occurred in literary attitudes toward extremes of individuality. The solipsism of fictional characters who rejected the social definitions of propriety to follow the bent of their "own peculiar Madness" somehow became heroic. In Mackenzie's *The Man of Feeling*, vacillating Harley was intended to be viewed neither as a comic eccentric nor as a pitiable neurotic but as an exemplar: a nonpolitical, catatonic Cato. During the 1760s and 1770s, emulation of sentimental conduct began to be expected of readers. It began to be assumed that every narrator imposed a private system, filtering every story through his peculiar consciousness. Objectivity was not only impossible but undesirable. *A Sentimental Journey* forces everything into Yorick's sentimental framework, and Sterne points out through Yorick that a recent travel book by Smollett had been just as one-dimensional, though its underlying principle had been ill temper rather than benevolence: "The learned SMELFUNGUS travelled from Boulogne to Paris—from Paris to Rome—and so on—but he set out with the spleen and jaundice, and every object he pass'd by was discoloured or distorted—He wrote an account of them, but 'twas nothing but the account of his miserable feelings" (p. 116). Inveterate ironist that he was, Sterne did not unequivocally support Yorick's claim to sentimental heroism in *A Sentimental Journey*. Yet he did concentrate more on the pleasures of his sentimental hobby horse. Yorick's relative isolation during his travels precludes the steady counterimposition of other hobby horses (Slop's Catholicism; Walter's pedantry) that adds up to fugal counterpoint in *Tristram Shandy*.[2] Sensibility is all Yorick and the reader have to go on in *A Sentimental Journey*.

Other writers made even stronger cases for the distorted viewpoints of their heroes. What is *Werther* but "the account of [the narrator's] miserable feelings," rendered convincing by Goethe's astonishing force of description? In a conversation recorded by Eckermann about the popularity of *Werther*, Goethe explained why people were moved by the sorrows of his hero:

> The much talked about "age of Werther," is not, strictly speaking, a mere historical event. It belongs to the life of every individual who must accommodate himself and his innate and instinctive sense of free-dom to the irksome restrictions of an obsolescent world. Happiness un-attained, ambition unfulfilled, desires unjustified are the defects not of any particular age, but of every individual human being.[3]

This eighteenth-century intimation of "Civilization and Its Discon-tents" is founded on the characteristic assumption of the age of sen-sibility that all are prone to view the social world as "obsolescent" (*veralteten*).[4] Sentimental protagonists like Werther define their hero-ism by the extent of their alienation. It is literally how they know themselves.

This new sentimental heroism was inner, not social. As with *Clar-issa*, *The Man of Feeling*, and most other novels of sensibility, *Werther* ended by describing the hero's death. To sentimental heroes, death was the only suitable climax to their sense of alienation. To choose death—or, in Clarissa's and Harley's cases, to meet it halfway—was to judge the world inadequate to the demands of selfhood. The "self" asserted in *Clarissa* has been earned, while Harley's is perhaps gratuitous; but for both, to die is to avenge the past and to transcend the "irksome restrictions" of society.

Goethe was aware of the morbid self-preoccupation that caused his hero's discontent with life. Pathological metaphors pervade even the early letters in *Werther;* from the beginning, Werther "treats his heart like a sick child" (p. 5). Schiller, whose brilliant analysis of sentimen-tality will be discussed in chapter 7, said of Werther's self-destructive chemistry:

> [He is] a personality who embraces the ideal with burning feeling and abandons actuality in order to contend with an insubstantial infinitude, who seeks continuously outside himself for that which he continuously destroys within himself, to whom only his dreams are the real, . . . who in the end sees in his own existence only a limitation, and, as is reason-able, tears this down in order to penetrate to the true reality—this dan-gerous extreme of the sentimental personality [has become Goethe's theme in *Werther*].[5]

In all literature, but especially in tragedy, characters who are too aggressive in defying social norms end by destroying themselves. During the sentimental era, readers and authors viewed this unbending defiance and eventual destruction as "reasonable," to use Schiller's expression. So the sentimental audience was not purged by observing Werther's death. On the contrary, the hero's discontent was supposed to sharpen the reader's alienation—to encourage him to make his own stand against the inexorable way of the world. Several *Werther* enthusiasts staged their own suicides to show how much the book meant to them. These sentimental martyrs asserted an "individual" will based on literal imitation of their hero Werther—an example of the paradoxical behavior encouraged by the cult of feeling.

The social alienation of sentimental protagonists stems from their essential commitment to their individual laws, their "own peculiar Madness." All action progresses from a private code, a hobby horse viewed unironically. In one sentimental best-seller, *Zeluco* (1786) by Dr. John Moore (the same Dr. Moore to whom Burns addressed his autobiographical letter), the principle of the protagonist's conduct is even lack of principle. In a foreword to this novel, Anna Barbauld complained: "The work is formed on the singular plan of presenting a hero of the story, if hero he may be called, who is a finished model of depravity. Zeluco is painted as radically vicious."[6] Zeluco is radically vicious, Smelfungus radically cranky, Harley radically aimless, and Werther (to borrow from Johnson) radically wretched. Schiller said of such one-dimensional concepts of self that "a continuous tendency to this . . . must, at the last, necessarily enervate the character and depress it into a condition of passivity out of which no reality at all can proceed, either for the inner [or] the external life."[7]

Ironically, this enervation of character encouraged by the cult of feeling was represented at the stylistic level by a rhetoric of aggression taken from John Milton. The sentimental hero, who often seems patterned after Milton's Satan, continually tests the declared boundaries of the "norm." Sentimental heroes consistently prefer ruling in the hell generated by their self-will to serving in a society upheld by a consensus of the vulgar, the timid, the law-abiding. Even before this theme emerged in fiction, the midcentury poets who emulated Milton had described the perilous relationship of self-expression to social alienation and eventual self-destruction. In "Ode to Fear" (1743), Collins had seen that the energy he wanted for his work was inextricably connected to insanity, yet still accepted this burden of wild energy—no matter what destiny it required him to follow.

One reason Collins's breakdown was widely publicized was that it seemed a consequence of the boundless energy he idealized in his poems. Many contemporary readers reacted against the vogue for sentimental heroes, fearing or mocking the extremes of self-expression they advocated. (Many of Johnson's literary judgments, as well as Jeffrey's condemnation of Burns's admiration of "thoughtlessness," show this reaction against sentimental attitudes.) Even in the heyday of Mackenzie's success, a portion of the literary public found *The Man of Feeling* hilarious rather than moving, and the resounding success of decadent *Werther* elicited perhaps as many scornful parodies as denunciations from the pulpit. Indeed, Goethe himself wrote several parodies of the novel. In one, a pilgrim to Werther's grave relieves himself on that hallowed turf, a concession to biological imperatives over sentimental awe reminiscent of an earlier literary epoch—for instance, of Pope's rude sequel to his worshipful praise of *Cato*, the burlesque "To a Lady who P——st At the Tragedy of *Cato*." Every literary triumph contains elements that make it vulnerable to parody, even within the mind of its own creator.

By the same token, every literary movement contains within itself the modalities which animate discussion of its merit and lead eventually to attacks on its supremacy. Diderot's *Rameau's Nephew* documents the polarization between feeling and doing which characterized—and to many minds, including Diderot's, undercut—the cult of sensibility. In a central episode the nephew performs a violin solo accompanied by soulful facial contortions, graceful arm movements, and virtuoso fingering. His performance is distinguished by every accessory to musical excellence except the one essential thing: the violin itself. This pantomime solo brings music to mind but refuses to translate allusion into sound. The nephew thus refuses to offer his performance up for common judgment.

Hannah More thought such sentimental egotism sacrificed substance for mere gesture: in feeling, she said, religion was reduced to "benevolence and benevolence to almsgiving."[8] During the late eighteenth century even incidental conversations such as those preserved in Boswell's journals show the vigor with which the comparative merits of feeling were debated at this time. James Macpherson, irritated by Gray's vindication of country folk in "Elegy in a Country Churchyard," snorted, "Hoot! . . . To write panegyrics upon a parcel of damned rascals that *did* nothing but plough the land and saw corn."[9] Gray's assertion of the significance of rustic obscurity seemed to Ossian to ask too much of readers: peasants were too ordinary in themselves to merit the extraordinary sympathy offered by the poem. (Macpherson evidently had not seen the central disunity in the "Elegy" between the rustic virtues overtly praised and the elegant self-absorption actually practiced by the doomed speaker in that poem.) In his own poetry, Macpherson was much more literal-minded than Gray. If he wanted a rhapsodic response from his readers he gave them rhapsodic characters in a wild, exotic setting. Indeed, Gray's public (with the notable exception of Johnson) was more apt to praise his sublime Pindarics than his many-leveled "Elegy." Boswell once told Goldsmith, "Well, I admire Gray prodigiously. I have read his odes till I was almost mad."[10]

Young Boswell followed the sentimental fashion in sharing Gray's rhapsodies almost to the point of taking on their ecstatic transport. Another contemporary, Christopher Smart (who will be discussed more fully in chapter 8), went beyond fashion and into clinical obsession in his pursuit of duty to a private God. The intellectual direction of the cult of sensibility was to exert individual pressure on the conventions of society, the boundaries of literary form: to get rid of the actual violin when it began to limit rather than amplify one's message. Or, to use Samuel Johnson's masterful summary of what made Dryden both erratic and superb: "to tread upon the brink of meaning, where light and darkness begin to mingle; to approach the precipice of absurdity, and hover over the abyss of unideal vacancy."[11] Johnson's remarks, though on a far from sentimental poet, apply a distinctly late-century perspective to Dryden's achievement. Johnson was no "man of feeling," but even he thought that consistency of formal control was not the main ingredient in great poetry.

Shaftesbury, with his definition of "natural and kind affection" as "the very principle of virtue,"[12] was an early spokesman for the systematic legitimization of individual impulse that was to dominate literature by the late eighteenth century. Writers of the generation born around the midcentury developed their own ways of showing the heroic dimensions of individual instinct; but this message—and an undermining of social conventions and norms that went along with it—was their common concern. Where this influence led its adherents varied. The sentimental mode could be brilliantly self-expressive (Boswell's journals) or shamelessly self-indulgent (the suicides of *Werther* enthusiasts). The importance to Burns of this elevation of private impulse was that it helped to build his confidence as a young poet. He was a poor man and a poor man's son, but a social disadvantage like poverty actually counted as a positive factor in the sentimental calculus. He would never be a "man of the world," but his early reading showed him that he could be proud of this separation from conventional status. To be outside social norms was the first requirement for heroism in the sentimental mode. The age of feeling supported the early writings of Burns when it evolved a definition of heroic genius that did not necessarily exclude him.

IN HIS AUTOBIOGRAPHICAL LETTER to Dr. John Moore, Burns revealed that most of his sentimental reading was done in late adolescence and that his education was capped at age twenty-three with *Tristram Shandy* and *The Man of Feeling,* his "bosom favorites."[13] *Rameau's Nephew* excepted, all the novels discussed in this chapter were read by Burns during those years.[14] Emulating the sentimental writers he admired, Burns began to cultivate his individual law, his "own peculiar Madness." In imitation of many sentimental heroes, he began to assume a satanic persona in his letters, an affectation that was to persist throughout his life. In 1787, he wrote: "I have bought a pocket Milton, which I carry perpetually about with me, in order to study the sentiments—the dauntless magnanimity; the intrepid unyielding independance; the desperate daring, and noble defiance of hardship, in that great personage, Satan" (*Letters,* 1:96–97). Like other contemporaries, including Blake, Burns rejected the conventional view of Satan as the embodiment of evil, preferring to study him as a spectacular example of sentimental alienation—he admired Milton's dramatic portrait of "the wild, broken fragments of a noble, exalted mind in ruins" (1:156).

Burns's poorest work has often been ascribed to sentimental excesses. If it be acknowledged, however, that failures like "The Vision" result from too literal an imitation of other writers, it could be said that the problem in such bad work is that Burns is not sentimental enough. In the first letter quoted above, Burns dwells on Satan's defiance of hardship rather than directly informing his correspondent of the nature of his own discontents. By such maneuvers, Burns evades self-expression at the same time that he asserts alienation. Similarly, in poems like "The Vision," he alludes to his passionate nature instead of showing it in action and announces that he is treading the brink of meaning when he is actually working with a net. When Burns imitates too closely, he fails to follow the "bent" of his own peculiar madness. To thus invoke consensus from a public is in fact to betray sentimentalism.

The differences between Gray's "Elegy" and the poems of "Ossian" have been mentioned above: their different approaches to sensibility correspond to the good and bad sides of the sentimental Burns. In his "Elegy" Gray takes the risk of exalting an ordinary group of peasants. The credit for the transcendence achieved by the poem goes wholly to Gray's transforming sensibility, which converts all those dead villagers into meaningful presences. In "Ossian," on the other hand, sensibility is the equal province of the author, audience, speakers, and "plot." Sensibility in "Ossian" is not allowed to settle: as Northrop Frye has noted, it is rather "diffused" throughout the Ossianic world. In Gray's "Elegy," emotion is just as important, but we never forget that one speaker's personal responses have originated these emotions. Feelings are concentrated in one speaker and ultimately are focused on that speaker's fate. This concentration makes the feelings seem both more finite and more real.

Burns's weaker work is like "Ossian's." He sets up an unvaryingly high pitch of feeling, and then casts about for images deep or vague enough to fulfill his transcendent design; it is in these Ossianic moods that Burns is most likely to recycle the transcendent images of some admired predecessor. In his better early poems, Burns is more like Gray in the "Elegy." A self-conscious poet trained in the sentimental mode and thus preoccupied with the imposition of his feelings on some convenient object, he nonetheless asserts those feelings gradually, taking up his subject in a casual way and ultimately infusing it with a private resonance. Burns's transforming sensibility, which makes beggars seem heroic and lice seem attractive, is the primary force to which readers respond in his good early work. This is not descriptive poetry; we do not so much focus on the objects themselves as on the originality and sensitivity with which the poet is making them palatable, then appealing, then instructive. Burns is at his best, then, when his talent for responding to things is all the reader can see between a humble, even depressing, subject and the existence of a fine poem. When Burns abandons the search for an appropriate personal voice and relies too much on sentimental models, he retards a reader's perception of his feelings.

Finally, it was the sentimental movement that freed writers, including Burns, to exploit their own peculiar madness. The cult of feeling encouraged poets to seize any means that could be used to elucidate their private feelings. Blake, whose early work I classify as sentimental, thought that even a grain of sand held a world of possibilities for the true poet. The sentimental movement encouraged (indeed, required) a reckless self-reliance. Burns once wrote that his notion of the merit of his poetry was settled during his midtwenties, before he had published or even widely circulated his work. It is no coincidence that this self-confidence was fixed during the time when he was most absorbed in sentimental reading.

Political liberalism and religious tolerance were among the other features of sentimentality that appealed to Burns. When he attacked righteousness there were more than local butts like Holy Willie to inspire him. Moore's *Zeluco* and Goethe's *Werther* were among the sentimental novels that encouraged Burns in his polemics. Indeed, these freer values were in the air throughout Scotland during the 1780's: Burns's attribution of virtue to frigidity in "Address to the Unco Guid" (1784–85) anticipates such passages in *Zeluco* (1789) as the following: "She was chaste, without being virtuous; because in her it proceeded from constitution, not principle. . . . She walked through life erect and steady to the dictates of decorum and self-interest, without slip or false step" (p. 8). In *Werther,* too, the narrator perceives in stability of purpose and deference to social convention only a constitutional coldness: "You moral creatures, so calm and so righteous! You abhor the drunken man, and detest the eccentric: you pass by like the Levite, and thank God, like the Pharisee, that you are not like one of them. I have been drunk more than once; my passions have always bordered on madness" (p. 48).

Even the poetry of Shenstone, whose influence on Burns has been universally deplored, served some purpose in supporting Burns's developing values. Burns's "On the Death of Sir J. Hunter Blair," his effort to reproduce Shenstone's elegiac diction, has always been taken by critics as sufficient proof that Shenstone passed on nothing of value to Burns. Yet underlying Shenstone's turgid diction was a value system Burns must have found particularly congenial in its elevation of friendship, tolerance, and freedom. Even a superficial reading of Shenstone's elegies turns up sentimental attitudes that Burns adapted to good purpose. The following lines from Elegy IX, for instance, seem to have suggested the train of images in Burns's first epistle to John Lapraik (quoted in chapter 3):

> Scorn'd be the wretch that quits his genial bowl,
> His loves, his friendships, e'en his self resigns;
> Perverts the sacred instinct of his soul,
> And to a ducat's dirty sphere confines.[15]

In Burns's lines we saw the same image of the "genial bowl," the same idea that pursuit of money indicates a perversion of the "sacred instinct of the soul," the same dialectic separation of good fellows from arid achievers.

In Elegy I, Shenstone's advice to poets also provided Burns with a suggestive metaphor: "Write from thy bosom—let not art control / The ready pen, that makes his edicts known" (p. 2). Burns converted this prose into poetry when he wrote: "Gie me ae spark o' Nature's Fire," and certainly his line far surpasses Shenstone's. (Certainly, too, there are other literary sources, including *Tristram Shandy*, for this sentiment.) But it is important to see that when Burns wrote in admiration of impulse and condemned the cultivation of artifice, he was defending a sentimental principle, not, like Sillar in the preface to his *Poems*, displaying himself as a sui generis phenomenon.

Burns saw in Shenstone a kindred spirit who held money in contempt and friendship in reverence. This "kinship" was illusory, of course, for Shenstone, writing in gentlemanly retirement at Leasowes, was only playing Horace when he criticized money; not, like Burns, being hounded from farm to ruinous farm. But the confidence of Burns's early work seems grounded in his assumption that behind him were a number of well-considered writers like Shenstone. Those liberal-minded thinkers helped to compensate for the conservative factions that dominated Burns's own locality.[16] Their beneficial influence on Burns, then, was more a matter of moral support than literary style. Generally speaking, Burns's praise of other writers tends to focus on them as brothers in feeling rather than masters in style. Though Burns read and enjoyed Smollett's novels, for instance, it was the abysmal "Ode to Independence" that he was fond of quoting in his letters:

> Thy spirit, Independance, let me share;
> Lord of the lion-heart, & eagle-eye!
> Thy steps I follow with my bosom bare,
> And brave each blast that sails along the sky![17]

That a master technician like Burns treasured such verses shows not his incomprehension of the subtle possibilities of English diction but the supportive and compensatory role performed by his reading.[18]

THOUGH RELIGIOUS TOPICALITY had seemed to Mauchline and southwest Scotland the most striking feature of Burns's first collection, it was his relevance to contemporary literature and his posture as sentimental hero that attracted the attention of Edinburgh intellectuals. Hugh Blair, the defender of "Ossian," whose lectures praised Shenstone at the expense of Johnson,[19] and Henry Mackenzie, who was still known locally as the "man of feeling" in deference to a bestseller written fifteen years earlier, were both enthusiastic about Burns's poems. This is not surprising: Burns's poems offered in a striking new form variations on sentimental themes that Blair and Mackenzie had helped to bring into fashion. The only poem Mackenzie quoted in full in his review of the Kilmarnock edition was the lachrymose "To a Mountain Daisy," one of the most Mackenzian poems Burns ever wrote. [20]

The chapters that follow will discuss the change in Burns's poems after his residence in Edinburgh; how, from late 1786 (the year of his first winter in the capital) and 1787 (the year of his tours of the Border and Highlands) Burns stopped writing the poems of direct address, vernacular epistles, and satires discussed in these chapters to concentrate instead on the revision of old Scots songs.

Generally speaking, I propose that when Burns encountered large numbers of admirers who not only agreed with his transcendent value for feelings but tried to compete with him on that basis, his writing lost the compensatory function it had served at Mossgiel and took a turn from the polemical to the purely lyrical. After Edinburgh, Burns continued to express the values of his sentimental education; and he kept his sense of alienation—his difficult position in society ensured that. But he ceased to value a benevolist pose as he had in his younger days. His Edinburgh experiences demonstrated to Burns's satisfaction that a coterie of the sentimental was no more likely to be admirable than a coterie of the rigidly righteous. From Edinburgh on, Burns separated himself from theories of merit, sentimental or otherwise, and organized his songs instead around a pragmatic description of the infinite shapes emotions could give to experience. He progressed from the implicit self-justification of poems like "The Vision" and "Love and Liberty" to the non-justifying and therefore less self-serving humaneness of "Tam o' Shanter" and the songs.

II

Burns at Edinburgh

And when proud Fortune's ebbing tide recedes,
And when it leaves me no unshaken friend,
Shall I not weep that e'er I left the meads,
Which oaks embosom, and which hills defend?
William Shenstone, Elegy VII

5

The Sentimental Critics

Seven years before Henry Mackenzie began his *Lounger* essay on Robert Burns with a discussion of the "divinity of genius,"[1] another peasant poet, Michael Bruce, had been praised in glowing terms in an earlier Edinburgh periodical, *The Mirror*.[2] A comparison of these essays in sentimental criticism may suggest how men of feeling extended patronage to admired poets and what factors in poems and poets stimulated this sentimental response.

Both periodicals were projects of the Mirror Club, an organization of influential lawyers and current Lords of Session whose literary activities were dominated by Mackenzie—also a lawyer, though better known as the author of *The Man of Feeling*. Both *The Mirror* (January 1779–May 1780) and *The Lounger* (February 1785–January 1787) were conceived as disseminators of cosmopolitan values in Edinburgh and throughout northern Britain, much as *The Spectator* had been for an earlier generation of readers in London and beyond.[3] Indeed, the most significant addition made by these periodicals to the canon of urbane virtues established by Steele and Addison can be seen in their essays on Bruce and Burns. These essays presented a new challenge to the person of culture, who not only had to be cosmopolitan and well-informed in the manner of *The Spectator*, but also highly responsive and benevolent. The vindication of neglected merit was the new, sentimental enterprise of the essayist and his public. The critic presented the claims of talent emanating from a rustic, obscure setting, and readers were expected to concede both the merit of the poet and—no less important—the virtuosity of the critic who had unearthed him. The quality of the poet's work was peripheral to this transaction between critic and reader, as peripheral as mad Maria in the relationship between Yorick and his readers in *A Sentimental Journey*. A poet's suffering, not a poet's work, was the basis of his attraction

59

for the critic—the factor that allowed both critics and the literary public to exercise their own benevolent natures.

In *A Sentimental Journey,* Yorick refuses the supplication of a mendicant monk but later, when there is an attractive female witness, becomes the monk's effusive benefactor. There is much of Yorick's combination of shame, atonement, pleasure in being observed in the exercise of benevolence, and complacent admiration of his own good feelings in the *Mirror* and *Lounger* essays that present Bruce and Burns as humble poets not unworthy of polite notice. That the genius of these men emanated from unglamorous and unlikely settings only gave more credit to their sentimental benefactors, who had penetrated the mean disguise of circumstance to find authentic merit.

Michael Bruce's is the first case in point. The major difference between Burns and Bruce was that Bruce was dead when the critics discovered his merits: the poems in question had been in print for nine years. The tendency of sentimental benevolence to perceive subjects as objects has been discussed in chapter 1: let it only be noted here that a late poet was more easily objectified than a live one. The author of the piece on Bruce could give fuller rein to sentimental fantasy since his subject could offer no resistance to sentimental amplification.

William Craig, author of the *Mirror* piece, was a friend of Mackenzie and an important man of affairs in Edinburgh. As one of the Lords of Session he wielded considerable personal power. His essay on Bruce, however, presents an unworldly persona, combining the gentle exploitation of pathetic detail that characterizes sentimental Sterne with the elegiac regard for disintegrating relics that preoccupies Harley in *The Man of Feeling.* The *Mirror* issue for 29 May 1779 begins with an epigraph from Gray's "Elegy" ("Some mute inglorious *Milton* here may rest") and advances by easy stages into rapt benevolist fantasy:

> For my own part, I never pass the place (a little hamlet skirted with a circle of old ash-trees, about three miles on this side of *Kinross*) where *Michael Bruce* resided; I never look on his dwelling,—a small thatched house, distinguished from the cottages of the other inhabitants only by a *sashed window* at the end, instead of a *lattice,* fringed with a *honey-suckle* plant, which the poor youth had trained around it;—I never find myself in that spot, but I stop my horse involuntarily;—and, looking on the window which the honey-suckle has now almost covered, in the dream of the moment I picture out a figure for the gentle tenant of the man-

sion; I wish, and my heart swells while I do so, that he were alive, and that I were a great man to have the luxury of visiting him there, and bidding him be happy. I cannot carry my readers thither; but, that they may share some of my feelings, I will present them with an extract from the last poem in the little volume before me, which from its subject, and the manner in which it is written, cannot fail of touching the heart of every one who reads it.[4]

Craig's reason for writing on Bruce is said to be so that readers "may share some of my feelings." His assumption seems to be that no reader can achieve the full response that Craig reserves for himself.

Adam Smith's *Theory of Moral Sentiments* (1759), a treatise on self-interest, benevolence, and society that was particularly influential in Scotland (Burns quoted from it in his *First Commonplace Book*), suggests one explanation for Craig's assumption that only a fraction of his feelings about Bruce could be shared by his readers:

Mankind, though naturally sympathetic, never conceive, for what has befallen another, that degree of passion which naturally animates the person principally concerned. That imaginary change of situation, upon which their sympathy is founded, is but momentary. . . . the thought that they themselves are not really the sufferers, continually intrudes itself upon them; and though it does not hinder them from conceiving a passion somewhat analogous to what is felt by the sufferer, hinders them from conceiving any thing that approaches to the same degree of violence. The person principally concerned is sensible of this, and at the same time passionately desires a more complete sympathy. He longs for . . . the entire concord of the affections of the spectators with his own. . . . But he can only hope to attain this by lowering his passion to that pitch, in which the spectators are capable of going along with him.[5]

Smith is discussing the social discomfort produced by individual grief; but his emphasis on the calculus of suffering—the efforts of the "person principally concerned" to modulate his expression of distress in order to stimulate concord among less involved spectators—captures perfectly the relationship between Craig, as the elegist for Bruce, and his readers.

In the *Mirror* essay, Craig, not Bruce, is the "concerned" person. Craig's feelings of frustrated benevolence, his manipulation of pathetic details like the honey-suckle, and his pensive musings are central in this passage. "I wish, and my heart swells while I do so, that he were alive." The amplification in the sentence pertains to Craig's swelling heart, not to the object of its pangs. Nonpathetic details of Bruce's life are omitted to facilitate the desired dolorous "concord." And, like Smith's principal actor in the passage from *The Theory of Moral Sentiments*, Craig assumes the lesser absorption of his readers in his subject but is determined to produce "somewhat analogous" elegiac feelings within them. Mercilessly, he milks the pathos of Bruce's early death:

> A young man of genius, in a deep consumption at the age of twenty-one, feeling himself every moment going faster to decline, is an object sufficiently interesting; but how much must every feeling on the occasion be heightened, when we know that this person possessed so much dignity and composure of mind as not only to contemplate his approaching fate, but even to write a poem on the subject!
>
> In the *French* language there is a much admired poem of the *Abbé de Chaulieu*, written in expectation of his own death. . . . *Michael Bruce*, who, it is probable, never heard of the *Abbé de Chaulieu*, has also written a poem on his own approaching death; with the latter part of which I shall conclude this paper. (*British Essayists*, 34:188–89)

This unmistakably sentimental mixture of compassion and self-congratulation would also characterize the critical reception of Robert Burns; though Burns, as I have said, was a living poet and potentially more resistant.

Craig's account of Bruce suppressed several details that would have done Bruce credit but which, in introducing admiration as a variant emotional response, also would have lessened the pathos of the essay. Craig presents him as a cottager who "never heard of the *Abbé de Chaulieu*"—implying that Bruce had been uneducated. In fact, though the son of a weaver, Bruce had been a precocious village scholar, and a small legacy received by his father had allowed him three terms of attendance at Edinburgh University. He had corresponded in Latin with his university friends and he probably had some exposure to modern languages as well. He had been a schoolmaster at Gairney Bridge while studying for the ministry. Bruce, in short, had worked hard to prize himself out of a rustic context, but Craig's essay works even harder to keep him in his victim's place.

In a similar way, Mackenzie's *Lounger* essay on Burns would paint its subject as a "Heaven-taught ploughman," emphasizing Burns's low social status so heavily that the competence of the poems begins to seem not so much admirable as miraculous. In fact, Burns was a tenant farmer, not a ploughman: a rent-payer, not a wage-earner. William Burnes (or Burness), the poet's father and (as Carlyle notes in his *Essay on Burns*) a remarkable man in his own right, did without needed extra income when he refused to hire his children out as laborers on other men's farms; poor as he was, he paid a schoolmaster to educate his children in his home.[6] Similarly, Bruce's father had spent a legacy to send his son to a university. Nonetheless, sentimental critics wrote of pathetic struggle, not achievement, when they wrote of peasant poets. The more necessary they felt to the success of the peasant poet's work, the better they felt. And yet the more creative the effort of the sentimental critic to bring about public support, the less real the poet became. Real people do not exhibit the consistency of dejection that Craig applied to terminal Bruce, any more than they snatch poems out of the rustic ozone—Mackenzie's theory of Burns's work. But the real poets were pawns sacrificed early in these sentimental games.

In a letter written in 1779 to his cousin Elizabeth Rose, Mackenzie transcribed the first draft of an elegy on Bruce. The egotism of the sentimental patron in this piece surpasses even the *Mirror* essay:

> Could this be mine, a Poet's decent pride
> To scorn the meanness of a titled name,
> To cast the pageants of the world aside
> And lead the blushing Virtues up to fame!
>
> Alas! to me hath Heaven denied the power
> Thus drooping worth with bounteous hand to cheer;
> Yet may I give them from my little store
> A verse to honour, to embalm, a tear.[7]

Heaven, though, was only biding its time. "Drooping worth," in the unlikely shape of Robert Burns, was waiting in the wings and would soon claim Mackenzie's—and Edinburgh's—support.

Both Craig's and Mackenzie's praise of Bruce shows one side of sentimental patronage—its eager championship of lost causes. As Burns's reception would show, however, where more substantial claims were made on the sympathies of the critics, praise was more guarded and patronage less cheerfully extended. Like a suddenly calculating Yorick weighing the comparative wretchedness of beggars, the sentimental critics hesitated before giving their approval to a living poet. Some months before Burns's first collection appeared, Mackenzie, departing from the benevolism of the elegy for Bruce, wrote a piece for *The Lounger* that says more realistic and far more skeptical things about patronage and native genius. In the paper for 6 May 1786, he outlines the hazards to social peace that a living genius represents. Men of superior talent, he notes, have a tendency to be unruly:

> Where genius is . . . found to languish in obscurity, or to pine in indigence, the world is not always to be blamed for its neglect. . . . Temper, moderation, and humility, a toleration of folly, and an attention to trifles, are endowments necessary in the commerce with mankind; often as useful, and generally more attractive, than wisdom, learning, eloquence, or wit, when attended with arrogance, ill-nature, an ungracious manner, or a forbidding address. (*British Essayists*, 37:93)

Boswell and a friend had once joked about "the style of genteel company. We agreed in calling it a *consensual obliteration of the human faculties*."[8] Boswell was demonstrating his usual acute ear for contemporary rhythms, and his witticism makes ironic a notion about society that Mackenzie's essay takes quite seriously. Society requires concord, and mediocre people are more likely to contribute to concord than people of great abilities, who will naturally want to exercise them and thus disrupt the ease of others.

So when Burns's Kilmarnock edition of *Poems, Chiefly in the Scottish Dialect* came to the attention of Mackenzie, the Man of Feeling was confronted with a paradoxical challenge. On the one hand, this peasant's work was brilliant, and genius in obscure situations called for his active patronage. It was Mackenzie's responsibility as a sentimental spokesman to be feelingly alive to the least likely sources of inspiration. On the other hand, who was Robert Burns?[9] It was rumored that he had just moved to Edinburgh. Would his undoubted "endowments" be accompanied by "arrogance, ill-nature, an ungracious manner, or a forbidding address"? Mackenzie's prophetic anxiety about disruptive genius undercuts his praise of Burns in the *Lounger* review and was shared by other Edinburgh literati whose reactions will soon be discussed. Those who concentrated on Burns's former poverty and obscurity hailed him with less reserve than those who wrote about his present fame and residence in Edinburgh. Both the enthusiastic and the skeptical modes of response were essentially sentimental, and both were present in Mackenzie's essay in *The Lounger* for 9 December 1786.

This essay is more concerned with the poems of Burns than Craig's had been with the work of Bruce, but it begins with a sentimental meditation that corresponds to Craig's opening gambit in *The Mirror* for 29 May 1776. Craig's essay began: "Nothing has a greater tendency to elevate and affect the heart than the reflection upon those personages who have performed a distinguished part on the theatre of life, whose actions were attended with important consequences to the world around them, or whose writings have animated or instructed mankind" (34:186). Mackenzie's review of Burns begins in a similar way. He stresses the pleasurable reverie genius produces in the mind of a spectator: "To the feeling and susceptible there is something wonderfully pleasing in the contemplation of genius" (37:300). Genius is to be welcomed for its utility to onlookers. Mackenzie continues: "In the view of highly superior talents, as in that of great and stupendous natural objects, there is a sublimity which fills the soul with wonder and delight. . . . investing our nature with extraordinary powers and extraordinary honours, interests our curiosity and flatters our pride."

The main function of genius, then, is to "flatter the pride" of the nongenius, who is reminded of the range of human capabilities by the brilliant achievement on which he meditates. But Mackenzie continues his preparation for discussion of Burns by noting that the public resists the acknowledgment of living geniuses:

> This divinity of genius, however, . . . is best arrayed in the darkness of distant and remote periods, and is not easily acknowledged in the present times, or in places with which we are perfectly acquainted. . . . There is a familiarity in the near approach of persons around us, not very consistent with the lofty ideas we wish to form of him who has led captive our imagination in the triumph of his fancy, overpowered our feelings with the tide of passion, or enlightened our reason with the investigation of hidden truths. (37:295–96)

The existence of a living genius is not "easily acknowledged," because the sentimental mind resists distraction from its self-absorption: "familiarity" with the genius in question interferes with the "ideas" the sentimental public "wish to form" about him. The relationship of a genius to his public is, then, a power struggle in which his sensibility has "overpowered" his public, "led captive" their imaginations, and triumphed over them by virtue of his superior sensitivity. Art is a battlefield on which only an author both strong and strategic can win over his readers. Mackenzie is shrewd in noting that strategic power is heightened by the antiquity of a poet (he is probably thinking of "Ossian").

Mackenzie's essay in *The Lounger,* having stated this competitive relationship between genius and reader, then warns of the danger of awarding honor to poseurs, poets whose assertions of creative dominance take in the public for a while, but whose claims do not hold up:

> We have had repeated instances of painters and of poets, who have been drawn from obscure situations, and held forth to public notice and applause by the extravagant encomiums of their introductors, yet in a short time have sunk again to their former obscurity; whose merit, though perhaps somewhat neglected, did not appear to have been much undervalued by the world, and could not support, by its own intrinsic excellence, that superior place which the enthusiasm of its patrons would have assigned it.
>
> I know not if I shall be accused of such enthusiasm and such partiality, when I introduce to the notice of my readers a poet of our own country, with whose writings I have recently become acquainted; but if I am not greatly deceived, I think I may safely pronounce him a genius of no ordinary rank. The person to whom I allude is ROBERT BURNS, an *Ayrshire* ploughman. (37:301)

In the three long introductory paragraphs that have led to the naming of Burns as his subject, Mackenzie has discussed primarily the pleasures and perils of patronage. Even in the paragraph that introduces Burns, Mackenzie's attention is devoted largely to vindication of his own taste. He hopes that he can "safely pronounce" Burns "a genius of no ordinary rank," if he is not "greatly deceived"—presumably by the wiles of the poet himself, whose adversarial relationship to the critic and the public has already been emphasized.

For a man who prided himself on his responsiveness to rising talent, Mackenzie hails Burns with a quite gingerly attention. Reservations about the man have made him cautious. Mackenzie warms to his subject considerably when he begins to quote from the poems: he praises their "uncommon penetration" and, in a section deleted after Burns's fall from public favor, objects to charges that Burns's poems are irreligious, preferring to call the satires justified attacks on rural fanaticism. But his attitude toward Burns as a person remains contradictory. His extension of patronage to Burns, for instance (and it was this review that launched Burns in fashionable society), concludes with a request that somebody come forth as his patron: "To repair the wrongs of suffering or neglected merit; to call forth genius from the obscurity in which it had pined indignant; and place it where it may profit or delight the world, these are exertions that give to wealth an enviable superiority, to greatness and to patronage a laudable pride" (37:307). Mackenzie cleverly evades the challenge of Burns's residence in Edinburgh: he praises the poet, but passes on to others the responsibility for maintaining support.

A slippery evasion of definitive support for Burns generally characterized the critical reaction to his first volume. Mackenzie's *Lounger* essay, self-serving as it was, still seems the warmest and best-informed of the early reviews. James Anderson's piece in *The Monthly Magazine* for December 1786 is enthusiastic but concludes with the advice that Burns abandon traditional Scots verse forms—counsel that shows how little the poems can have been appreciated on their own merits. Anderson wanted to groom Burns as a model poet: in Mackenzie's terms, Anderson resisted the excellence of the poems themselves, holding out for a closer approximation of Burns's work to his own standards:

> The modern ear will be somewhat disgusted with the measure of many of these pieces, which is faithfully copied from that which was most in fashion among the ancient Scottish bards; but hath been, we think with good reason, laid aside by later Poets. . . . But if ever [Burns] . . . should think of offering any thing more to the Public, we are of opinion his performances would be more highly valued were they written in measures less antiquated. The few Songs, Odes, Dirges, &c. in this collection, are very poor in comparison of the other pieces. The Author's mind is not sufficiently stored with brilliant ideas to succeed in that line. (Low, *The Critical Heritage*, p. 74)

Such interjections as "we think with good reason" and "we are of opinion" show Anderson in a competitive relationship to his subject. He is more emphatic about the merits of his advice than about the merits of Burns's poems.

John Logan contributed an interesting early review of Burns's first volume to *The English Review*. Writing in London at a safe distance from the scene of the vogue for Burns that had already swept Edinburgh, Logan dismissed the notion that Burns had been "heaven taught," noting that "he is better acquainted with the English poets than most English authors that have come under our review" (p. 77n). Like Mackenzie's, Logan's review is prefaced by a discussion of poseurs; but although Logan accepts this poet as authentic, he cannot resist the temptation to condescend:

> In an age that is satiated with literary pleasures nothing is so grateful to the public taste as novelty. . . . Whatever excites the jaded appetite of an epicure will be prized, and a red herring from Greenock or Dunbar will be reckoned a *Délice*. From this propensity in human nature a musical child, a rhyming milkwoman, a learned pig, or a Russian poet will "strut their hour upon the stage," and gain the applause of the moment. From this cause, and this alone, Stephen Duck, the thresher, and many other *nameless* names have glittered and disappeared like those bubbles of the atmosphere that are called *falling* stars.
>
> Robert Burns, the Ayrshire ploughman, whose Poems are now before us, does not belong to this class of *obscurorum virorum*. Although he is by no means such a poetical prodigy as some of his *malicious* friends have represented, he has a genuine title to the attention and approbation of the public, as a *natural*, though not *legitimate*, son of the muses. (p. 76)

Logan courts the public less than Mackenzie or Anderson. Their taste is mocked, along with the poet's apparent acquiescence to a "heaven taught" posture. Logan is seizing all the status in his essay, putting both Burns and the literary public in their places and forcing his readers to admire his own wit. Interestingly enough, Logan's first literary responsibility had been to publish Bruce's poems posthumously; whereupon he had probably stolen Bruce's three best poems to print later, with improvements but without acknowledgment, as his own work. Plagiarism is one of the possible extremes of literary competitiveness, that equivocal trait so central to the sentimental era.

Critics of all eras, of course, must consider the flaws in a writer's work. But the tendency of the sentimental era was for all people to assume the rectitude of their responses, regardless of their ear for poetry. This was especially true of the response to Burns because the extent of his formal education was generally underestimated. Everybody had a theory about his probable future as a poet, and everybody urged that theory without much tact.

The careless presumption of critical authority is one target of William Blake's satire on polite discourse, written around 1784 and entitled "An Island in the Moon" by his editors. Blake's attack on critical incompetence provides a parallel for Burns's disenchantment with his critics, soon to be discussed. Blake's piece offers a series of interchanges among a group of self-absorbed dilettantes whose discourse reveals their corruption of taste and whose opinionated ignorance is used to mock the complacency of all minor literati:

> Then Sunction Ask'd if Pindar was not a better Poet than Ghiotto was a Painter.
> "Plutarch has not the life of Ghiotto," said Sipsop.
> "No," said Quid, "to be sure, he was an Italian."
> "Well," said Suction, "that is not any proof."
> "Plutarch was a nasty ignorant puppy," said Quid. "I hate your sneaking rascals. There's Aradobo in . . . ten or twelve years will be a far superior genius. . . ."
> "Ah!" said Sipsop, "I only wish Jack Tearguts had had the cutting of Plutarch. He understands anatomy better than any of the Ancients. He'll plunge his knife up to the hilt in a single drive, and thrust his fist in, and all in the space of a Quarter of an hour. He does not mind their crying, tho' they cry ever so. He'll swear at them & keep them down with his fist, & tell them that he'll scrape their bones if they don't lay still & be quiet. What the devil should the people in the hospital that have it done for nothing make such a piece of work for? (*Complete Works*, pp. 49–50)

Blake's mixture of surgical and critical metaphors underscores the bloodthirsty ardor of contemporary critics and the literary public. Writers under discussion in those days were often comparable to charity patients under the knives of impetuous surgeons, and Burns's reception by the sentimental public did suggest in some ways Plutarch's sad treatment at the hands of Jack Tearguts in the passage above. Some of the letters written by residents in Edinburgh that describe Burns's reception suggest the more predatory aspects of the sentimental public's response.

6

Sentimental Civilization and Its Discontents

When Burns came to Edinburgh in 1786 he became an urban phenomenon. It was impossible for the public to champion rustic obscurity in the way that Mackenzie and the other early reviewers had suggested. Almost unanimously, the literati worked out a new approach: praise for Burns's authenticity of manner combined with a warning about the danger of being ruined by the blandishments of civilized life. As though he were a country cheese, they talked about "spoilage." Alison Cockburn, a minor poet, wrote to a friend in December 1786: "The town is at present agog with the ploughman poet, who receives adulation with native dignity, and is the very figure of his profession, strong and coarse, but has a most enthusiastic heart. . . . The man will be spoiled, if he can spoil, but he keeps his simple manners, and is quite sober."[1] Andrew Dalzel, professor of Greek at the university, strikes a similar tone of admiration, but his description is even more class conscious than Cockburn's:

We have got a poet in town just now, whom everybody is taking notice of—a ploughman from Ayrshire—a man of unquestionable genius, who has produced admirable verses, mostly in the Scottish dialect, though some nearly are in English. . . . He runs, however, the risk of being spoiled by the excessive attention paid him just now by persons of all ranks. Those who know him best, say he has too much good sense to allow himself to be spoiled. . . . He behaves wonderfully well; very independent in his sentiments, and has none of the *mauvaise honte* about him, though he is not forward. (Quoted by Snyder, *The Life of Robert Burns*, pp. 196–97)

The possessiveness of Dalzel's account—"We have got a poet . . . whom everybody is taking notice of"—shows the proprietary way in which Burns was "noticed" by these literati. Burns may have been the famous poet, but they were the ones who "had" him. Writing of Burns's season of glory in Edinburgh, Robert Heron, in an erratic but often shrewd early *Memoir* of the poet, noted: "Everyone wondered that the rustic bard was not *spoiled* by so much caressing, favour and flattery as he found: and every one went on to *spoil* him: by continually repeating all these, as if with an obstinate resolution they should, in the end, produce their effect" (Hecht, *Robert Burns,* p. 337).

Discussion of "To a Mouse" in chapter 1 showed the sentimental basis for the attention Burns's speaker devotes to the mouse. The Edinburgh public reacted to Burns as he had reacted to his mouse—with benevolent condescension. He was from a stratum of society which most of them considered infinitely beneath them; the course of his life, they knew, had not run parallel to theirs. Initially, this was all the more reason to flatter and notice him: sentimentality thrived on the egotistical assimilation of out-of-the-way phenomena. To remain in the good graces of the sentimental public, however, Burns would have to remain in the subordinate role which they considered appropriate. Too blatant a servility would be *mauvaise honte* and unbecoming in a poet of genius; but too independent a spirit would also diminish sentimental regard, which wanted to fix its attention on objects lower than eye level. At the beginning of Burns's stay in Edinburgh, his public assumed that he would be grateful to enter the polite world on any terms—even those which required that he always be placed in the role of an inferior. Burns's public would define as spoilage any defiant or aggressive action that spoiled their contemplation of him as an interesting object. Burns was bound eventually to resist this sentimental notice. As Mackenzie said in his *Lounger* essay on Burns, even the most pliable living genius was bound to interfere at some point with the "ideas" his public "wished to form" about him, and Burns was not especially pliable to begin with.

Sentimental scrutiny of the ploughman-poet was focused on his conduct in society. Although virtually every contemporary account of Burns acknowledges his abilities as a poet, descriptions of Burns stress chiefly his behavior to others. Because the literary public viewed his success as a consequence of their notice, which had drawn him out of his low condition in society, they watched him carefully to see how he would react and if he would abuse their indulgence.

Robert Couper (who produced his own vernacular collection in 1804) was coldly dismissive, rather in the vein of Miss Caroline Bingley speaking of Miss Elizabeth Bennet in *Pride and Prejudice:* "He was loquacious and was unable to discriminate between easiness of Manners and something bordering too much on forwardness and coarse familiarity."[2] Other writers, such as Robert Anderson, were as conscious as Couper of Burns's independent manner but judged that this was a good social posture for a man in Burns's unique position somewhere between field hand and man of letters:

> His behaviour was suitable to his appearance: neither awkward, ar-
> rogant, nor affected, but decent, dignified, and simple. In the midst of
> a large company of ladies and gentlemen assembled to see him, and
> attentive to his every look, word, and motion, he was no way discon-
> certed, but seemed perfectly easy, unembarrassed, and unassuming.
> He received me with particular attention, as the editor of the Poems of
> Graeme. (Quoted in Burns, *The Poems and Songs*, 3:1536)

As with the concern for spoilage, this concentration on Burns's social address was produced by the concern of the sentimental public over what effect they were producing on him.

This concern is even more clear in the unanimous verdict of contemporaries that Burns did not pay enough attention to advice. In 1797 the antiquarian Lord Buchan offered two reasons for failing to become a patron of Robert Burns. He had feared that Burns was already overpatronized, and he had not approved of Burns's stubborn adherence to native meters: "when Burns made his first appearance at Edinburgh (where I then was) I rather thought they were spoiling him and clogging the wings of his Muse with too much patronage and festivity. . . . Burns appeared to me a real *Makar* a *Creator* a *Poet* & I wished him to assume the language as well as the character of a Briton & to throw off the masquerade garb of Allan Ramsay, whom, he so greatly surpassed" (letter to James Currie, 14 September 1797, Cowie Collection, Mitchell Library, Glasgow). Buchan's admiration is clear, but what also strikes the modern reader is his assurance that he could claim a superior taste over Robert Burns. The poet's insensibility to the promptings of his public was universally noticed and criticized by his contemporaries:

> He did not endure contradiction with sufficient patience. (Burns, *The Poems and Songs*, 3:1544; quoting Sir Samuel Egerton Brydges)

> If there had been a little more of gentleness and accommodation in his temper, he would, I think, have been still more interesting; but he had been accustomed to give the law in the circle of his ordinary acquaintance, and his dread of anything approaching to meanness or servility, rendered his manner somewhat decided and hard. (3:1534; quoting Dugald Stewart)

> When I asked him whether the Edinburgh Literati had mended his poems by their criticisms, "Sir," said he, "these gentlemen remind me of some spinsters in my country, who spin their thread so fine, that it is neither fit for weft or woof." He said he had not changed a word except one, to please Dr. Blair. (3:1539–40; quoting Ramsay of Ochtertyre)

The observers of Burns assumed that the role the public would play in his life would be major. This explains the careful record they kept of their own effect on him. If his inferiority in this relationship were not also assumed, they would not have insisted so eagerly that he correspond to their own notions of proper behavior and, worse, literary quality. The proprietary nature of their regard is clear in a letter from Hugh Blair to Burns, dated 4 May 1787:

> The success you have met with I do not think is beyond your merits; and if I have had any small hand in contributing to it, it gives me great pleasure. I know no way in which literary persons who are advanced in years can do more service to the world than in forwarding the efforts of rising genius, or bringing forth unknown merit from obscurity. I was the first person who brought out to the notice of the world the poems of Ossian.[3]

This is Shaftesbury's hedonistic benevolence with a vengeance. A pleasurable consciousness of his own role in Burns's success dominates Blair's praise. Such notice from the polite world was possessive and intrusive. In his letter, Blair is mainly concerned with Blair and makes no effort to disguise his self-congratulation even with a little tact. No wonder Burns soon enough became notorious for his refusal to play sentimental games with his admirers. No wonder his Edinburgh commonplace book recorded the following resentful comment on Blair:

> When he descends from his pinnacle and meets me on equal ground, my heart overflows with what is called, *liking:* when he neglects me for the meer carcase of Greatness, or when his eye measures the difference of our points of elevation, I say to myself with scarcely any emotion, what do I care for him or his pomp either? . . . Natural parts like his are frequently to be met with.[4]

Of course, Blair's was not the only eye "measuring the distance" between Burns's creative vantage point and their own more solid social positions. Sentimental notice was dependent on continuous calibration of this sort, and Burns must have encountered a measuring glance a dozen times a day. Even his biographer Robert Heron, a hack writer none too high himself on the ladder of literary or social status, observed of Burns in Edinburgh: "Burns . . . led a life differing from that of his original condition in Ayrshire, almost as widely as differed the scenes and amusements of London, to which OMIAH was introduced, under the patronage of the Earl of SANDWICH, from those to which he had been familiar in the Friendly Isles" (Hecht, *Robert Burns*, p. 336). As Heron was aware, Omiah had contracted smallpox as a result of his association with the English: the brush with sophistication had been fatal.

For all the pleasure they derived from their notice, and for all their flattery, Burns's public feared—while they urged—their effect on him. They wanted to make him conform more to polite notions of creative worth—Buchan, for instance, wanted more neoclassical poetry from him. At the same time, they were afraid of the spoilage which their own influence might induce. Writing after Burns's death, Mackenzie deplored the effects of his celebrity on Burns as a fatal contamination; it seems that Mackenzie lived to regret the effects of a patronage he himself had initiated: "Alas! it was the Patronage and Companionship which Burns obtained, that changed the Colour of his later life; . . . notice . . . flattered his vanity, and in some degree unsettled his religious faith. . . . Dugald Stewart who first introduced him to me, told me latterly, that his Conduct and Manners had become so degraded that decent persons could hardly take any notice of him" (Burns, *The Poems and Songs*, 3:1538). It is hard to avoid forming a suspicion that Burns's conduct after a while must have been calculated to drive off the notice of "decent" people and produce a little peace and privacy for himself. In any case, Mackenzie demonstrates here a sentimental compulsion to seek a pattern of decline in Burns's life. He assumes that when Burns arrived in Edinburgh at age twenty-eight, author of a number of salty and even seditious poems, he was an untouched innocent; exposure to patronage ruined his manners and destroyed his religious faith. In fact, as his poems show, Burns held unorthodox religious views long before he became a literary celebrity.

Still, Burns was not quite the same after being so widely noticed. Egerton Brydges, briefly quoted from earlier, recorded one encounter with Burns that indicates the encroachments of Burns's public and the defenses Burns learned to employ against his self-styled patrons. Brydges describes arriving uninvited at Burns's farm Ellisland a short time after Burns had left Edinburgh and married. Brydges remains wholly unaware of his own intrusion, ascribing Burns's resistance to his presence to the poet's moody temper:

> I was aware he was a person moody and somewhat difficult to deal with. I was resolved to keep in full consideration the irritability of his position in society. . . . On arriving at his humble cottage, Mrs Burns opened the door; she was the plain sort of humble woman she has been described; she ushered me into a neat apartment, and said that she would send for Burns, who was gone for a walk. In about half an hour he came. . . . At first I was not entirely pleased with his countenance. I thought it had a sort of capricious jealousy, as if he was half inclined to treat me as an intruder. I resolved to bear it, and try if I could humour him. I let him choose his turn of conversation. . . . It was now about four in the afternoon of an autumn day. While we were talking, Mrs Burns, as if accustomed to entertain visitors in this way, brought in a bottle of Scotch whisky, and set the table. I accepted this hospitality. I could not help observing the curious glance with which he watched me at the entrance of this signal of homely entertainment. He was satisfied; he filled our glasses: "Here's a health to auld Caledonia!" The fire sparkled in his eye, and mine sympathetically met his. He shook my hand with warmth, and we were friends. (Burns, *The Poems and Songs*, 3:1543–44)

Brydges' description of this encounter shows the influence of sentimental tactics on both Brydges and his object. Brydges, apparently a kind of minor-league Boswell, is determined to create a relationship between himself and Burns and ignores the poet's resistance to his overtures. Also in sentimental fashion, Brydges seems more self-important than kind. "Humble" is used condescendingly twice in his account: once to describe the poet's wife and once to describe his house. Brydges observes the different expressions of Burns's face closely, but files them away in the context he has already concluded upon—poetic moodiness—rather than acknowledging their obvious intention of communicating to him his own unwelcome presence. Brydges relates Burns's ultimate capitulation into friendship as a personal triumph. The defenses of his object have been overborne; he has made contact in spite of his quarry's initial reluctance.

This strategic concept of discourse was characteristic of the sentimental era. Many of the conversations in Boswell's *Life of Johnson* are arranged to show the way colliding individuals attempt to "win" in conversation. The pattern of aggression, resistance, and eventual acquiescence to a friendly interchange is as characteristic of Johnson's meeting with Wilkes as of Brydges' meeting with Burns. In his *London Journal*, Boswell recorded a compliment from a friend that captures perfectly the contemporary notion that skillful participants could manipulate each other into brilliant discourse: "Erskine and I walked down the Haymarket together, throwing out sallies and laughing loud. 'Erskine,' said I, 'don't I make your existence pass more cleverly than anybody?' 'Yes, you do.' 'Don't I make you say more good things?' 'Yes. You extract more out of me, you are more chemical to me, than anybody'" (p. 98).

The difference between the social encounters engineered by James Boswell and those endured by Robert Burns is that Burns's position was so circumscribed by the sentimental disposition of his public to perceive him as an interesting object that he was given little leeway in discourse. In their eagerness to experience Burns as a poet of nature, his admirers ignored Burns's efforts to assert an articulate critical authority. Burns was "chemical" to others because his creative-peasant status was generally intriguing. But others were not chemical to him. Burns expected little from the literati in his later years: what novel traits could they "extract" when the conversation was always structured by the efforts of his admirers to confirm their condescending preconceptions? In this respect, the encounter of Brydges with Burns was typical. Brydges, though initially stating that he "let" Burns "choose" the subjects of discourse, actually limited the range of top-ics: "I carefully avoided topics in which he could not take an active part. Of literary gossip he knew nothing, and therefore I kept aloof from it: in the technical parts of literature his opinions were crude and uninformed; but whenever he spoke of a great writer whom he had read, his taste was generally sound" (Burns, *The Poems and Songs*, 3:1544).

Brydges—like Buchan, Blair, Mackenzie, Stewart, and a host of other intellectuals and noblemen of the officious type Burns sar-castically designated "Great Folk"—wanted to preserve Burns's char-acter as a rustic oddity. Try as he might, Burns would never impress these people with his critical abilities, though they would be ready enough to use his opinions to support their preconception of Burns's gifted-but-ignorant status. In the passage quoted above, Brydges is ready enough to admit that Burns had a sound natural taste; but he dismisses the poet's discourse on "the technical parts of literature" as "crude and uninformed."

Burns was in fact an articulate man, but most of the contemporary public preferred watching to listening. The cross-purposes which con-sistently thwarted his conversations—his own wish to dominate dis-course versus the wish of his preceptors to instruct him in the ways of culture—must have been the catalyst for the nasty rejoinders which contemporaries always record in their descriptions of his conversation. When Brydges noted at the conclusion of his visit with Burns that "I thought I perceived . . . the symptoms of an energy which had been pushed too far," he was attributing to lawless poetic energy the "symptoms" of a pressure he had undoubtedly introduced into the atmosphere at Ellisland with his own patronizing notice. Like Bos-well and many others caught in the strategic toils of contemporary social intercourse, Burns paid the price of a constant maneuvering for power: a chronic anxiety.

Women were the only admirers whose notice Burns could comfort-ably accept. It is well known that Burns liked women generally, but such literary friends as Maria Riddell became especially important in his later years, when his residence at Dumfries removed him from the "patrons" who had begun his vogue at Edinburgh. Like Burns him-self, Maria Riddell and his other important female friends, Frances Wallace Dunlop and Margaret Chalmers, were self-taught students of literature, trying to navigate without the benefit of the classical learning and university attendance which were considered indispensable to critical sophistication. Like Burns, they had to base their literary judgments on their fund of reading and their confidence in their own taste. Unlike the men of letters who took up Burns's cause and then cooled when he refused to heed their advice, these were fairly steady friends. Margaret Chalmers, with whom Burns was friendly during the late 1780s, was a gentleman farmer's daughter only slightly higher than Burns in social class. But Mrs. Riddell and Mrs. Dunlop were both gentlefolk (the social class whose male half Burns had come to distrust). Burns enjoyed a relationship with these two women based on their acquiescence to his authority in intellectual and aesthetic matters. (As Sir Walter Scott perceptively noted, "in female circles . . . the respect demanded by rank was readily paid as due to beauty or accomplishment" [Low, *The Critical Heritage*, p. 202]: polite deference to his female acquaintances did not threaten Burns's pride.) Burns lost touch with Margaret Chalmers after her marriage, and he quarreled with both his other woman friends (the source of disagreement was political with Mrs. Dunlop and probably sexual with Mrs. Riddell). But by comparison to his friendships with intellectual men, these relationships with literary women seem to have been among the most solid that he enjoyed in later life.

Mrs. Dunlop's friendship was epistolary and maternal: the mother of thirteen children and a proud descendant of the Scottish hero William Wallace, she first encountered Burns's Kilmarnock edition during a depression caused by her husband's death, her eldest son's treacherous marriage, and his subsequent sale of the ancestral estate. Burns's poems took her mind off these family troubles; she purchased half a dozen copies and wrote him a grateful letter. Mrs. Dunlop's letters, though full of bad advice (she thought "Tam o' Shanter" was shocking), allowed Burns the pleasure of arguing his methods with someone who eventually could be counted on to concede his superiority. The only problem in their friendship was Burns's enthusiasm for the French Revolution. Mrs. Dunlop had four sons and a grandson in the British army preparing to fight against France; two of her daughters had married French refugees. Still, for all his Jacobin talk, Burns himself joined a volunteer regiment when French invasion seemed imminent, and Mrs. Dunlop wrote to him during his last illness to affirm their friendship despite their political differences.

Maria Riddell's notice was even more important than Mrs. Dunlop's, because Mrs. Riddell had some literary flair of her own and was a more intelligent critic of his work. She was a neighbor at Dumfries and saw much of Burns socially during his last years. When Burns died, Maria Riddell produced a character sketch that showed she had listened to as well as watched the poet. Alone among the early biographers, Riddell would forego the opportunity to talk of spoilage, coarseness, and turpitude; with genuine perceptiveness, she spoke not of decline but of aggression produced by "almost habitual disappointments":

> His wit . . . had always the start of his judgment, and would lead him to the indulgence of raillery uniformly acute, but often unaccompanied with the least desire to wound. . . . He paid for this mischievous wit as dearly as anyone could do. "'Twas no extravagant arithmetic" to say of him, as was said of Yorick, "that for every ten jokes he got an hundred enemies"; but much allowance will be made by a candid mind for the splenetic warmth of a spirit whom "distress had spited with the world," and which, unbounded in its intellectual sallies and pursuits, continually experienced the curbs imposed by the waywardness of his fortune. The vivacity of his wishes and temper was indeed checked by almost habitual disappointments, which sat heavy on a heart, that acknowledged the ruling passion of independence, without having ever been placed beyond the grasp of penury. (Low, *The Critical Heritage*, p. 103)

Incidentally, Mrs. Riddell shows real fortitude in this vindication of Burns's explosive temper, for she herself had been subject to its whims. (Item 438 in Kinsley's edition of Burns is a hyperbolic celebration of her birthday; item 446 several pages later is a spiteful bit of doggerel condemning her rattling tongue and "rotten . . . heart.")[5]

In any case, her description of Burns's "almost habitual disappointments" brings the central paradox of sentimental celebrity to mind. For all their notice, Burns's sentimental public never afforded him a steady support. A crowded subscription list for the 1787 Edinburgh edition of Burns's poems was the only patronage he ever received from the literary public at large. A name on a subscription list does indicate a financial commitment to a poet; also, of course, it allows the patron to be publicly identified: some of the poet's glory is shared. Indeed, in one review of the Edinburgh edition, in the *Gentleman's Magazine* for July 1787, attention is actually focused not on Burns's poems but on the brilliance of his subscription list.[6] Very few patrons went beyond the gesture of subscription.

One who promised well but died young was the Earl of Glencairn. Robert Graham of Fintry, a commissioner of the Scottish Board of Excise, was also a serious and steady supporter: he offered Burns a position as part-time officer. Another active friend was Patrick Miller, a banker and something of a projector, who offered a farm—Ellisland—which was in the process of being "improved" (modernized), at what he thought was a fair rent. Burns, who knew all he needed to about the difficulty of improving farmland and the strain of meeting rent payments, favored the position with the Excise as a better source of income and advancement.[7] His own inclination, however, was overborne by the advice of men like Hugh Blair, whom Burns disliked but did not then want to offend. Most people who gave Burns's alternatives any thought considered farming the better choice: the "heaven-taught ploughman" had produced his early work in that setting and should return to the soil to ensure a creative future. Burns finally chose both alternatives: he signed a lease on Ellisland and took a part-time job with the Excise.

I mention Burns's career choices in this chapter on sentimental notice because aside from subscription to his Edinburgh edition, the two offers that he accepted were the sum of assistance he ever received from his public. (Personal friends he made during his employment with the Excise assisted his advancement there.) Also, ironically enough, when he became a full-time exciseman (giving up Ellisland as "a ruinous affair . . . let it go to hell!" [Burns, *Letters*, 2:1]) he lost all subsequent claim to the interest of the polite world. A ploughman had been low enough to be "interesting," but a collector of customs duties and taxes was an impossibly prosaic object for sentimental scrutiny. Indeed, even a tenant farmer would have retained only tenuous claims to attention. In 1786 Mackenzie might have called Burns a ploughman to make him seem more vulnerable and exposed: a farmer is difficult to imagine as an interesting victim. As Austen's Emma Woodhouse observes to Harriet Smith in an apposite reflection on Robert Martin:

> A young farmer . . . is the very last sort of person to raise my curiosity. The yeomanry are precisely the order of people with whom I feel I can have nothing to do. A degree or two lower, and a creditable appearance

might interest me; I might hope to be useful to their families in some way or other. But a farmer can need none of my help, and is therefore in one sense as much above my notice as in every other he is below it.[8]

And if patrician Emma's remarks on "the yeomanry" are cool, those of people like Robert Couper on Burns's position as a tax collector are positively icy:

> The Bard might have been at this day a growing honour to his country but . . . the baneful interference of Harry Dundas[9] . . . brought him forward at the expense of his talents and reputation. He was addicted I find to low company . . . and George the third in his great munificence and to foster something like a credit to his reign made a Gauger of him which whatever his Majesty or Mr. Dundas may think . . . rendered him unfit for any Gentlemans Society. (Letter to James Currie, 23 November 1798, Cowie Collection, Mitchell Library, Glasgow)

Couper here demonstrates the circular reasoning typical of the contemporary public. The poet's debased job made him unfit for any gentleman's society, but Burns is simultaneously criticized for seeking the alternative society of nongentlemen. Burns's post with the Excise was all wrong for sentimental celebrity: too "low" for competitive envy and too "high" for pity.

As a "gauger," Burns actually achieved a subtle revenge on the polite world, as he confiscated or taxed the luxury goods of which the upper classes were major consumers. In any case, his Excise position made his public conscious of the lack of common sympathy between themselves and Burns; as though Burns's mouse, on having her nest turned up by the plow, had turned and bitten the farmer. Even the friendliest notice conferred on Burns after he became a tax collector came to be circumscribed by reservations about his glamorless job: "Seeing him pass quickly, near Closeburn, I said to my companion, that is Burns. On coming to the inn, the ostler told us he would be back in a few hours to grant permits; that where he met with anything seizable, he was no better than any other gauger; in everything else, that he was perfectly a gentleman" (Burns, *The Poems and Songs*, 3:1543; quoting Ramsay of Ochtertyre). As an exciseman, Burns found himself in a profession so despised that even ostlers could comment on his dubious status. And like Robert Couper, most people who rejected Burns the exciseman were calling Burns a debased man when a major source of opprobrium was the debased job their own lack of patronage had compelled him to accept. Class hatred, perhaps even more than priggishness, was behind the discontinuation of notice.

When John Logan criticized Burns's songs about drinking and love in 1786, it was on the grounds that "no man should avow rakery who does not possess an estate of £500 a year" (Low, *The Critical Heritage*, p. 79). Logan's was an early version of the mass rejection which occurred after Burns found his niche with the Excise. His last literary associate, the impossible George Thomson (editor of the *Select Collection* series of songbooks), declared in his obituary for Burns in the *London Chronicle* that Burns's own deficiencies were to blame for his lack of advancement. His patrons were not to be considered remiss: "at last one of his patrons procured him the situation of an Exciseman, and an income somewhat less than 50£ per ann. We know not whether any steps were taken to better this humble income. Probably he was not qualified to fill a superior station to that which was assigned him. We know that his manners refused to partake the polish of genteel society" (Low, *The Critical Heritage*, p. 100).

William Blake once wrote that "the Enquiry in England is not whether a Man has Talents & Genius, But whether he is Passive & Polite & a Virtuous Ass & obedient to Noblemen's Opinions in Art & Science. If he is, he is a Good Man. If not, he must be Starved" (*Complete Writings*, p. 452–53). For all the benevolent posture of the sentimental critics and public, Burns's life shows that this was the "Enquiry" in Scotland as well. The discomfort of the "Passive & Polite" role conferred on Burns by his "noticers" is summarized in an acute essay by Thomas De Quincey on patronage and Burns's attitudes toward it. While still a schoolboy, De Quincey had been a peripheral member of the literary coterie in Liverpool that had revolved around the poet Roscoe and that had helped James Currie with the first edition of Burns's complete works. He recalled:

> I heard every one . . . heartily agreeing to tax Burns with ingratitude and with pride falsely directed, because he sate uneasily or restively under the bridle-hand of his noble self-called *"patrons."* . . . For my part, . . . when all the world was reading Currie's monument to the memory of Burns . . . I felt and avowed my feeling most loudly—that Burns was wronged. . . . A £10 bank note, by way of subscription for a

few copies of an early edition of his poems—this is the outside that I could ever see proof given of Burns having received anything in the way of *patronage*. . . . I stood alone in remembering, the very remarkable position of Burns: not merely that, with his genius, and with the intellectual pretensions generally of his family, he should have been called to a life of early labour, . . . but also that he, by accident about the proudest of human spirits, should have been by accident summoned, beyond all others, to eternal recognitions of some mysterious gratitude which he owed to some mysterious patrons little and great, whilst yet, of all men, perhaps, he reaped the least . . . benefit from any patronage that has ever been put on record. Most men, if they reap little from patronage, are liberated from the claims of patronage, or, if they are summoned to a galling dependency, have at least the fruits of their dependency. But it was this man's unhappy fate—with an early and previous irritability on this very point—to find himself saddled, by his literary correspondents, with all that was odious in dependency, whilst he had every hardship to face that is most painful in unbefriended poverty. (Low, *The Critical Heritage*, pp. 428–29)

De Quincy has captured the essence of Burns's equivocal status. But although he is certainly correct in assuming that this officious but sentimentally dysfunctional patronage must have been a constant irritation to Burns, it is also true that very fine poetry—the late songs and "Tam o' Shanter"—was the result of this discomfort. Burns was led by his perception of the self-serving behavior of his sentimental public to rethink some of his own early values. After Edinburgh and a short period of adjustment, he began to concentrate on songs; and he produced them in an idiom free of sentimental cant. Remedial benevolence ceased to be a central strategy of his writings—and when Burns circumvented this convention for expressing feelings, he achieved his greatest authenticity. How Burns managed this transition from announced to experienced sympathy will follow in the next chapter's concluding discussion of Burns's relationship to his public.

7

Naive and Sentimental Burns

The notice of Burns by his public—and Burns's eventual reaction against it—can be illuminated, like much of "feeling," by reference to Shaftesbury. In the "Inquiry Concerning Virtue or Merit," Shaftesbury had written: "We cannot doubt of what passes within ourselves. Our passions and affections are known to us. They are certain, whatever the objects may be on which they are employed. Nor is it of any concern to our argument how these exterior objects stand: whether they are realities or mere illusions; whether we wake or dream" (Shaftesbury, *Characteristics*, 1:336–37). Following Shaftesbury, "feeling" was oddly incurious about the real identity of its object, though intense in its cultivation of that object. Selfishness, that universal bias in human personality, was regarded by Shaftesbury as paradoxically an aid to benevolence; for good conduct made people feel good about themselves. Moral strictures and prescriptive religious dogma were not central to Shaftesbury's theory of virtue. It was an innate, cultivated taste—an instinct to harbor and express good feelings—that moved Shaftesbury's ideal person:

> In a creature capable of forming general notions of things, not only the outward beings which offer themselves to the sense are the objects of affection, but the very actions themselves, and the affections of pity, kindness, gratitude, and their contraries, being brought into the mind by reflection, become objects. So that, by means of this reflected sense, there arises another kind of affection towards those very affections themselves. (1:251)

Important studies by R. S. Crane, Donald Greene, George A. Starr, G. S. Rousseau, and Jean Hagstrum have debated the historical and philosophical origins of the cult of feeling, and perhaps these critics would object to any placement of Shaftesbury as the sole figure.[1] Yet in specific terms of Scottish literary culture during the eighteenth century, his influence seems indubitably major. Francis Hutcheson, Shaftesbury's brilliant disciple, trained a generation of midcentury Scottish students at Glasgow University—including Adam Smith. In addition, Shaftesbury's emphasis on instinctive virtue seems to have had special appeal to intellectuals in Scotland, who often sought escape from Calvinism's gloomy insistence on original sin.

At any rate, Shaftesbury's vision of a human instinct—considered universal and innate—toward good feeling combined with other cultural influences to encourage such diverse phenomena of the late eighteenth century as the vogue for a ploughman-poet in Edinburgh and Blake's *Songs of Innocence* (1789), which implicitly celebrate Shaftesbury's "affection . . . towards affection" in such poems as "The Divine Image":

> To Mercy, Pity, Peace and Love
> All pray in their distress;
> And to these virtues of delight
> Return their thankfulness.

Indeed, the optimism encouraged by Shaftesbury's philosophy seems also to have encouraged the smugness that accompanied the sentimental movement. If it is natural and instinctive to be good, then those who reject the "virtues of delight" are base and unnatural. Skeptics about human nature only show their own degeneracy: Jonathan Swift is one example of a writer neglected during the sentimental era. James Beattie, in a letter to Bishop Porteus, derided voyage four of *Gulliver's Travels* as "a satire on human nature"—as though to write a satire on human nature were somehow reprehensible. As for Swift's repellent Yahoos, Beattie followed a conventionally anti-Swiftian argument when he called them blasphemous: "an oblique censure of Providence itself in the formation of the human body."[2]

Indeed, Beattie—self-appointed defender of Christianity against the bland assaults of David Hume—is an interesting case in the annals of the Scottish age of feeling. In his essay "On Poetry and Music as They Affect the Mind," Beattie demonstrates a thoroughgoing commitment to the optimistic moral doctrine of Shaftesbury while showing also its weak point in failing to offer any explanation for non-benevolent conduct:

> The human mind, unless debased by passion or prejudice, never fails to take the side of truth and virtue. . . . To favor virtue, and speak truth, and take pleasure in those who do so, is natural to man; to act otherwise, requires an effort, does violence to nature, and always implies some evil purpose in the agent. The first, like progressive motion, is easy and graceful; the last is unseemly and difficult, like walking sideways, or backwards. The one is so common, that it is little attended to. . . . the other has a strangeness in it, that provokes at once our surprise and disapprobation.[3]

Feeling produced very different artifacts—"To a Mouse," *The Life of Johnson, La Nouvelle Héloïse*—but in all cases the effect of Shaftesbury was to turn the attention inward. Delight in one's own good feelings predisposed men of feeling to shocks of "surprise and disapprobation" at shortcomings in others or in society.

And in the day-to-day pressures of social life, carefully cultivated inward affection tended to evolve into affectation. The attention to personal instinct, which often had a liberating effect on philosophers and writers, just as often had grotesque effects on social life, as in contemporary descriptions of such men of feeling as James Boswell and Oliver Goldsmith. Most of the cultivated benevolist eccentricities of the time (the list is endless, but Burns's reception in Edinburgh has been discussed) were characterized more by posture than by authenticity.

As late at 1805, Sir Samuel Egerton Brydges applied a noble-bandit metaphor to Burns, thrusting a thoroughly fictive sinister significance upon him: "We can almost suppose in [Burns's] athletic form and daring countenance, had he lived in times of barbarism, and been tempted by hard necessity to forego his principles, such an one as we behold at the head of a banditti in the savage scenery of Salvator Rosa, gilding the crimes of violence and depradation by acts of valour and generosity!" (Low, *The Critical Heritage*, 170). Such flights on the part of Burns's public were common. Considering the passion of these times for cultivating one's individual responses, whatever their "object," distorting descriptions like Brydges' are not at all surprising. It is surprising, however, on first reading the letters of Burns, to observe how indefatigably Burns himself indulges in bizarre sentimental postures with his correspondents. Known for abrupt and somewhat explosive candor in discourse and for a self-sufficient and therefore successful adaptation of sentimental techniques in his early poetry, Burns is consistently, disappointingly, and derivatively sentimental in nearly all his letters.

THE REACTION of posterity to the self-directed pity of most of Burns's correspondence has run the gamut from Keats's rueful verdict: "He talked with Bitches—he drank with Blackguards, he was miserable—We can see horribly clear in the works of such a man his whole life, as if we were God's spies"[4] to William Maginn's more visceral—and typical—response: "His Letters are enough to make a dog sick" (p. 328). In truth, Burns's letters, like Goldsmith's and Boswell's manners in company, were products of his vast social unease. They exhibit practically none of the charm to be found in such abundance in his poetry and song, and their awkwardness is not just the fault of Burns's English diction (the usual theory introduced to explain their failure to evoke the Burns we know from other contexts). The fretful egotism of Burns's letters is an effect of his sentimentally veering modes of self-definition. Franz Kafka once wrote that "every human being is unique, and designed to be useful by virtue of his individuality, but he must find that individuality to his taste."[5] In his letters—like Boswell and Goldsmith in their social lives—Burns never quite composed a persona to suit his taste: he kept shifting ground. Generally speaking, he alternated between a pose of passive aggression borrowed from Mackenzie's Harley and a Miltonic defiance heightened by a violent self-pity like Werther's.

> It never occurred to me, at least never with the force it deserv'd, that this world is a busy scene, and man, a creature destined for a progressive struggle; and that, however I might possess a warm heart and inoffensive manners (which last, by the by, was rather more than I could well boast), still, more than these passive qualities, there was something to be *done*. (Burns, *Letters*, 1:48)

> No! if I must write, let it be Sedition, or Blasphemy, or something else that begins with a B, so that I may grin with the grin of iniquity, & rejoice with the rejoicing of an apostate Angel— "All good to me is lost, / Evil be thou my good!" (2:323)

Neither pose expresses Burns with the distinction of his best poetry.
  Burns, like Boswell and Goldsmith, wanted to seize attention on his own terms. Also like them, he was not consistent as to what his

own terms were. Unlike them, Burns had no Johnson—no respected supplier of certainty and support; and unlike them he was considered semiliterate by many of the people with whom he corresponded. In his letters, Burns attempted to overcome the probable resistance of his correspondents; to establish his authority by structuring his own assertions around quotations rifled from prestigious authors. As in some of his weaker poetry, he aligned himself with powerful allusions rather than expressing himself directly.

The paradigm for all of Burns's sentimental correspondence is the epistolary relationship he established with Agnes McLehose during his second winter in Edinburgh. Confined to his lodgings by an injured knee, Burns diverted himself with a brief but intense flirtation with Mrs. M'Lehose, alias "Clarinda." She was a newly met acquaintance, an attractive woman, a dabbler in verse writing, and in the interesting situation of having been abandoned by her husband (he had thrown off his financial and family obligations by emigrating to Jamaica). When "Clarinda" met Burns she had been separated from her husband for eight years; she and her three children were being supported by Lord Craig, a wealthy cousin. Given her attentive solicitude for Burns and the discomfort of her marital situation, Burns's interest in Mrs. M'Lehose was inevitable: it was not often that he encountered people in social positions more equivocal and embarrassing than his own. But his letters to her are deadened by excessive literary allusion:

> You have converted me, Clarinda (I shall love that name while I live: there is heavenly music in it!). Booth and Amelia I know well. Your sentiments on that subject, as they are on every subject, are just and noble. "To be feelingly alive to kindness and to unkindness" is a charming female character. (1:160–61)

> I like to have quotations ready for every occasion.—They give one's ideas so pat, and save one the trouble of finding expression adequate to one's feelings.—I think it is one of the greatest pleasures attending a Poetic genius, that we can give our woes, cares, joys, loves &c. an embodied form in verse, which, to me, is ever immediate ease.—Goldsmith says finely of his Muse—"Thou source of all my bliss and all my woe; / Thou found'st me poor at first, and keep'st me so."(1:164)

> I have been this morning taking a peep thro', as Young finely says, "the dark postern of time long elaps'd"; and you will easily guess, 'twas a

rueful prospect.—What a tissue of thoughtlessness, weakness and fol-
ly! My life reminded me of a ruin'd temple: what strength, what pro-
portion in some parts! . . . I kneeled down before the Father of mer-
cies. . . . I rose, eased and strengthened.—I despise the superstition of
a Fanatic, but I love the Religion of a Man.—The future, said I to
myself, is still before me: there let me—"On Reason build Resolve, /
That column of true majesty in Man!" (1:166)

In the correspondence with Clarinda, Burns quotes from sources as
various as Alexander Pope (repeating lines from "Eloisa to Abelard"
several times), Oliver Goldsmith, the Song of Solomon, the Book of
Job, the Acts of the Apostles, John Locke, Thomas D'Urfey, John
Milton, Edward Young, St. Luke, Joseph Addison, "Ossian," Thomas
Gray, James Thomson, Thomas Southerne, and the Book of Prov-
erbs.[6] Even the name he gave her was appropriated from another
poet: "Clarinda" had been Allan Ramsay's name for the Duchess of
Queensberry.

Burns used literary allusions in his letters, as he says above, to
"save" himself "the trouble of finding expression adequate" to his
feelings. As in duan 2 of "The Vision," this dependence on other
writers ("They give one's ideas so pat") prevents Burns from explor-
ing his own feelings. Where there is leisure for quoting from *Night
Thoughts*, as Johnson might have remarked, there can be no passion.
Even in a description of Agnes M'Lehose to Captain Richard Brown,
an old comrade in dissipation to whom Burns might have been expected to unbend a little, Burns still introduces the topic of his new
flirtation with a literary allusion, and assumes a familiar sentimental
pose in describing the relationship: "Almighty Love still 'reigns and
revels' in my bosom; and I am at this moment ready to hang myself for
a young Edin[r] widow, who has wit and beauty more murderously fatal
than the assassinating stiletto of the Sicilian banditti, or the poisoned
arrow of the savage African" (1:152). There is that Sicilian bandit
again—a sure sign that the man of feeling is ascendant.

A preference for picturesque imagery and inflated language characterizes Burns's correspondence generally. Even in relationships less
superheated than that with Clarinda, Burns tried to get the upper
hand of his correspondent by using a barrage of virtuoso allusion. In
March 1787, for instance, Burns wrote in response to a letter from an
old friend, James Candlish, that he had delayed writing for some time

because "I was determined to write [you] a good letter, full of argument, amplification, erudition and, as Bayes says, *all that*" (1:79). Two things are striking about Burns's approach to Candlish in that sentence. First, Candlish was a student at Glasgow University, and Burns is addressing him in technical terms that he regards as appropriate. Burns, in short, is somewhat defensively implying his command of what he supposes to be Candlish's erudite context. This is reminiscent of the Goldsmith who "once at the exhibition of the *Fantoccini* in London, when those who sat next him observed with what dexterity a puppet was made to toss a pike, . . . could not bear that it should have such praise, and exclaimed with some warmth, 'Pshaw! I can do it better myself' " (Boswell, *Life of Johnson*, 1:414). Burns is less blatant than Goldsmith, of whom every contemporary noted that he "could not bear" to be excluded from a position of authority in any situation, and thus talked with great confidence and frequent absurdity on any and all topics.[7] But Burns is also implicitly saying to Candlish, "Pshaw! I can do it better myself."

The second striking feature of Burns's approach to Candlish could be used to suggest the radical difference between his letters and his verse (especially his later songs). Burns attributes the phrase "*all that*" to Bayes, the Dryden caricature in Buckingham's *Rehearsal*, rather than to the more homely context in which it was also familiar to him: the Scots folk tradition, in which "a' that" was used to promote double entendre in the refrains of bawdy songs. Burns could seldom be casual and homely in his letters, however, any more than Boswell or Goldsmith could be relaxed in company. The expression, assigned to wicked, witty Buckingham, helps establish for Burns's letter a formally ironic and self-consciously "literate" mood. When he uses "a' that" in "For a' that and a'that" (one of his best-known songs) on the other hand, the phrase creates exactly the opposite effect of conversational ease:

> A prince can mak a belted knight,
>   A marquis, duke, and a' that;
> But an honest man's aboon his might,
>   Gude faith he mauna fa' that!
> For a' that, and a' that,
>   Their dignities, and a' that,
> The pith o' Sense, and pride o' Worth,
>   Are higher rank than a' that.—
>   (2:763)

The focal points of Burns's letters and Burns's poetry, particularly in his later years, were entirely different. The letters aimed at a tone of conscious superiority; the later poems and songs at a tone of casual empathy. The relationship with Agnes M'Lehose that produced letters at once febrile and unauthentic produced also the song "Ae Fond Kiss," in which "Clarinda" becomes "Nancy," and an unconvincing epistolary passion boils down to genuine affection:

> I'll ne'er blame my partial fancy,
> Naething could resist my Nancy:
> But to see her, was to love her;
> Love but her, and love for ever.—
>
> Had we never lov'd sae kindly,
> Had we never lov'd sae blindly!
> Never met—or never parted,
> We had ne'er been broken-hearted.—
>
> Fare-thee-weel, thou first and fairest!
> Fare-thee-weel, thou best and dearest!
> Thine be ilka joy and treasure,
> Peace, Enjoyment, Love and Pleasure!—
>
> Ae fond kiss, and then we sever!
> Ae fareweel, Alas, for ever!
> Deep in heart-wrung tears I'll pledge thee,
> Warring sighs and groans I'll wage thee.—
>
> (2:592)

Significantly, Burns speaks mostly of "I" in his letters to Clarinda and mostly of "we" in his song to Nancy. Sympathy and tenderness are not so much asserted as demonstrated.

AN OVERLY EMPHATIC SELF-CONSCIOUSNESS in Burns's letters can be put into context by referring again to Adam Smith's *Theory of Moral Sentiments*. Smith observed that communication of one's "situation" to "spectators" involves a continual revision of presentation to accommodate their external perspective. Thus, instead of attempting candid and direct presentation of one's feelings, the "sufferer" continually tries to calculate which pose will be least resisted by the spectators; which metaphors will get through most quickly. And Smith not only notes this existence of posture in social relationships; he recommends it.

In order to produce . . . concord, as nature teaches the spectators to assume the circumstances of the person principally concerned, so she teaches this last in some measure to assume those of the spectators. As they are . . . placing themselves in his situation, and thence conceiving emotions similar to what he feels; so he is . . . placing himself in theirs, and thence conceiving some degree of that coolness about his own fortune, with which he is sensible that they will view it. . . . he is constantly led to imagine in what manner he would be affected if he was only one of the spectators of his own situation. (pp. 23–24)

Burns's letters do seem to presuppose a "coolness" in the recipients that he is all too determined to overcome. Smith ends this analysis of social transactions with the optimistic conclusion: "Society and conversation, therefore, are the most powerful remedies for restoring the mind to its tranquillity" (p. 25). For men of feeling, tranquillity was undermined by the pressure of these highly competitive contemporary social stratagems.[8] The constant need to anticipate one's effect on others—and the continual need to revise one's "affect" in order to secure sympathetic scrutiny—created stress, not peace, for sentimental writers.

Smith published his treatise in 1759, before the crest of the sentimental movement. Perhaps its early date accounts for its optimism. A later essay on contemporary aesthetics, Friedrich von Schiller's *Naïve and Sentimental Poetry* (1795–96), appeared during the wane of the sentimental cult and supplies a less benign perspective on the social effects of the movement.

Schiller's thesis divides literature into two dialectic types: the direct, unreflective and apparently artless "naive," and the oblique, conscious and deliberate artful "sentimental." Says Schiller, "The poet . . . either *is* nature or he will *seek* her. The former is the naive, the latter the sentimental poet" (p. 110). This thesis is illustrated chiefly by reference to *Werther* and other contemporary German writings (Schiller lived from 1759 to 1805), but British authors such as Sterne, Young, "Ossian," and Fielding also are discussed. Schiller does not discuss Burns (whom he had, however, read with interest), but his comments on contemporary letters and society illuminate the social difficulties experienced by all contemporary writers and also will help to introduce the topic of my final chapters: Burns's concentration on song revising during his later career.

Schiller's view of art and morals is as much as extension of Shaftesbury as was Smith's *Theory of Moral Sentiments.* Smith's teacher at Glasgow University had been Francis Hutcheson, Shaftesbury's first apologist. Hutcheson and—through him—Shaftesbury influenced Smith's optimistic theories of human nature. Schiller's descent from Shaftesbury, though less lineal than Smith's, is evident in such statements as "[there is an] incipient impulse for truth and simplicity which, like the moral tendency from whence it derives, lies incorruptible and inalienable in every human heart" (p. 103). What has vanished in Schiller is the faith of Shaftesbury and Smith in society and socialization. Smith, like Shaftesbury, wrote that social discourse burnished people's minds and was good for them. Shaftesbury had even said that "out of . . . community . . . arise more than nine-tenths of whatever is enjoyed in life" (1:299). Shaftesbury stressed that social life is a source of good feelings and hence a means to goodness itself. Smith reduced that emphasis somewhat but still praised social interaction as therapeutic. Shaftesbury differed from his chief adversary, Mandeville, who held that society was governed by self-interest and greed and that the best hope for civilization was to be found in a renewed attention to the Bible. Shaftesbury, on the other hand, attributed the rise of society to our human refinements on the "herding" instinct of the animal world (1:74; 2:83–84) and in this way argued that altruism as well as self-protection was at the basis of the social contract: "Even the swinish kinds want not common affection" (2:83–84). Love bound families together and—said Shaftesbury—also societies.

Schiller, as convinced as Shaftesbury of the innate moral impulses of mankind, took a more skeptical view of the tendencies of society. Social life involved a "timid propriety" because social animals had become dependent on their armor. Socialization had weakened them:

> Because we have fallen . . . short from simplicity and strict truth of expression in life in society . . . our easily wounded guilt, as well as our easily seduced powers of imagination, have made a timid propriety necessary. Without being false, one often speaks otherwise than one thinks; one is forced into periphrasis in order to say things which could cause pain only to a sick egotism or danger to a perverted fantasy. (p. 99)

Schiller attributed the contemporary interest in landscape and child psychology to a widespread need to counterbalance the polished stratagems of contemporary socialization: he said that people of the modern age sought "such objects as . . . [offered] a retrospective view" of themselves and "[revealed] . . . more closely the unnatural" in them (p. 86). But only artists could do much more than look at such interesting natural objects as children and meadows. Only the creative mind assimilated the object in the process of observing it; only the poet knew how to transmit his sense that objects signified ideals. Schiller wrote that all of contemporary culture indicated a painful need for a return to nature; but he insisted that polite society's requirement of continual maneuvering held most people back from ever achieving a more natural condition. Even the artist, in addressing himself to others rather than to his art, was forced by decorum into "falseness." Impulses that literary synthesis might have wrought into meaning were drained off by social pressures into defensive small talk. Schiller concluded that "to be true to humanity one must be far from men" (p. 132).

Schiller's analysis of the conflict between creative impulse and the social requirements of the sentimental era helps to explain the disparity between the luminous presence of Boswell and Goldsmith in their writings and the distracted and inconsistent impression of their personalities that emerges from contemporary descriptions of their social conduct. It also suggests an explanation for Burns's failure to emerge as himself in most of his letters. "Forced into periphrasis" might well be the epigraph to the two volumes of Burns's correspondence, so well does it describe the impression created by his defensive, overwritten letters. Their failure does seem related to their distance from humanity and their proximity to men, priggish men like Hugh Blair. Burns appears constantly to "speak" otherwise than he "thinks" in his letters—even to reassuring allies such as Frances Dunlop. Presumably to avoid offending others (something he was always forgetting to do in conversation), in his letters he refrains from the direct expression of honest feelings that—as Schiller said—"could cause pain only to a sick egotism."

Schiller wrote that no writer—naive or sentimental—could work within society. The literary public, however reflective and sensitive it proclaimed itself to be, was satisfied by conventions in a way that no artist could ever accept, while an artist was motivated by challenges and ideals that the public at large could never be expected to appreciate. Schiller said that for both artist and public, art was recreation

(*Erholung*);[9] but the public expected it to be recreation in the sense of relaxing fun, while for the artist it was recreation in the sense of radical regeneration. The public could respond to art only according to its capacity, which, Schiller said, was never profound: "[In picking up a poem] they [expect] recreation . . . but a recreation . . . in accordance with their feeble notion, and they discover with dismay that they are now first expected to put out an effort of strength for which they might lack the capacity even in their best moments" (p. 171). Like Mackenzie in his *Lounger* review of Burns, Schiller defines as inescapable the adversarial relation of contemporary artists to contemporary society. Indeed, in *Naive and Sentimental Poetry*, Schiller sees a conflict not only between his two poetic archetypes but also between the opposing requirements of society and creativity. And although Schiller praises both naive and sentimental types of art in his treatise, he is uniformly hostile to society, extending his disapprobation to critics as well. He writes that criticism operates—as society does—on principles of clarification and limitation and is therefore opposed to the transcendence and simplicity of art:

> The understanding of the schools, always fearful of error, crucifies its words and its concepts upon the cross of grammar and of logic, and is severe and stiff to avoid uncertainty at all costs, employs many words to be quite sure of not saying too much, and deprives its thoughts of their strength and edge so that they may not cut the unwary. . . . [In criticism, unlike poetry,] the sign remains eternally heterogeneous and alien to the thing signified. (p. 98)

Schiller's dislike of criticism is allied to his dislike for the reductive strategies required by polite discourse: in both cases, his view is curiously similar to Blake's. Like the Nurse in *Songs of Experience* (1789–94), Schiller is equally dissatisfied with the thoughtless games of children and the conscious games of adults. Where Blake warns: "Your spring & your day are wasted in play, / And your winter and night in disguise" (*Complete Writings*, p. 212), Schiller first denigrates children ("their perfection is not to their credit, because it is not the product of their choice" [p. 85]) and later speaks grimly of "maturity," of "artificial man entoiled by civilization" (p. 111). Like Blake, Schiller idealizes individual energy and has little but scorn for polite convention. Like Blake's system, Schiller's is an extension of the Genesis myth of the Fall and is developed more metaphorically than analyt-

ically. Schiller separates his naive and sentimental archetypes by the
very factors that separate Blake's famous lyrics—by innocence and
experience. In Schiller, as in Blake (and Genesis), experience is a
fallen state; the loss of grace (innocence) can only become a fortunate
fall if the individual can retain his individual energies against the assaults of society and civilization.

To expand these points: the naive artist is the "innocent" in
Schiller; he "*is*" nature (pp. 106, 110). He enjoys a subconscious
(even preconscious) rapport with his subject like the unity with the
created world that Adam enjoyed in Eden. By contrast, this "harmony" has been "withdrawn" from the sentimental writer, who feels a
postlapsarian disjunction between the disillusioned social creature
that he is and the child of nature that he wishes to become again. The
sentimental poet sees nature "only *ideally* . . . as an idea still to be
realized, no longer as a fact in his life" (p. 111). Although Schiller
thought no modern writer could be entirely naive (free of the self-
consciousness produced by society), he did think that his friend and
rival Goethe seemed little touched by social pressures or by personal
feelings of guilt and inadequacy, and thus approached a naive condition. He said that although *Werther* treated the sentimental themes of
alienation and despair, Goethe told his story with the same indifference to the sensibilities of his readers that characterized naive art.

What impressed Schiller about Goethe was what impressed him in
all naive art—the lack of anxiety, the apparent spontaneity. Schiller
himself worked with painful deliberation and revision, and he seems
wistful as he dwells on the "calm" of nature and of the naive writing
which is at one with nature. Homer, to use another of Schiller's naive
exemplars, described heroic deeds with calm concentration, "as
though he possessed no heart in his bosom" (p. 109). The ancient
bard, Schiller observes, "does not seem to make any distinction between those [objects] which appear of themselves, and those which
arise as a result of art or the human will; . . . he does not cling to
[Nature] . . . with fervor, with sentimentality, with sweet melancholy, as we moderns do" (p. 102). By contrast, sentimental writers
like Schiller were fervid; they did experience "a pressing need for
objects in which [they] might find [Nature] again" (p. 104).

So what separated the sentimental from the naive artist was his
experience of civilization, which had made him self-conscious and
thus undermined his union with Nature: "At one with himself and

happy in the sense of his humanity, [the naive poet remains] with it as his maximum and assimilate[s] all else to it; whereas *we* [modern, sentimental poets], not at one with ourselves and unhappy in our experience of mankind, possess no more urgent interest than to escape" (p. 104). In his discussion of Shakespeare, Schiller indicates the effect of a naive poet upon a sentimental one:

> When, at a very early age I first made the acquaintance of [Shakespeare] . . . I was incensed by his coldness, the insensitivity which permitted him to jest in the midst of the highest pathos, to interrupt the heartrending scenes in *Hamlet*, in *King Lear*, in *Macbeth*, etc., with a Fool; restraining himself now where my sympathies rushed on, then coldbloodedly tearing himself away where my heart would have gladly lingered. Misled by acquaintance with more recent poets into looking first for the poet in his work, to find *his* heart, to reflect in unison with *him* on his subject matter, in short, to observe the object in the subject, it was intolerable to me that here there was no way to lay hold of the poet, and nowhere to confront him. (p. 106–7)

Schiller's discussion of naive Shakespeare is applicable to Burns's song revising, just as his discussion of the sentimental is applicable to Burns's early poems.

To state the case briefly and paradoxically, Burns changed after Edinburgh from adapting sentimental themes of benevolent encounter and redemptive feeling to adapting, in his later song revising, naive ones (he worked with folk song and, in "Tam o' Shanter," folktale). The catalyst for change, as in Schiller, was experience: his exposure in Edinburgh to sentimental civilization and his resultant acquisition of its discontents. Burns's ultimate concentration on song revising—at first glance, a "naive" enterprise—was in Schiller's sense sentimental, because it developed as a result of his disillusionment with society and his subsequent wish to recapture simplicity. Also in sentimental fashion, when Burns revised folk songs, he did so self-consciously, restructuring them to support his private values.

Yet the effect of these sentimental motives still is basically naive: Burns's songs are more elegant and orchestrated than the folk sources, but they still impress by virtue of their seeming artlessness. The songs seem more anonymous, less directed to a specific purpose, than Burns's early poems; these qualities, too, Schiller had defined as naive. In discussing Shakespeare, Schiller noted that it was "impossible to find the poet in his work, to find *his* heart": Burns's heart, too, is fairly underground in his songs, especially by comparison to his early poetry. There is no clear "way to lay hold of the poet" in "Tam o' Shanter," especially by contrast to "Love and Liberty" or "To a Mouse," where Burns's alliances are firmly emphasized. And how do we "confront the poet" who abandoned such self-revealing literary forms as verse-epistle and satire in order to revise—often anonymously—old Scottish songs?

Schiller's essay provides us with clues. In describing Homer's naive treatment of the episode in the *Iliad* in which Glaucus and Diomedes exchange armor to reaffirm an old exchange of hospitality between their fathers, Schiller marvels at the "dry truthfulness" with which Homer reports, noting "it would hardly be possible for a *modern* poet . . . to have waited . . . before expressing his pleasure at this action" (p. 109). The "modern poet," then, would exploit an emotion in a situation where Homer merely presents an action. Burns's songs are "modern" in Schiller's sense, and do not demonstrate the pure "dry truthfulness" of Homer; yet they do avoid the overt manipulation of the reader's sympathy and the personal expressions of "pleasure" in benevolence that characterize narrative in most contemporary literature, and certainly in much of his own early work.

"Tam o' Shanter" and a selection of Burns's songs will be discussed at length in chapters 9 and 10. Here I will take up a single song in order to clarify the interplay between sentimental motive and naive effect in the song revisions of Burns. "The bonie lass made the bed to me" is Burns's recreation of a Restoration ballad, "The Cumberland Lass." As usual in Burns's adaptations, his version achieves an emotional coherence lacking in the bawdy original; also as usual, his revision, though more generalizing than its source, in no way bleeds the song of authenticity or charm. Burns is implicitly sentimental, but refrains from the open manipulation of feeling. The result is what Schiller suggests is the ultimate goal both of naive and sentimental poetry: the expression of feeling "*poetically*" but "completely humanly" (pp. 156–57):

> Her hair was like the links o' gowd,
>   Her teeth were like the ivorie,
> Her cheeks like lillies dipt in wine,
>   The lass that made the bed to me.—

Her bosom was the drifted snaw,
   Twa drifted heaps sae fair to see;
Her limbs the polish'd marble stane,
   The lass that made the bed to me.—

I kiss'd her o'er and o'er again,
   And ay she wist na what to say;
I laid her between me and the wa'
   The lassie thought na lang till day.—

Upon the morrow when we rase,
   I thank'd her for her courtesie:
But ay she blush'd, and ay she sigh'd,
   And said, Alas, ye've ruin'd me.—

I clasp'd her waist and kiss'd her syne,
   While the tear stood twinklin in her e'e;
I said, My lassie dinna cry,
   For ye ay shall mak the bed to me.—

She took her mither's holland sheets
   And made them a' in sarks to me:
Blythe and merry may she be,
   The lass that made the bed to me.—

                                    (2:856)

Sentiment is pervasive in this song, but anxious sentimentality is present not in the protestations of the speaker but in the blushes, tears, sighs, and recriminations of the lass, whose anxieties are easily allayed. In this song, as in so many others, Burns achieves a charming synthesis between the artful pathos of the sentimental and the dry truthfulness of the Homeric naive. In naive fashion, Burns interrupts the proposal scene to describe the shirts made for her lover by the lassie from her mother's sheets.[10] The poet, then, does not linger to "express his pleasure" at the events described. On the other hand, the tenderness of the song does indicate implicit pleasure at the events described in it, and in the first two stanzas quoted here, Burns is evidently using the diction of the Song of Solomon in his description of the lass; unlike a naive poet, he applies an outside literary perspective on his subject.

Like most of Burns's song revisions, then, "The bonie lass" is a complex mixture. It demonstrates a sentimental value for feelings—

the lover's feeling eliminates the lassie's anxiety and is the agent that resolves the song—but Burns suggests rather than parades his values.

Schiller distinguished between the gross "actual" nature commonly perceptible and the net "real" nature to be discovered in the course of poetic synthesis, whether of the naive or the sentimental type. Burns's songs generally evoke "real" nature in Schiller's sense; they transform what often seems a scarcely untouched "actual" nature in his folk sources. Schiller's terms provide a metaphor for the process by which Burns changed traditional bawdy fragments like "Duncan Davidson" from graphic jokes to complex lyric statements like "Mary Morison."

After Edinburgh and "notice," Burns broke faith with conventionally sentimental benevolism only to find in his work with song revising a way to assert feeling less restrictively. From the inert objects of sentimental scrutiny and the finite opinions of his speakers, Burns transferred feeling away from objects and into his subject.[11] His early poems, successful though they often are, tend to concern themselves with eccentricity. His early narrator, "Silly Rab," extends himself in a parody of virtuoso responsiveness to a succession of small mammals, beggars, vermin, fallen women, quacks, devils, fanatics. The later poems, by contrast, seldom involve eccentric encounter (though "Tam o' Shanter" is a sort of exception soon to be discussed): they deal not with lice or Scotch drink but with friendship, courtship, marriage. Burns's songs involve feeling necessarily—it is implied in their subjects, by contrast with such poems as "To a Mouse," where the emotion is not intrinsically called for by the situation in the poem, and where Burns's intensity seems incongruous (this creates the gently comic tone of the poem). Generally speaking, in the later songs emotions vindicate themselves, not just Robert Burns. The poet writes not so much of the movement of transcendent feeling within himself as of its power in the world at large.

III

Burns as Bard

For who has mind to relish, Minos-wise,
The Real of Beauty, free from that dead hue
Sickly imagination and sick pride
Cast wan upon it?

John Keats,
"Sonnet on Visiting the Tomb of Burns"

8

Paradoxes of Self-Expression and Tradition after 1740

Burns wrote his first song at fifteen to impress his partner in the harvest, Nellie Kilpatrick. In his autobiographical letter to Dr. John Moore, he described why he had felt capable of suiting his words to Nellie's favorite tune:

> I was not so presumtive as to imagine I could make verses like printed ones, composed by men who had Greek and Latin; but my girl sung a song which was said to be composed by a small country laird's son, on one of his father's maids, with whom he was in love; and I saw no reason why I might not rhyme as well as he, for excepting smearing sheep and casting peats, his father living in the moors, he had no more Scholar-craft than I had.—
> Thus with me began Love and Poesy. (1:108)

Burns composed or revised verses to fit Scottish airs throughout his life after beginning with "Handsome Nell." Although these chapters will stress Burns's immersion in lyric writing and revising as the culmination of his career as a poet, it must also be said that the difference between his early and late songs consists only in Burns's attitude toward them, which changed after he left Edinburgh.

By 1786 Burns had produced such brilliant lyrics as "Mary Morison" and "Green grow the Rashes," but none of these was included in his major early publication, the Kilmarnock edition of 1786. Burns included only three songs in that volume and only one of them—to the tune "Corn rigs are bonie"—is among his finest early efforts. At that stage in his career, Burns clearly thought that his poems were more impressive than his songs; the Kilmarnock edition was designed to emphasize his narrative, comic, and satiric talents. By October

103

1787, however, Burns's sense of priorities had changed. In a letter to Reverend John Skinner, author of "Tullochgorum" (Burns's own favorite song), Burns spoke of song writing with a new enthusiasm:

> The world may think slightingly of the craft of song-making, if they please, but . . . let them try. There is a certain something in the old Scotch songs, a wild happiness of thought and expression, which peculiarly marks them. . . . I have often wished, and will certainly endeavour, to form a kind of common acquaintance among all the genuine sons of Caledonian song. The World, busy in low prosaic pursuits, may overlook most of us; but "reverence thyself." The world is not our *peers*, so we challenge the jury. . . . There is a work going on in Edinburgh. . . . An engraver . . . has set about collecting and publishing all the Scotch songs, with the music, that can be found. . . . I have been absolutely crazed about it, collecting old stanzas, and every information remaining respecting their origin, authors, &c., &c. (1:133–34)[1]

The collection to which Burns refers above was James Johnson's *Scots Musical Museum* (1787–1803), for which Burns eventually contributed more than two hundred songs.[2] This was unpaid labor, much of it performed during Burns's earliest years with the Excise, when his duties (as a part-time rider) required supervision of twelve parishes and horseback travel of more than two hundred miles a week.[3]

During the 1790s, Burns also began to collect and produce songs (over one hundred in all) for George Thomson's *Select Collection of Original Scotish Airs* (1793–1826). Like Allan Ramsay's *Ever Green*, neither of these collections achieved much success in the literary marketplace, but working on such projects was, Burns wrote to Thomson, "positively [an] . . . addition" to his "enjoyments":

> I shall enter into your undertaking with all the small portion of abilities I have, strained to their utmost exertion by the impulse of Enthusiasm.—Only, don't hurry me: "Deil tak the hindmost" is by no means the Cri de guerre of my Muse.—Will you . . . let me have a list of your airs, with the first line of the verses you intend for them, that I may have an opportunity of suggesting any alteration that may occur to me—you know 'tis in the way of my trade. . . .—I say, the first line of the verses, because if they are verses that have appeared in any of our Collections of songs, I know them. . . . As to any remuneration, you may think my Songs either *above*, or *below* price; for they shall absolutely be one or the other—In the honest enthusiasm with which I

embark in your undertaking, to talk of money, fee, hire, &c. would be downright Sodomy of Soul! . . . P.S. I have some particular reasons for wishing my interference to be known as little as possible. (2:122–23)

This letter to Thomson summarizes Burns's late preoccupations: his identification of his own work with the anonymous Scottish bardic tradition and his increasing desire to keep a low public profile—to ensure that his own revisions be "known as little as possible."

His contributions to these two songbook series almost entirely engrossed Burns during the last ten years of his life. Neither Johnson nor Thomson was an ideal collaborator for Burns, but their deficiencies, in an odd way, complemented one another. James Johnson, by profession an engraver, was uneducated and disorganized, but he offered Burns a creative control rare in the eighteenth century. Burns wrote songs by memorizing the traditional tune and then fitting new words to the music; Johnson adhered to Burns's choices, both of words and of music. A major disadvantage, however, was the shoddy appearance of Johnson's series: he engraved the songs on cheap pewter plates (instead of on the customary copper or steel)—and the cost-cutting showed. In addition, scholars are still puzzling out the chaotic "coding" system by which Johnson's contributors were identified. (No songs were signed, but those entirely by Burns were supposed to be marked "R," "B," or "X"; traditional texts lightly altered by Burns were supposed to be marked "Z." Probably because of Johnson's editorial carelessness, many of Burns's contributions were not marked at all.)

George Thomson, by contrast, was an all-too-organized meddler with a grandiose conception of his series; he often substituted his own choice of tune for the originals that Burns submitted. Thomson was also an incurable anglicizer of Burns's diction. He did have his fleeting moments of insight: the air he selected for "Auld lang syne" has become standard, replacing the traditional tune from which Burns had originally worked (and which Johnson had faithfully printed in his series). Perhaps the chief benefit of Burns's association with Thomson was their correspondence: the fifty-six letters written between 1792 and 1796 in which Burns was forced to articulate his theories about folk song in order to argue, usually without effect, that his songs be printed as submitted, without editorial interference from Thomson. (Thomson's passion for tinkering was not limited to Burns alone.

Later in the series, he attempted to "correct" a song submitted by Beethoven and was duly snubbed.)

In any case, the association with Johnson produced the most reliable texts; the association with Thomson produced the most illuminating letters. The chapters that follow will rely chiefly on Johnson's series because of the difficulties involved in determining the extent of George Thomson's meddling (most volumes in his *Select Collection* were issued after Burns's death). In addition, many of the songs published in Johnson's series were annotated by Burns in an "interleaved" copy of *The Scots Musical Museum*. For songs printed in Johnson's books we have the widest spectrum of information, often including Burns's comments on the original texts and tunes, his opinion of his own version, and his own words as to the exact extent of his revisions.

Before discussing specific songs and revisions by Burns, however, it may be useful to link his preoccupation with revising later in his career to the careers of other mid and late century "bards." Burns's decade of immersion in song revising has often been viewed as a marginal enterprise, when in fact nothing could be more characteristic of major contemporary poetry than the use of traditional material both as a refuge and as a paradigm.

MANY POETS besides Burns used a bardic persona during the age of sensibility. Broadly defined, a bard is a poet whose insights convey a national perspective and for whom self-expression simultaneously involves cultural definition. The major difference between Burns and other eighteenth-century bards is that he was really from the Scottish culture his bardic personae speak for. Other poets who used bards appropriated them from historically remote or exotic cultures, so that their urgent nationalism served symbolic (or decorative) rather than authentically cultural purposes. A bard speaks the truths of his nation in midcentury writings as diverse in locale as Thomas Gray's "The Bard" (1757) and Joseph Warton's "The Dying Indian" (1755). In both poems, a haughty narrator upholds the values of a doomed society. Gray's Welsh bard mourns the death of his country's freedom, and Warton's dying Inca advises his son to stay away from European invaders.

These bards are related to the heroes of sentimental fiction discussed earlier in their alienation from the contemporary world, though in the writings of the bards this alienation takes a more covert form. Sentimental heroes announce their personal rejection of the contemporary world; bardic writers, on the other hand, rather than directly articulating their private values, array them in exotic costume and present them as the values of an entirely different society, usually one that flourished and died in an earlier age. Like sentimental heroes, then, bards reject the norms of the contemporary world, and they often indulge in heroic posture. Unlike them, however, bards seek to articulate a social context—in some earlier place or time—that was admirable. The sentimental hero's defiance of society becomes, for bards, an urgent nostalgia for other countries, other times.

The midcentury "bards" also bear an interesting relationship to their Augustan predecessors. While proceeding from an assumption inherited from Augustanism that "imitation" is a good route to self-expression, they selected as their models the verse forms and mannerisms of archaic texts. Thomas Warton chose the Elizabethans, Beattie and others imitated Spenser, Percy collected English folk songs and Shenstone (and Johnson) urged him to publish them, Smart emulated the King James translation of Biblical psalms, Chatterton became the medieval monk Rowley, and Macpherson stunned the world (chiefly western Europe) with primeval "Ossian." Even Alexander Boswell, dour parent of James, collated manuscripts of Anacreon in his leisure hours. How far back one went for a literary model seems to have depended on how discontented one was with the status quo: Blake went back to Genesis. In 1700 Dryden had said that "the Genius of our Countrymen in general [is] rather to improve an Invention, than to invent themselves,"[4] and several generations of poets succeeding him concentrated on "improving" the "inventions" of other, older writers.

Subsequent discussion will demonstrate that even writers of the mid and late eighteenth century who avoided the nationalism of a bardic voice used preexisting literary models as the armatures around which they "invented themselves," to misquote Dryden. The neoclassical emphasis on pointed expression is not characteristic of these writings, although the neoclassical policy of imitation has preserved a historical context to support the "free" utterances of the bard. The creators of bards all wished to integrate their personal message with an admired cultural or textual model. But the selection of an ideal culture and text was to be determined by each poet on his own. Pindar and Spenser have little in common except an unmistakable idio-syncrasy of style. Gray's *The Progress of Poesy* (1757) is his effort to recapture in English the sublime "voice" of Pindar, and Beattie's *The Minstrel* (1771–74) also uses a verse form strongly associated with its creator—the Spenserian stanza—as the vehicle for expressing his own notion of creativity, or what Beattie's subtitle identifies as "The Progress of Genius."

Writers of sentimental prose had tried to evolve unique forms to embody the unique qualities of their fictional heroes (for example, *Tristram Shandy* and *The Life of Johnson*). During the sentimental era, the fictional form most commonly used was the epistolary novel, which encouraged the intense involvement of readers with the charac-ters' feelings. The bards, on the other hand, although they selected their textual ideals self-consciously, adhered closely to their model once chosen, using its traditional images yet hoping to infuse into those images a personal resonance. Direct contact with the poet's feelings becomes difficult.

This somewhat fugitive quality in their self-expression is charac-teristic of mid and late eighteenth-century poets generally. Johnson found the diction of Gray's odes cumbrous, and he saw the poseur lurking behind the bard when he read "Ossian"; but his own poetry relies on Augustan conventions as thoroughly as Macpherson's relies on Highland folklore or Gray's *Progress of Poesy* on Pindar. All poets use tradition, of course, but mid and late eighteenth-century poets drew on an unusually diverse array of traditions. There was no com-munity of assumptions about which tradition produced the best poems. Another odd feature of the age was the way bards and non-bards alike seemed to subordinate themselves rather excessively to their chosen model. Thus, poets of this era seem often not so much to be emerging from traditions as to be hiding in them. Chatterton and Macpherson are the most striking instances of writers who lost them-selves in a "voice." A better poet, Thomas Gray, seems in his "Ele-gy" to achieve a distinctive tone; but in other poems, working from models as diverse as Pindar, Norse sagas, Celtic myth, and Dryden's "Alexander's Feast,"[5] he throws himself into the spirit of his models so energetically that in sections of them Gray seems to have vanished without a trace.

In his essay "Towards Defining an Age of Sensibility," Northrop Frye calls the impulse of mid and late eighteenth-century poets gen-erally an "interest in the poetic process as distinct from the product":

Where the emphasis is on the communicated product [as in Augustanism], the qualities of consciousness take the lead; a regular metre, clarity of syntax, epigram and wit, repetition of sense in antithesis and balance rather than sound. . . . Where the emphasis is on the original process, the qualities of subconscious association take the lead, and the poetry becomes hypnotically repetitive, oracular, incantatory, dreamlike and in the original sense of the word charming. The response to it includes a subconscious factor, the surrendering to a spell. In Ossian, who carries this tendency further than anyone else, the aim is not concentration of sense but diffusion of sense.[6]

Frye's account of the "voice" of sensibility de-emphasizes the extent to which this poetry was based on formal models (and perhaps neglects the influence of nonclassical factors on poets of "product"—John Dryden much preferred Chaucer to Martial). But Frye's is still a convincing analysis of our response to the "diffusion" and repetition of these bardic poems. And his point that we "surrender" to the oracular rhythm of Rowley and Ossian can be expanded: the poets' surrender to their personae is at least as marked as ours.

What was explicit imitation in Augustan writings (Pope's Horatian epistles, Swift's poems in imitation of Juvenal, and Johnson's *London* all announce in their title or subtitle their subordination to a model) became forgery—"pseudoepigraphia," as Frye calls it—for a significant number of mid and late eighteenth-century poets. The adversarial relationship between contemporary writers and their public discussed earlier can thus be seen in the contemporary relationship between the "bards" and their readers. James Macpherson produced an apocryphal version of primitive Highland culture which most of his Scottish readers took to be authentic. (Indeed, belief in the authenticity of Ossian is not unusual even today in Scotland.) Robert Burns, too, used imitation in this self-concealing way. His songs, usually reconstructed and revised from fragments, were often sent to his editors as untouched material Burns had merely collected: "Auld lang syne" is one example of a song largely written by Burns that Burns himself disclaimed, calling it the work of a nameless ancient bard. This self-concealing use of imitation argues a strong degree of dissociation between the private selves and public roles of contemporary poets.

William Cowper did not consider himself a bard, yet he too was a poet of his time in his retreat from society and also in the somewhat fugitive relationship in his poetry between self-expression and tradition. Whereas the bards selected some archaic or exotic culture to speak for, Cowper selected the traditional images of Scripture. Unlike the poseur bards, however, Cowper never entirely hid behind a persona. He often connected his feelings explicitly to his subjects, the most famous connection appearing in book 3 of *The Task* (1785):

> I was a stricken deer, that left the herd
> Long since; with many an arrow deep infixt
> My panting side was charg'd, when I withdrew
> To seek a tranquil death in distant shades.[7]

Yet it is not independently that Cowper reveals himself in metaphor; it is, as Patricia Spacks has noted in *The Poetry of Vision*,[8] through conventions associated with Scripture—Biblical images, parables such as the stricken deer, or hymns:

> To me, the waves that ceaseless broke
>   Upon the dang'rous coast
> Hoarsely and ominously spoke
>   Of all my treasure lost.
>
> Your sea of troubles you have past,
>   And found the peaceful shore;
> I, tempest-toss'd, and wreck'd at last,
>   Come home to port no more.
>
> (p. 308)

Like the Psalmist of the Bible, Cowper uses images of deluge and storms to express the hazards of faith and the fear of loss of identity. Cowper's use of such images, however, is often personal and subversive. In the poem just quoted, the speaker does not express a fear of drowning in order ultimately to be reconfirmed in faith (as in a Psalm); he expresses a fear, and then he does drown.

"The Castaway" also draws connotative power from the Psalms that express this fear of deluge and from the story of Jonah. Cowper describes the fate of a sailor swept overboard during a storm who had drowned while his helpless friends looked on; and Cowper is moved to compare this man's doom explicitly to his own:

> No voice divine the storm allay'd,
>   No light propitious shone;
> When, snatch'd from all effectual aid,
>   We perish'd, each alone:

> But I beneath a rougher sea,
> And whelm'd in deeper gulphs than he.
>
> (p. 432)

Psalms may begin in doubt ("the waters are come in unto my soul. / I sink in deep mire, / Where there is no standing: / I am come into deep waters, / Where the floods overflow me" [Psalm 69]), but they characteristically end in praise ("For the Lord heareth the poor, / And despiseth not his prisoners. / Let the heaven and earth praise him, / The seas, and everything that moveth therein" [69]). In "The Castaway," on the other hand, the imagery associated with traditional psalms has been employed finally to insist on the poet's despair. In Cowper's use of the tradition, the psalm becomes an antipsalm.

A subversion of the emulated ideal can also be seen in Samuel Johnson's last English poem (November 1784), where he translates Horace's list of heroes and gods who failed to surmount mortality. Despite its Augustan model and its conventional elegiac meter, Johnson's poem is more abrupt than urbane, alternating between the perfunctory ("The sprightly nymph and naked grace / The mazy dance together trace") and the trenchant ("Who knows if Jove who counts our score / Will toss us in a morning more?") and modulating to a conclusion remarkable for its tense economy of expression:

> Not you, Torquatus, boast of Rome,
> When Minos once has fix'd your doom,
> Or eloquence, or splendid birth,
> Or virtue shall replace on earth.
> Hippolytus unjustly slain
> Diana calls to life in vain,
> Nor can the might of Theseus rend
> The chains of Hell that hold his friend.[9]

Johnson employs the closed rhyme scheme of octosyllabics and the elegant closure of Horace, yet neither wholly steadies an anxious undercurrent in the verses. Although I do not depart here from the view that Johnson remained an Augustan throughout his life, I see Johnson as a poet of his time in the way he freights conventional models with a heavy cargo of private feeling and also in his tendency to apply Augustan rhetoric to emotionally charged or pathetic subjects (as in *The Vanity of Human Wishes*). The Augustan conventions thus seem more moving when they appear in Johnson's work. As with Cowper in "The

Castaway," then, Johnson in his last Horatian imitation adheres closely to a textual model; yet paradoxically, that convention becomes a
medium for expressing not stability but tension.

Both for Cowper and Johnson, reverence for sanity and tradition
was not accompanied by any sustained confidence in their ability to
achieve them as goals. Perhaps it is the stress reflected in their poetry
that makes it so much more interesting than that of the poseur bards:
Beattie's relationship to Spenser was both easier and more facile than
Cowper's relationship to Scripture. In any case, the ideal cultural or
textual model emulated by each poet is a source of alternating hope
and despair in the best poetry of the mid and late eighteenth century,
a conflict which has been documented in several classic critical
studies.[10]

William Collins may not have been haunted like Cowper and Johnson by the *Dies Irae*,[11] but he did have to contend with the ghosts of
Shakespeare, Spenser, and the Milton of "Il Penseroso." Indeed, in
"Ode on the Poetical Character," Collins confesses he feels ill-
equipped even to follow Waller: "With many a view from hope's aspir-
ing tongue, / My trembling feet his guiding steps pursue: / In vain—."[12]
Collins felt reduced in stature by the very excellence of the literary
models he pursued, a state of mind that corresponded to Johnson's
inertia in the performance of religious duties he theoretically took
seriously, as well as to Cowper's despairing view of his unregenerate,
doomed, yet God-given nature. For all three poets, self-doubt led to a
tense sort of poetry, self-attentive although seldom independently self-
expressive, and never self-approving. In his fragmentary "Lines
Addressed to a Fastidious Critic," Collins at once suggests his high standard for excellence and his own depressed condition: "But Black-
[well's] self might doubt if all of art / Were self-produced in one
exhaustless heart" (p. 537). Mid and late century poets all assumed that
art could not be "self-produced." They commonly selected some spec-
tacularly successful traditional model to embody their sense of the
heroic possibilities of poetry while helping them also to amplify their
message, using the resonance of the chosen tradition.

The worst danger inherent in this method of compositon was obsession, and Christopher Smart's poetry provides an example of it. In his
later work, Smart began to associate his own poetic life with that of the
poet-king David. Parts of *Jubilate Agno* and all of *A Song to David* celebrate the diverse achievements of his hero, who was king, prophet,

musician and poet—demonstrating rapport with divine, political and aesthetic orders. In the impressive figure of David, Smart found an ideal to challenge him, but also a challenge that humbled him. In "A Song to David," the poet-king is his "peril" as well as his "prize."[13] The relationship of Smart to David was like that of Collins to Shakespeare or Cowper to the Psalmist. The very transcendence of the chosen ideal could threaten to preempt the poet in his own poem.

The common use of the image of a "mine" by these writers suggests their ambivalence and also demonstrates the rich vein of ambiguity and submerged self-reference in their work. Johnson, Cowper and Smart all used the figure, which connotes danger, suffocation, and imprisonment on the one hand, and untapped wealth on the other. "Mine" is also the first person singular of the possessive pronoun. "Hope's delusive mine" was Johnson's metaphor for every human consciousness in his elegy "On the Death of Mr. Robert Levet" (1784). Self-awareness is the "mine" in which all are condemned to toil, seeking delusive hopes as though they were real objects. This is a strong, and inherently joyless, image of individual consciousness. (Johnson will subsequently counter this image with the better way of life pursued by Levet—one of selfless service to others.) Christopher Smart uses the image of a "mine" in a defensive self-justification: "For there is silver in my mines and I bless God that it is rather there than in my coffers."[14] In one of Cowper's most famous Olney hymns, the "unfathomable mine" is said to be lighted up with the workings of divine ingenuity:

> Deep in unfathomable mines
> Of never failing skill;
> [God] treasures up his bright designs,
> And works his sovereign will.
>
> (p. 455)

The poet's personal view of creativity can only be calculated by reduction of what he says about the "bright designs" of his Creator. In this, Cowper is similar to Christopher Smart, whose personal values pervade the pseudo-Scripture of *Jubilate Agno*, though Smart seldom refers directly to himself.

George Eliot praised Cowper's "calm gladness that springs from a delight in objects for their own sake, without self-reference."[15] Yet

Cowper's sympathy for humble objects was extended more for pity's sake than for "their own." And the "calm gladness" of *The Task* is a constructed, not an innate, serenity; like *Jubilate Agno*, Cowper's poem was undertaken as therapy, and the tranquil order it describes was not to Cowper so much a fact as an embodied wish. Self-reference is usually accomplished in Cowper and Smart through Biblical allusion; the paucity of direct self-expression, however, indicates not apathy but ambivalence, which shows itself within the poem as subterranean, unrefined ore. In *Jubilate Agno* Smart remarks with his usual pithy ambiguity: "For I have seen the White Raven & Thomas Hall of Willingham & am myself a greater curiosity than both" (p. 45). We are left to infer whether Smart is labeling himself a prodigy or merely a freak, and this dubious consciousness of curious gifts was shared to some extent by most poets of Smart's day.

"The Snail," a translation by Cowper from the French of Vincent Bourne, offers perspective—cloaked by metaphor—on how one of these poets viewed the relationship of "self" to "form." Cowper's description of the self-sufficient, "self-collecting" snail, whose security and uniqueness is provided by its shell, suggests his own tendency (and I would say the tendency of his age) to seek in tradition a formal shell for the poet's self:

> To grass, or leaf, or fruit, or wall,
> The snail sticks close, nor fears to fall,
> As if he grew there, house and all
> > Together.
>
> Within that house secure he hides,
> When danger imminent betides
> Of storm, or other harm besides
> > Of weather.
>
> Give but his horns the slightest touch,
> His self-collecting power is such,
> He shrinks into his house with much
> > Displeasure.
>
> Where'er he dwells, he dwells alone,
> Except himself has chattels none,
> Well satisfied to be his own
> > Whole treasure.

Thus, hermit-like, his life he leads
Nor partner of his banquet needs,
And if he meets one, only feeds
                    The faster.

Who seeks him must be worse than blind
(He and his house are so combin'd)
If, finding it, he fails to find
                    Its master.
                    (p. 560)

Cowper is working here from another poet's concept—Bourne's French poem; but the view of form implied here seems to me generally suggestive of the age in which these poets lived. The snail's shell is the inorganic "house" of the living snail. Yet, though composed of heterogeneous materials, snail and shell are so "combin'd" that to "find" the house is to "find"—if not fully to see—its "master." A form is something in which to "collect" the self—to Bourne, as to Cowper, it is a place into which the self "retreats."

Literary forms were to many contemporary poets a protective husk more than a transparent medium. This is a different idea of creative expression from the organic relationship between poet and verse form that Wordsworth suggested in the preface to *Lyrical Ballads* and Coleridge later codified in *Biographia Literaria*. Cowper suggests that the snail is connected to its shell (the living self to form) not by identity but by proximity. They are "stuck close," not united—a mixed combination (snail and housing) and not a single entity. And Cowper's view is no more like the Augustan ideal of perfection through form than it is like the Romantic ideal of organic expressiveness. It approaches the ironic self-deprecation of Wallace Stevens: "The truth itself, the first idea becomes / The hermit in a poet's metaphors,"[16] but Cowper's religious obsession precluded any tendency toward the modern poet's irony.

In any case, two generalizations can be drawn from discussion of these mid and late eighteenth-century poets. They commonly show subservience to pre-existing, ideal models, and they commonly attempt to reanimate those ideals by relying on conventional images already associated with them. Finally, all tend to subvert those revered models by the implicit self-reference in which they covertly indulge. The poets discussed so far—the forgers Macpherson and Chatterton, the simple bards and folklore buffs such as Beattie, the Wartons and Bishop Percy, and the complex poets Johnson, Cowper, Smart, and Collins—all displayed different measures of confidence in their ability to recapture their traditional model. But they commonly subordinated each poem they wrote to the demands of some transcendent value.

Chapter 9, which will analyze Burns's revisions of Scottish songs, will also discuss the procedures of a poet who saw in his literary project a challenge that exceeded any means he could invent to fulfill it. In his letters, Burns sometimes says that his interest in song collecting is a simple matter of a Scotsman wishing to help preserve the native music of his country. While that simple motive was in part responsible, discussion of the song revisions will show how self-preservation was also among Burns's motives as he revised traditional material. His private values are consistently—if covertly—conveyed in most of his song revisions. Burns's role as a bard is not one in which he utters the values of his country as naively and naturally as he breathes. Rather, he is, like Cowper or Smart, a complex poet who subordinates himself to a tradition he himself regards as transcendent, so that his own compatible ideals can be amplified to seem the values of a whole country. Burns's reliance on the traditional images of Scottish song is as thoroughgoing as Cowper's on Biblical images; and Burns's praise of the old Scots bards has in it a compensatory element similar to, though less stressful than, Smart's hero worship of King David.

Scottish song fragments were the formal shell into which Burns chose to retreat after Edinburgh. He promised friends who were concerned about his immersion in revision (thinking such work too easy for Burns) that he would try his hand at epics, novels, or plays; but all he wanted was to continue as a bard. Smart uses Biblical allusions in such a personal way that, though familiar, they regain power in his highly private synthesis. Burns demonstrates a similar paradox, for, though consciously subordinating himself to preexisting texts, he generally substituted his own values for theirs as he revised, thus making them his own. Hugh MacDiarmid, who tried all his life to reclaim Scottish vernacular poetry from the shadow of Burns, rightly noted that Burns's revisions do considerable violence in many cases to the spirit of his originals.[17] The negative way in which he expresses his insight is, though understandable, unfortunate. Indeed, like

Smart's piety, Burns's patriotism has been a highly problematic thing for posterity to understand.

In *The Songs of Robert Burns* (1903), J. C. Dick suggests that traditional Scots song might have perished altogether through the tinkerings of genteel editors had it not been for Burns's project of creating good "polite" verses for them that perpetuate the tunes by accurately indicating the native stresses in the music.[18] Yet Dick gives Burns credit for singlehandedly saving some forty-five of the airs in *The Scots Musical Museum* when many of the airs had already been published in the songbooks of Alexander McGlashan (1780–81, 1786) and James Aird (1782–99). Burns's contributions as an antiquarian, in short, were not considerable. William Stenhouse's notes to Johnson's *Scots Musical Museum*, which predate Dick's work, point out many of the published sources of the tunes Burns used and thus reduce Burns's status as a preserver of oral traditions.[19] At least one modern editor, G. Legman, accuses Burns of bowdlerization:

> It may come as a surprise to the reader to learn that Burns appears to have been one of the most important bowdlerizers and expurgators of folk-song, on a wholesale basis, of whom any record exists. Were any poet of lesser stature to engage today in even a tenth of the revision and castration of folk-collected originals that Burns considered to be his "patriotic" duty, no folklorist—and almost no literary critic—would hesitate to assail him as a forger. . . . In the case of a great poet like Burns one would hesitate, of course, to apply such words as "forgery," and his revisions are to be gratefully accepted as what they are: the product of his genius influenced by folk materials.[20]

Though ultimately Legman finds Burns not guilty as charged, his ambivalence about Burns's revisionary procedures is clear. Yet assailing Burns for changing "John Anderson my jo" is exactly as sensible as accusing Chatterton of pretending to be a medieval poet named Rowley. Legman concludes in a later section of his introduction to Burns's *Merry Muses* that Burns's song revising was a "failure"—on which Burns "threw away" ten years of effort—because Burns's versions are not preferred to the older forms in folk performance (p. xli). This is like calling *Jubilate Agno* a waste of Smart's time in confinement because its theology has never become part of the Anglican canon.

Perhaps on some purely folk level, Burns's songs have gone un-

used—though this neglect might be explained in some part by
Burns's preference for fiddle tunes as the basis for many songs. (The
violin has a wider range than most voices; Burns's songs are often
vocally unattainable by untrained singers.) It is in any case undenia-
ble that when a musician performs a song by Burns it is in tribute to
Burns himself, not to the collective tradition of folklore. On the other
hand, it is also true that to the popular mind outside of Scotland,
Burns's songs simply are the Scottish folk tradition. Emerson said in
1859 that Burns's work "offers the only example in history of a language made classic through the genius of a single man" (Low, *The
Critical Heritage*, p. 435). This is one of the things Burns accomplished
through his song revising, for it was his songs that disseminated Scots
vernacular into the vocabulary of the world. To paraphrase Johnson
writing on Pope: if that be failure, where is success to be found?

It is in Burns's popularity—in the success of his synthesis of personal values and Scottish tradition—that he differs significantly from
such mid and late eighteenth-century poets as Smart and Collins,
whose allegiance to more esoteric models makes them obscure. But
like those poets, Burns subjected every song he wrote to a comprehensive ideal standard. Burns's ideal was Scottish song, and his heroes
were the old Scottish bards. His "textual" model was the existing
music and the fragments of verse for each song. Burns considered
individual songs to be only "vehicles to the music."[21] In his annotations to *The Scots Musical Museum*, Burns refers mostly to the sources of
tunes he used and hardly at all to his own verses, unless to apologize
for their deficiencies: "Here, once for all, let me apologize for many
silly compositions of mine in this work. Many beautiful airs wanted
words; in the hurry of other avocations, if I could string a parcel of
rhymes together any thing near tolerable, I was fain to let them pass"
(p. 24).

As with his contemporaries, Burns's acceptance of a role subordinate to his model was at best a way to relax into powerful creative
expression; at worst, it was an obsession that frustrated him by the
very magnitude of the task it set. Cowper drew both his conventional
imagery and his powerful sense of personal destiny from the Bible; in
its own way, Scots song performed this focusing function for Burns.

Like other contemporary poets, too, Burns chose conformity to a
preexisting tradition not out of a conservative love of form for its own
sake but out of a strong private idealism that required support from

some transcendent source. Burns's reverence for the old bards was centered around the way that—submerging himself in the traditions they had established—he could still see himself in the values they expressed: "Bards . . . described the exploits of Heroes, the pangs of disappointment, & the meltings of Love, with such fine strokes of Nature. . . . O ye illustrious names unknown! the last, the meanest . . . one who though far inferior to your flights, yet eyes your path. . . . pays this sympathetic pang to your memory."[22] Like Collins's regard for his predecessors, Burns's avowed reverence for ancient Scottish bards (and his respects are paid to individuals, however anonymous; not to a collective folk tradition) was partly pure admiration and partly a way of working depressed creative energies up to a competitive pitch. His enthusiasm for the bards did not prevent him from altering their texts if he decided their "strokes of Nature" were not "fine" enough.

As a bard, Burns could work with the preexisting music and even with traditional images worn thin from use. Burns's heroes, the Scottish bards, had used them and even the commonplaces seemed to Burns suggestive of values he wanted to embody within this tradition he trusted. In *Jubilate Agno*, when Smart reveals why he loves God, he says it is because God signifies love ("For L is love. God in every language." [p.107]). And like Smart's God, Burns's folk song signified love, which signified everything: "Love is the Alpha and Omega of human enjoyment. . . . It is the emanation of Divinity . . . Without it, life would be a damning gift" (*Glenriddle Manuscripts*, p. 23). Chapter 9 will discuss how Burns adapted old songs to express his sense of the "Alpha and Omega" of human life.

9

The Songs

Of Burns's 330 songs, some are wholly original and others almost wholly traditional. Like the ratio of vernacular Scots to standard English in Burns's poetic language, the ratio of traditional to new material in Burns's songs varies considerably. The task of determining the extent of Burns's contributions is, however, simplified by the existence of an "interleaved" copy of Johnson's *Scots Musical Museum* that Burns annotated, often recording the traditional stanzas he had worked from and discussing his reasons for altering them. Most of the songs discussed in this chapter received this special attention from Burns, or are texts for which the extent of Burns's contribution has been otherwise determined.

There are other unusual problems posed by Burns's songs. Some lyrics that work beautifully on the page are ill-matched to their tunes and cannot be regarded as great if strictly considered as songs (for example, "Mary Morison"). Other songs that may seem on the page to verge on doggerel rhythm are set to intricate tunes and are brilliantly fluid in performance (such as "Sodger laddie," the song from "Love and Liberty" discussed in chapter 2). Songs that may seem rather slight on the page achieve an exquisite simplicity when heard with their perfectly matched melodies; "The bonny wee thing" is one such song. Finally, many of Burns's finest songs are set to dance and fiddle music (instrumental "reels," "jigs," and such that Burns slowed to adapt them to lyric stanzas): it is a matter of interpretation just how slowly Burns intended his songs to be performed. Thus, not only Burns's words but also the "airs" to which he set the words offer a spectrum of interpretative possibilities. For some sense of how broad that spectrum is, the spare, powerful recordings of Burns's songs made by Ewan MacColl may be compared to the more elaborate arrangements of Jean Redpath (whose more studied versions are, incidentally, probably closer to what Burns intended when he set out to provide "drawing room" verses for the old airs of Scottish bawdry).

The most comprehensive treatment of Burns as a lyric writer is Thomas Crawford's *Society and the Lyric;* and the best discussion of the musical quality of the songs is Cedric Thorpe-Davie's "Robert Burns, Writer of Songs." The discussion that follows will, by contrast, be selective rather than exhaustive. I will focus on a wide range of songs, of high literary quality, that we know Burns revised. The consistency and coherence of Burns's mature aesthetic can only be understood fully in terms of how and why he changed traditional folk material.

In one of his annotations to Johnson's *Scots Musical Museum,* Burns said of the air "Corn rigs are bonie" that "there must have been an old song under this title, the chorus of it is all that remains":

> O corn rigs and rye rigs,
> O corn rigs are bonie;
> And whene'er ye meet a bonie lass,
> Preen up her cockernony.[1]

In Stenhouse's commentary to James Johnson, another version of "Corn rigs" current in Burns's day is cited, Allan Ramsay's conclusion to *The Gentle Shepherd:*

> Let maidens of a silly mind
> Refuse what maist they're wanting;
> Since we for yielding are design'd,
> We chastely should be granting;
> Then I'll comply, and marry Pate,
> And syne my cockernony,
> He's free to touzle, air or late,
> Where corn-riggs are bonny.[2]

One would never know from Ramsay's rhetorical version that he was not one of Edinburgh's literary lawyers. His shepherdess, with her syllogistic assent to Pate, is wholly unlike Burns's heroine in his version. Burns wrote the following stanzas in the earliest stage of his career, between 1774 and 1784:

> It was upon a Lammas night,
>   When corn rigs are bonie,
> Beneath the moon's unclouded light,
>   I held awa to Annie:
> The time flew by, wi' tentless heed,
>   Till 'tween the late and early;
> Wi' sma' persuasion she agreed,
>   To see me thro' the barley.
> ....
>
> I hae been blythe wi' Comrades dear;
>   I hae been merry drinking;
> I hae been joyfu' gath'rin gear;
>   I hae been happy thinking:
> But a' the pleasures e'er I saw,
>   Tho' three times doubl'd fairly,
> That happy night was worth them a',
>   Amang the rigs o' barley.
>
> *Chorus*
> Corn rigs, an' barley rigs,
>   An' corn rigs are bonie:
> I'll ne'er forget that happy night,
>   Amang the rigs wi' Annie.
>
>   (1:13–14)

This very early song shows an already mature lyric ability. Like most of Burns's early work, "Corn rigs are bonie" sounds auto-biographical, but except for this self-reference, it can be compared to his later revisions. Notable throughout Burns's songs, early and late, is the absence of a double standard for sexuality. Annie agrees "wi' sma' persuasion"—Burns does not present the "happy night" so much as a seduction as an episode involving mutual agreement. The fragment of the folk stanza quoted above is impersonal and anecdotal, as the old fragments often are. "Whene'er ye meet a bonie lass / Preen (pin) up her cockernony (hair)" is a rather crude parody of a proverb. Burns's "I held awa' to Annie," on the other hand, introduces two individuals into the setting of the harvest fields and makes a story out of a piece of gnomic advice. Allan Ramsay took from the old fragment only the harvest setting and the idea of tousling the girl's hair (he applied the image more literally than in the folk chorus, where double entendre was intended).

In the second and third stanzas of his version, Burns develops the harvest theme simultaneously with the theme of mutual pleasure by alternating his rhymes: the fruition of the environment is juxtaposed to the fulfillment of the lovers' feelings:

> The sky was blue, the wind was still,
>   The moon was shining clearly;
> I set her down, wi' right good will,
>   Amang the rigs o' barley:
> I ken't her heart was a' my ain;
>   I lov'd her most sincerely;
> I kiss'd her owre and owre again,
>   Amang the rigs o' barley.
>
> I lock'd her in my fond embrace;
>   Her heart was beating rarely:
> My blessings on that happy place,
>   Amang the rigs o' barley!
> But by the moon and stars so bright,
>   That shone that hour so clearly!
> She ay shall bless that happy night,
>   Amang the rigs o' barley.
>
>   (1:14)

The first stanza concentrates on the speaker's feelings, describing them in concert with the blue sky, still wind, and clear moon of the environment; the second describes Annie's, again in harmony with the natural setting. The speaker blesses "that happy place" while avowing that Annie herself will always bless that "happy night." Happiness links the characters to their environment and to each other. Burns's version of "Corn rigs" is designed to convey a totality of happy emotions; it blends description and appraisal, avoiding both the baldness of the folk source and the rhetorical excesses (emotional falseness) of Ramsay's version.

In a letter of April 1793 to George Thomson, Burns tried to persuade the editor to insert his version of "Corn rigs are bonie" into the *Select Collection* in preference to Ramsay's: "[His version] is surely far unworthy of Ramsay, or your book.—My Song, 'Rigs of barley,' to the same air, does not altogether please me; but if I can mend it, & thresh a few loose sentiments out of it, I shall submit it to your consideration" (*Letters*, 2:166). Thomson, however, continued to prefer Ramsay's song (in a typical demonstration of his tastelessness), and Burns's version went to Thomson's rival editor, James Johnson. (It had appeared, without musical notation, in the Kilmarnock edition of his *Poems.*) Burns's statement that "Corn rigs" was not yet pulled together to his satisfaction (some "loose sentiments" remained to be "threshed out") indicates the high standard to which he submitted his work.

This standard was a matter of delicate balance between the natural and the artificial, and Burns's view of the dynamic requirements of good lyric writing seems to have been shaped to some extent by the work of John Aikin (1747–1822), a man he admired as "a great Critic . . . on songs" (*Letters*, 2:284). In his *Essays on Song Writing* (1772), Aikin—a physician and brother of Mrs. Barbauld—had separated songs into several types:

> The rude original pastoral poetry of our country . . . [is] ballads. These consist of the village tale, the dialogue of rustic courtship, the description of natural objects, and the incidents of a rural life. . . . Nature, further refined, but still nature, gives the second class of pieces containing the sentimental part of the former, abstracted from the tale and rural landscape, and improved by a more studied observation of the internal feelings of passion and their external symptoms. It is the natural philosophy of the mind, and the description of sensations.[3]

Aikin's first and most primitive song type, the ballad, primarily tells a story. His second, the sentimental song, primarily conveys a feeling. Both song types confine themselves to a rustic subject matter; what separates the two is the level of emotional integration. Aikin's sentimental song is in fact an internalized "refinement" and "improvement" on the ballad: the ballad's emphasis on narrative has become subordinated to the expression of some powerful feeling.

It was, of course, Aikin's sentimental song that corresponded to Burns's own revisions, virtually all of which are "abstracted" from tales of "rural life" but "improved by a more studied observation of . . . feelings." Burns loved the old Scots airs exactly as they were, but considered the fragmentary existing verses fair game for refinement and improvement. Like Aikin, Burns distinguished between ancientness and authenticity as lyric effects and aimed his own revisions toward the latter. There is every evidence that Burns, like Aikin, without actually wishing to suppress older verses, considered many of them too "rude" to deserve preservation. In one letter, for instance, he dismissed the traditional stanzas to "The posie": "it is well known in the West country, but the old words are trash" (*Letters*, 2:266).

In his introduction to *Notes on Scottish Song*, J. C. Dick cites Joseph Ritson's "Historical Essay," prefixed to the collection *Scotish Songs* (1794), as the first real history of Scots lyric writing ever to appear. Dick does not also mention Burns's dislike of some of Ritson's ideas. Burns's resistance has its bearing, however, on his support of Aikin's theories and his attitude toward song revising. Ritson (1752–1803) was a folklorist, vegetarian, and polemicist who had written on English lyric tradition before turning to Scottish song. What immediately struck Ritson was the prevalence of revisionism among the Scottish bards. Ritson was annoyed at the "impunity" with which such poets as Ramsay had rewritten old song fragments. Ritson's view was that "modern taste" was inimical to the pith of realism that animates old texts; and his annoyance is expressed in the introduction to *Scotish Songs* in highly sarcastic passages: "Why the Scotish literati should be more particularly addicted to literary imposition than those of any other country, might be a curious subject of investigation for their new Royal Society. . . . The history of Scotish poetry exhibits a series of fraud, forgery and imposture, practiced with impunity and success."[4]

Ritson included two songs by Burns in his collection: "When *Guilford* good our Pilot stood" and "Willie brew'd a peck o' maut." Neither is an especially lyrical lyric: Ritson's selections show his antiquarian and anthropological orientation. A pioneer collector of Robin Hood legends and English fairy tales, Ritson seems to have been rather insensitive to lyric poetry, judging by his verdicts both on Robert Fergusson and Robert Burns: "Robert Fergusson . . . is the author of two tolerably pretty love-songs. . . . Robert Burns, a natural poet of the first eminence, does not, perhaps, appear to his usual advantage in song: *non omnia possumus*" (pp. lxxiv–lxxv). A man who could miss Fergusson's comic genius and print "two tolerably pretty" love songs and then question Burns's talent for lyric composition was bound to irritate Burns. Most interesting is Burns's accusation in a letter to George Thomson that Ritson sent his unretouched songs "naked into the world": "A lady of my acquaintance, a noted performer, plays, 'Nae luck about the house,' & sings it at the same time so charmingly, that I shall never bear to see any of her songs sent into the world as naked as Mr. What-d-ye-call-um has done in his London Collection" (*Letters*, 2:267).[5] Burns is criticizing Ritson's omission of music from his English songbook; but both the lack of musical accompaniment and the purist approach to the old song fragments signified to Burns a museum-piece attitude toward what Burns liked to regard as a malleable living tradition. Indeed, as a folklorist, Ritson's chief interest necessarily was in Aikin's primitive first category of song— the rude ballad. And though Burns thought Ritson's critical approach in the English songbook "interesting," he resented Ritson's apparent view in the Scottish collection that Robert Burns should be grouped with the primitives: "The legion of Scotish Poetasters of the day, whom your brother Editor, Mr Ritson, ranks with me as my coevals, have always mistaken vulgarity for simplicity; whereas Simplicity is as much eloignée from vulgarity, on the one hand, as from affected point & puerile conceit, on the other" (2:276). "Vulgarity" on the one hand and "puerile conceit" on the other were the two extremes between which the lyric writer of Aikin's "natural" but refined second category had to steer his songs; and Burns could be a harsh judge if he perceived too much of either quality in a composition. One of his own revisions, "The last time I came o'er the moors," was ultimately rejected on the grounds of "affected point": "On reading over this song, I see it is but a cold, inanimate composition" (2:173). He criticized vulgarity elsewhere, criticizing Thomson's selection of one popular old text, for instance, as "foolish": "I am out of temper that you should set so sweet, so tender an air, as 'Deil tak the war,' to the foolish old verses" (2:272).

Burns's concept of lyric simplicity is, then, Horatian: a bard mediates between the two undesirable extremes of "vulgarity" on the one hand and frigid "affected point" on the other. To Burns, a bard's relationship to tradition was properly self-conscious, not naive: the texts to songs, old or new, should measure up to a high standard of emotional coherence and expressiveness. Thus, Burns greatly differs from Ritson (and the folkloric or anthropological approach to song collecting) and corresponds closely to Aikin.

Both Burns and Aikin valued what they called a realistic effect, yet both saw realism to result from an emphasis on feelings. Ritson and other antiquarians, on the other hand, perceived "realism" to be that shaggy, brusque effect often created by the interplay of different "voices" within the collective repository of the folk text. To Ritson, whatever parts of songs showed integration of personal statement were immediately to be suspected as forgeries. To Aikin and Burns, however, integration of emotion within a single speaker was the sole purpose of that second, sentimental category of lyric writing. As Aikin writes:

> The lover . . . must seek . . . . to express the emotions of his mind. He must *burn* with desire, and *freeze* with disdain; rage with the *ocean*, and sigh with the *zephir*. . . . The effects which the passions produce upon the body . . . also prove a happy source of the description of emotions. Thus the fluttering pulse, the changing colour, the feverish glow, the failing heart and the confused senses, being natural and invariable symptoms of the passion of love . . . successfully heighten his description. Hitherto all is simple and natural, and poetry so far from being the art of fiction, is the faithful copyist of external objects and real emotion. (pp. 5–6)

Aikin's requirement that his second category of songs be "simple and natural" is actually rigorous, because in his view this naturalness was a result of the adept recreation of "real emotions." And as his own cliché-ridden list of possible tropes indicates, "real" emotion is not that easy to express in words. Burns, a poet rather than a doctor, avoided Aikin's clinical approach to describing the "symptoms" of passion; and even in his adaptation of one set of old verses in which the speaker is experiencing something like Aikin's "freezing disdain," Burns is able to authenticate the commonplace:

> Oh, open the door, some pity to shew,
>   If love it may na be, Oh;
> Tho' thou hast been false, I'll ever prove true,
>   Oh, open the door to me, Oh.
>
> Cauld is the blast upon my pale cheek,
>   But caulder thy love for me, Oh:
> The frost that freezes the life at my heart,
>   Is nought to my pains frae thee, Oh.
>
> The wan moon sets behind the white wave,
>   And time is setting with me, Oh:
> False friends, false love, farewell! for mair
>   I'll ne'er trouble them, nor thee, Oh.
>   (2:681–82)

Burns's original touches to this old Irish song constitute the finest lines: the last two of the second stanza and the first two of the third, for instance, are by Burns. W. B. Yeats singled out the beginning of stanza three in a discussion of poetic diction:

There are no lines with more melancholy beauty than these by Burns—

> The white [sic] moon is setting behind the white wave,
> And time is setting with me, O!

and these lines are perfectly symbolical. Take from them the whiteness of the moon and of the wave, whose relationship to . . . time is too subtle for the intellect, and you take from them . . . their beauty. . . . All sounds, all colours, all forms, either because of their pre-ordained energies or because of long association, evoke indefinable and yet precise emotions, or, as I prefer to think, call down among us certain disembodied powers, whose footprints over our hearts we call emotions.[6]

Like Burns and Aikin, Yeats saw reality in poems to be a matter of the emotional intensity conveyed. What Yeats called "symbolism," Burns, following Aikin, called "simplicity." When Burns praised an old Scots air, it was often in terms highly similar to Yeats's praise above of Burns's lines. In one letter to Frances Dunlop, for instance, he defined a song's symbolic power: "Notwithstanding its rude simplicity [it] speaks feelingly to the heart" (*Letters*, 2:4). And when Burns sought to expand the emotional significance of conventional figures or old texts, he tended, like Yeats, to stress "colors," "forms," "precise yet indefinable" feelings. As other critics have observed, one of his most famous songs, "A red red Rose," is distinguished largely by the inspired repetition of "red" in the first line, which encourages the reader or listener to see the rose—reanimating a too-familiar image.

Even in his comic songs or densely vernacular lyrics, Burns's chief concern was to use his folk models expansively—to show characters who embody certain emotions. Modern critics writing on Burns have tended to overstress the songs' "realism"; actually, Burns's song revisions are both more and less than "real." Burns's sturdy and impulsive heroines, for instance, though thoroughly appealing, do not sustain the claims of several critics that Burns was a "master of feminine psychology."[7] His women speakers are indeed, as Thomas Crawford calls them, "the feminine equivalent of the 'man o' independent mind'" that Burns saw as the masculine ideal. But the wholly positive attitude of his heroines to sexual experience is essentially supported by their complacent attitude toward unwanted or unwed pregnancy; and this has more to do with the wishes of Burns that with the psychology of women. To be candid, even feckless, in one's emotional responses was central to Burns's idea of being heroically human (as later discussion of "Tam o' Shanter" will show). But no real woman has ever combined an independent mind with the total lack of rancor shown by the abandoned narrator of "Here's his health in water":

> Although my back be at the wa',
>   And though he be the fautor,
> Although my back be at the wa',
>   Yet here's his health in water.—
>
> O wae gae by his wanton sides,
>   Sae brawly's he could flatter;
> Till for his sake I'm slighted sair,
>   And dree the kintra clatter:
> But though my back be at the wa',
>   Yet here's his health in water.—
>
>   (2:868)

Burns had a prototype for a tolerant female temperament in his own wife, Jean Armour—by all accounts a paragon either of magnanimity or passivity. But Jean lacked the spirit of Burns's song heroines: she had forbearance but was easily bullied, or so it appears from Burns's descriptions of her in letters to friends around the time of their marriage. Burns's heroines, like his songs themselves, were symbolic more than descriptive—they were collages of traits he liked in different women. Much like his male characters, they seem simultaneously lifelike and larger than life. All Burns's speakers display an unclouded vehemence of opinion and heroic consistency of attitude: even his bawdry emphasizes the dominant personalities of his characters—the power of their feelings—rather than just their biological destinies.

Indeed, though the Scottish folk tradition has a reputation for cheerful sensuality largely because of Burns's dominance of it, the sexual attitudes conveyed by old bawdry often seem more ambivalent than those in Burns's genial adaptations:

> The modiewark has done me ill,
> And below my apron has biggit a hill;
> I maun consult some learned clark
> About this wanton modiewark.
>   (*Merry Muses*, p. 68)

In this old stanza, with which Burns was familiar (*Merry Muses*, p. 193), the attitude toward sex is more ironic than that to which the reader of Burns is accustomed. Moles and molehills are the metaphors, and the four stanzas dwell on this equivocal image, with its connotations of blindness, creeping, and darkness. When Burns took up the "modie-wark" metaphor (Kinsley, at any rate, endorses this as Burns's work; the authorship of many pieces in *The Merry Muses of Caledonia* [a collection of bawdry collected and partially written by Burns] is difficult to determine), he used it briefly, and only to highlight his speaker's frank enthusiasm for sex:

> The Mouse is a merry wee beast,
>   The Moudiewart wants the een;
> And O' for a touch o' the thing
>   I had in my nieve yestreen.
>   (*The Poems and Songs*, 1:177)

Even in bawdry, Burns orchestrated his materials for expressive rather than purely graphic ends: characters and what they stand for dominate and integrate the descriptions.

Burns's set of "polite" verses to the tune "Moudiewort" is a courtship rather than an erotic song, but its speaker demonstrates the forcefulness typical of all Burns's characters:

> And O, for ane and twenty Tam!
>   An hey, sweet ane and twenty, Tam!
> I'll learn my kin a rattlin sang,
>   An I saw ane and twenty, Tam.
> ....
> A gleib o' lan', a claut o' gear,
>   Was left me by my Auntie, Tam;
> At kith or kin I need na spier,
>   An I saw ane and twenty, Tam.
>   An O, for etc.

They'll hae me wed a wealthy coof,
  Tho' I mysel' hae plenty, Tam;
But hearst thou, laddie, there's my loof,
  I'm thine at ane and twenty, Tam!
    An O, for etc.

                                    (2:626–27)

Burns's speaker seems positively to enjoy the prospect of fighting
with her family for the three years that remain until she can claim her
inheritance and marry penniless Tam. It is not surprising that a poet
whose heroines declare sentiments like "I'll learn my kin a rattling
sang" was unmoved by Richardson's *Clarissa*, a novel Burns dismissed
in a letter to Dr. John Moore as an entertainment suitable only to
"captivate the unexperienced, romantic fancy of a boy or a girl" (*Letters*, 2:58).

One of Burns's most famous character sketches is his portrait of an
old Scots woman in his "polite" version of "John Anderson my Jo."
The oldest verses to this tune had appeared in Percy's *Reliques:*

> *Woman.*
> John Anderson my jo, cum in as ze gae bye,
> And ze sall get a sheip's heid well baken in a pye;
> Weel baken in a pye, and the haggis in a pat;
> John Anderson my jo, cum in, and ze's get that.
>
>   (3:1334)

Kinsley's note to Burns's version indicates that the text Burns worked
with was probably not the Percy fragment, but a later and less ellip-
tical set of erotic stanzas to the tune. Legman's note to this bawdy
version in *The Merry Muses* indicates that Burns's source is still popular
in Scotland:

> John Anderson, my jo, John,
>   I wonder what ye mean,
> To lie sae lang i' the mornin',
>   And sit sae late at een?
> Ye'll bleer a' your een, John,
>   And why do ye so?
> Come sooner to your bed at een,
>   John Anderson, my jo.
> ....

> I'm backit like a salmon,
>   I'm breastit like a swan;
> My wame it is a down-cod,
>   My middle ye may span:
> Frae my tap-knot to my tae, John,
>   I'm like the new-fa'n snow;
> And its a' for your convenience
>   John Anderson, my jo.
>
> (pp. 53–54)

In this version the neglected wife progresses through a succession of moods: loneliness, reminiscence, desire, and finally a threat of infidelity. Unlike most of the songs in *Merry Muses*, this is not bawdry dependent on punch lines; it is a dramatic monologue with some good poetry in it. (The imagery of the second stanza above is similar to images occurring in the well-known song "Annie Laurie.") When Burns worked up "drawing room" stanzas for "John Anderson my Jo," he kept its monologue form and the reflective mood of its speaker (reverie is in any case well-suited to the slow sadness of the tune). He changed the topic from sex specifically to marriage generally, and he equalized the ages of John Anderson and his wife. Burns adapted the "plot" so that the speaker can describe John Anderson's decline from youth but share in it. Complaint is changed to tolerance:

> John Anderson my jo, John,
>   When we were first acquent;
> Your locks were like the raven,
>   Your bony brow was brent;
> But now your brow is beld, John,
>   Your locks are like the snaw;
> But blessings on your frosty pow,
>   John Anderson my Jo.
>
> John Anderson my jo, John,
>   We clamb the hill the gither;
> And mony a canty day, John,
>   We've had wi' ane anither:
> Now we maun totter down, John,
>   And hand in hand we'll go;
> And sleep the gither at the foot,
>   John Anderson my Jo.
>
> (2:528–29)

In the bawdy source the endearment "jo" is applied sarcastically. Burns's speaker uses it unironically, to affirm her affection despite John's age and their mutual decline. Burns took several images from the older version but changed their import by applying them commonly to the couple rather than invidiously only to John. "We clamb the hill the gither" is a different application of a climbing metaphor than "I've twa gae ups for ae gae-down, / John Anderson my jo," which is an accusation, not a reminiscence. In the bawdy version, too, physical description of John is negative while the speaker insists on her own beauty. In Burns's version, the speaker concludes her description of John with a benediction intended to compensate for her insistence on John's decline; and the second stanza emphasizes what the couple has done and will do together.

"John Anderson my Jo" bears an interesting relationship to Burns's other revisions of bawdry—it is one of few cases where his effort does not work so well as the original. It is a matter of the reader's mood whether the last three lines of Burns's version—as expressive and economical a conclusion as he ever wrote—redeem earlier lines that border on mawkishness. "Totter down," for instance, seems too self-consciously pathetic for it to accord well with the speaker's otherwise consistent mood of practical sturdiness; and the character who would begin her reminiscence with the reticent "when we were first acquent" would probably not indulge in a sudden effusion like "But blessings on your frosty pow." Burns's song is largely successful, but there are inconsistencies within it; and the bawdy source remains the more integrated lyric. This is not the case with other revisions, such as the transformation of the bawdy stanzas of "Duncan Davison" into Burns's lovely early song "Mary Morison," written to the same tune.

Although there was a Mary Morison living in Mauchline during Burns's residence at nearby Mossgiel, most scholars agree that Burns's choice of her name had more to do with its euphonious sound and compatibility with his air than his feelings for her (he was in love at that time with a girl of invincibly prosaic surname: Begbie):

> Yestreen when to the trembling string
> The dance gaed through the lighted ha',
> To thee my fancy took its wing,
> I sat, but neither heard, nor saw:

> Though this was fair, and that was braw,
>   And yon the toast of a' the town,
> I sigh'd, and said amang them a',
>   "Ye are na Mary Morison."
>
>   (1:42)

Hugh MacDiarmid called that last line, "Ye are na Mary Morison," the "most powerful" that Burns ever wrote.[8] The way Burns works up to the line is just as impressive. Having assigned to nameless females the usually desirable attributes of beauty, fashion, and popularity, the speaker simply rejects these qualities as having any part in Mary Morison's appeal. The conventional adjectives of love lyrics, then, are introduced not to explain Mary Morison's attractiveness but to affirm her transcendence of merely conventional standards. She is the center of specific gravity in the song: Mary Morison is the only proper noun in it, and reference to other girls is not even expressed in common nouns but in impersonal pronouns—"this," "that," and "yon." Yet Mary Morison remains partly unknown. The speaker can only be sure of what she is not: not subject to the usual standards of female excellence, not in love with him, but—he hopes—not capable of outright cruelty:

> If love for love thou wilt na gie,
>   At least be pity to me shown;
> A thought ungentle canna be
>   The thought o' Mary Morison.
>
>   (1:43)

"Mary Morison" is one of Burns's best evocations of tenderness as an adjunct to sexual attraction, and the tenderness is entirely Burns's contribution to the text. Unlike "John Anderson my Jo," which owes its reflective mood to its bawdy source, his "Mary Morison" owes none of its tender inflections to "Duncan Davidson," which is crude and jocular:

> There was a lass, they ca'd her Meg,
>   An' she gaed o'er the muir to spin;
> She feed a lad to lift her leg,
>   They ca'd him Duncan Davidson.
>   Fal, lal, etc.

Meg had a muff and it was rough,
  Twas black without and red within;
An' Duncan, case he got the cauld,
  He stole his Highland p——e in.
    Fal, lal, etc.

Meg had a muff, and it was rough,
And Duncan strak tway handfu' in
She clasp'd her heels about his waist,
  "I thank you Duncan! Yerk it in!!!"
    Fal, lal, etc.

Duncan made her hurdies dreep,
  In Highland wrath, then Meg did say;
O gang he east, or gang he west,
  His ba's will no be dry to day.
                    (*Merry Muses*, p. 59)

The distance between Burns's version and its folk-collected source
was often similarly astronomical.

David Herd's *Ancient and Modern Scots Songs* (1769) was headed by a
brief preface, in which Herd called the characteristic effect of Scottish
song "a forcible and pathetic simplicity, which at once lays strong hold
upon the affections: so that the heart may be considered as an *instru-
ment*, which the bard or minstrel harmonizes" (Herd's italics).[9] Herd's
view of the bard or minstrel as an orchestrator of emotions is similar to
Aikin's view of refined lyric and corresponds closely to Burns's attitude toward his sources. Burns in theory revered them and relied on
the tunes and traditional metaphors of the folk tradition, but when he
worked with them it was usually to introduce more expressiveness
into them—to enlarge their evocative possibilities.

In his notes to Johnson's *Scots Musical Museum* Burns recorded political stanzas to an old version of "To daunton me" that he thought had
"some merit":

To daunton me, to daunton me,
O ken ye what it is that'll daunton me?
There's eighty eight and eighty nine,
And a' that I have borne synsyne,
There's cess and press and Presbytrie,
I think it will do meikle for to daunton me.

> But to wanton me, to wanton me,
> O ken ye what it is that wad wanton me,
> To see gude corn upon the rigs,
> And banishment amang the Whigs,
> And right restor'd where right sud be,
> I think wad to meikle for to wanton me.
>
> (*Notes on Scottish Song*, p. 56)

When Burns worked his own version of "To daunton me," he expanded the emotional power of the melody's defiant self-assertion by changing the context from politics to courtship. In Burns's version a young girl is declaring herself unmoved by the proposal of an older man:

> The blude-red rose at Yule may blaw,
> The simmer lilies bloom in snaw,
> The frost may freeze the deepest sea,
> But an auld man shall never daunton me.—
>
> (*The Poems and Songs*, 1:398)

Kinsley's note to Burns's version states that other courtship stanzas had been fitted to the tune, but that no parallel exists for Burns's first stanza quoted above. The significant and characteristic trait of this stanza is the way it states the girl's defiance in terms at once metaphorical yet unequivocal. "Precise yet indefinable emotion," Yeats's notion of the stuff of poetry, is at the center of the young girl's speech. Her pride suffuses the song. She does not specifically call herself a rose, a lily, or a sea—yet in declaring she is even less likely to betray her own nature than these other beautiful phenomena, she symbolically asserts the resemblance.

A similar instance of Burns's use of first stanzas to enlarge the emotional expressiveness of his source occurs in "Ay waukin O." Herd's collection of manuscripts preserves the old text from which Burns probably worked:

> O wat, wat—O wat and weary!
> Sleep I can get nane
> For thinking on my deary.
> A' the night I wak,
> A' the day I weary,

> Sleep I can get nane
> For thinking on my dearie.
> (3:1330)

The fragment, like the dramatic tune to which it is set, is expressive as it stands. When Burns adapted it, however, he intensified the mood by deferring the specific complaint of the lover until the second stanza. As is characteristic of Burns's songs of lamentation, a context stanza is provided to extend into Nature the echoes of the narrator's melancholy:

> Simmer's a pleasant time,
>   Flowers of every colour;
> The water rins o'er the heugh,
>   And I long for my true lover!
>
> *Chorus*
> Ay waukin, Oh,
>   Waukin still and weary:
> Sleep I can get nane,
>   For thinking on my Dearie.—
>
> When I sleep I dream,
>   When I wauk I'm irie;
> Sleep I can get nane,
>   For thinking on my Dearie.—
> (2:510)

Burns's economy of expression (what he called "simplicity") creates an effect of conclusive alienation between the "pleasant" season and the weariness of the speaker and does it with a masterful reticence.

"O saw ye bonie Lesley" was written in 1792 for an acquaintance of Burns, Miss Lesley Baillie of Mayfield:

> O saw ye bonie Lesley,
>   As she gaed o'er the Border?
> She's gane, like Alexander,
>   To spread her conquests farther.
>
> To see her is to love her,
>   And love but her for ever;
> For Nature made her what she is
>   And never made anither.
> ....

> The deil he could na scaith thee,
>   Or aught that wad belang thee:
> He'd look into thy bonie face,
>   And say, "I canna wrang thee!"
>   (2:596–97)

Burns exploits the implicit irony of hyperbole in the first and third stanzas quoted. In stanza 1, Lesley is a female conqueror, Alexander the Great on the march; then, in a reversal, she is seen as charmingly helpless—the disarming potential victim of the "deil" (devil) himself. Lesley's beauty is celebrated both in the reference to classical Alexander and the folk-mediated "deil": she is made relevant to both worlds, to all worlds. The irony inherent in Burns's gentle exaggerations does not undercut, but rather heightens, our sense of Lesley's all-encompassing charm. Irony's edge, however, touches the speaker himself. He is clearly among her already conquered victims, sharing the "deil's" attraction to her with all its diabolical potential (the "wrang" he cannot do her). Irony seems to be a vehicle for distancing the poet away from the direct expression of his feelings. In their indirect (ironic) presentation, the attraction of one man for one woman (and a woman inaccessible because of a disparity in their social classes) becomes an expression of wonder at the chastening power of beauty. The song, then, expands a restricted and exclusive subject (pretty Lesley) into an expression of illimitable feeling (the power of beauty). As Thomas Crawford notes in writing of this song, "In the early poems . . . positive value had resided in strong drink, or comradeship, or "generous love"; now, it is inherent in Beauty" (*Burns: A Study of the Poems and Songs*, p. 272). As has been mentioned, the later songs characteristically reject the sentimental preoccupation with eccentricity, turning instead to the expansive evocation of commonly felt emotions. Even songs addressed to women Burns knew personally follow "bonie Lesley's" pattern of universalization.

"The bonie wee thing," praised both by Thomas Crawford and Cedric Thorpe-Davie as one of Burns's finest songs, was inspired by Miss Deborah Duff-Davies—like Lesley Baillie, a young acquaintance of Burns:

Chorus
Bonie wee thing, canie wee thing,
    Lovely wee thing, was thou mine;

> I wad wear thee in my bosom,
>   Least my Jewel I should tine.—
>
> Wishfully I look and languish
>   In that bonie face o' thine;
> And my heart it stounds wi' anguish,
>   Least my wee thing be na mine.—
>   Bonie wee etc.
>
> Wit, and Grace, and Love, and Beauty,
>   In ae constellation shine;
> To adore thee is my duty,
>   Goddess o' this soul o' mine!
>   (2:618)

Attraction to Miss Davies, as in the "deil" stanza of "bonie Lesley," becomes subsumed in a mood of protectiveness. The song turns a limitation and potential flaw—the girl's tiny stature—into the basis of her claim to tender protection. By the concluding stanza, she has become a fixed "constellation" of lovely qualities, a paradigm. As in "bonie Lesley," then, a finite (in this case, literally tiny) heroine becomes the basis for an idealized projection of feeling.

The later songs are not always tender, of course: some of the best focus on other feelings. The Jacobite songs often rearrange traditional material to create powerful expressions of anger and despair. "Here's a Health to them that's awa" is one example of brilliant generalization based on the amplification of an older source. Kinsley (3:1412) quotes the old song from which Burns may have worked:

> Here's a health to them that's away,
> Here's a health to them that's away,
> Here's a health to him that was here yestreen,
>   But durstna bide till day.
>   O wha winna drink it dry?
>   O wha winna drink it dry?
> Wha winna drink to the lad that's gane,
>   Is nane o' our company.

This stanza, with its anticlimactic final line, stands in marked contrast to Burns's revision, in which every stanza builds to a crescendo of defiance:

> Here's a health to them that's awa,
> Here's a health to them that's awa;
> Here's a health to Charlie, the chief o' the clan,
> Altho' that his band be sma'.
> May Liberty meet wi' success!
> May Prudence protect her frae evil!
> May Tyrants and Tyranny tine i' the mist,
> And wander their way to the devil!
>
> Here's a health to them that's awa,
> Here's a health to them that's awa;
> Here's a health to Tammie, the Norland laddie,
> That lives at the lug o' the law!
> Here's freedom to him that wad read,
> Here's freedom to him that wad write!
> There's nane ever fear'd that the Truth should be heard,
> But they whom the Truth wad indite.
>
> (2:663)

The song's specific subject—Jacobite rebellion and allegiance to the Stuart kings—expands outward into a protest against all political oppression. The traditional source makes no effort to draw in the unconverted; rather, it specifically excludes from the company all who reject the Stuart kings. Burns's version, on the other hand, retains the peculiar vehemence of partisan expression but attaches that vehemence to values (for freedom, for the brave defiance of tyranny) that anyone not utterly insensible would instinctively embrace. Through Burns's amplification of his source, the partisan feeling becomes an emotional universal.

In "I hae a wife o' my ain," a song written in 1792, pride is the feeling Burns amplifies. Quoting Stenhouse, Kinsley cites the "trifling verses" that probably were Burns's source:

> I hae a wife o' my awn,
> I'll be haddin to naebody;
> I hae a pat and a pan,
> I'll borrow frae naebody.
>
> (3:1395–96)

Burns's adaptation brings the traditional speaker's self-sufficiency to the edge of misanthropy, an effect heightened in performance by the somewhat rigid and implacable tune to which it is set:

I hae a wife o' my ain,
   I'll partake wi' naebody;
I'll tak Cuckold frae nane,
   I'll gie Cuckold to naebody.—

I hae a penny to spend,
   There, thanks to naebody;
I hae naething to lend,
   I'll borrow frae naebody.—

I am naebody's lord,
   I'll be slave to naebody;
I hae a gude braid sword,
   I'll tak dunts frae naebody.—

I'll be merry and free,
   I'll be sad for naebody;
Naebody cares for me,
   I care for naebody.—

               (2:624)

Crawford, following his theory that Burns is generally auto-biographical, discusses this song as a humorous self-portrait:

> Now, Burns is the independent small farmer *par excellence*, beholden to no feudal superior or bureaucratic caste, and resentful of supervision and control, however paternally exercised; he is the small owner in love. Nowhere in literature, perhaps, is there a more succinct, more engaging, more sympathetically humorous presentation of a *petit bourgeois* attitude. . . . By thus giving expression to what millions of lower-middle-class people have known, he makes us feel for and with them as *people*, so that we glory in their essential humanity. (pp. 283–84)

While the song does embody a doughty middle-class independence, it does not seem to me to do so with humor. Crawford's interpretation fails to acknowledge the hostility that is surely the primary feeling conveyed by the song. Suspicious alienation, an emotional reality for more than just members of the "lower middle class," is the amplified extreme of the independence expressed by Burns's source. However negative, this feeling nonetheless is felt occasionally by everyone. The song, then, like many of Burns's most powerful, addresses itself to reawakening feelings already in the emotional repertoire of the listener. Its effect is more immediate and powerful than the effect of material primarily biographical or autobiographical, in which the listener feels the emotions as those of another person. Self-sufficiency—and misanthropy—are human universals; and the powerful resonance of such universals seems to me to be the primary focus of Burns's later songs.

One of Burns's most simple and powerful lyrics was written about a month before he died. He was being nursed by Jessie Lewars, the young sister of a friend who worked with him at the Excise; and Burns's gratitude for the girl's help to his family (his wife Jean was experiencing a difficult pregnancy, and Jessie was tending the children as well as Burns) was expressed in "Oh wert thou in the cauld blast," an exceptionally fine song. He asked the girl to play her favorite tune for him and then worked new stanzas to it in her honor. The consensus of biographers has been that Jessie chose "The robin came to the wren's nest" set to the air "Lenox love to Blantyre" (see Snyder, *The Life of Robert Burns*, pp. 385–86). Ironically, "The Wren's Nest" had already been refurbished by Burns himself in the *Scots Musical Museum* volume for 1796:

> The Robin cam to the wren's nest
>   And keekit in and keekit in,
> O weel's me on your auld pow,
>   Wad ye be in, wad ye be in.
> Ye'se ne'er get leave to lie without,
>   And I within, and I within,
> As lang's I hae an auld clout
>   To row you in, to row you in.
>
>   (2:834)

Allan Cunningham's *Songs of Scotland* (1825) presents as "early" two additional stanzas to the song which, if authentic, bear an interesting relationship to the symbols used in Burns's version. Before quoting these stanzas, however, I should mention that Cunningham is notorious for inventing many of his "ancient" texts:

> The robin came to the wren's nest,
>   And gae a peep and gae a peep—
> Now weels me on thee, cuttie quean,
>   Are ye asleep, are ye asleep?

The sparrow-hawk is in the air,
  The corbie-craw is on the sweep;
An' ye be wise, ye'll bide at hame,
  And never cheep, and never cheep.

The robin came to the wren's nest,
  And keekit in, and keekit in—
I saw ye thick wi' wee Tam-tit,
  Ye cuttie quean, ye cuttie quean,
The ruddy feathers frae my breast
  Thy nest hae lined, thy nest hae lined;
Now wha will keep ye frae the blast,
  And winter wind, and winter wind?[10]

Cunningham's note to "The Wren's Nest" calls it "so simple and absurd, so foolish and yet so natural, that I know not whether to reject or retain it" (p. 350), a cool appraisal it seems unlikely he would have applied to an interpolation of his own. In any case, when Burns worked from the old texts he abandoned their central feature, the use of the robin and wren. Speaker and addressee become "I" and "thee" and the whimsy of the original vanishes. Burns retained and expanded, however, the mood of endearment and protectiveness:

Oh wert thou in the cauld blast,
  On yonder lea, on yonder lea;
My plaidie to the angry airt,
  I'd shelter thee, I'd shelter thee:
Or did misfortune's bitter storms
  Around thee blaw, around thee blaw,
Thy bield should be my bosom,
  To share it a', to share it a'.

Or were I in the wildest waste,
  Sae black and bare, sae black and bare,
The desart were a paradise,
  If thou wert there, if thou wert there.
Or were I monarch o' the globe,
  Wi' thee to reign, wi' thee to reign;
The brightest jewel in my crown,
  Wad be my queen, wad be my queen.
                                      (2:813)

This song shows the features typical of Burns's best revisions from folk sources. He simplified the "plot" by substituting people for talking birds; yet he retained and exploited figurative connotations from the old sources: the offer of shelter and sacrifice, for instance, and the wistful status of "robin" (Burns's nickname) as an outsider. Burns's song is in the subjunctive throughout; not an indication of merely rhetorical emotion but rather the sign of a reticence that generally characterized his songs to very young women. Most interesting of all, though the song sounds "real," the situation it describes was exactly opposite to the relationship that inspired it. The song offers the speaker's protection to Jessie in various threatening situations; when he wrote it, however, it was he who was receiving the help his song hypothetically showers on Jessie. Burns probably transferred his own jeopardized situation to her in order to imagine a reciprocity in their friendship: he offers an equal support throughout vicissitude and in the final quatrain extends his pledge to assert that the girl would be prized above all even were he "monarch o' the globe." "Oh wert thou in the cauld blast" is characteristic of Burns as a bard in the way it abstracts from a painful situation and a fragmentary old text a powerful, transcendent feeling. The concluding line, however, implies reality in its stress on the subjunctive "wad" (would). Jessie "wad be" his queen if life worked like lyric poetry. The moving connotation—and the plain fact—is that life does not.

James Beattie's *The Minstrel; or, The Progress of Genius* (1771–74) offers some fascinating parallels to Burns's career as a bard. Beattie's poem, for one thing, furnished Mackenzie with the fatal epithet "heaven-taught," which occurs in stanza 7; and *The Minstrel* provided Burns himself with some of his favorite all-purpose quotations. (His early letters frequently refer to the "malignant star" that dogged his life—that phrase occurs in Beattie's first stanza, though it is also congruent with Tristram's sense of fated failure in *Tristram Shandy*.) More important, *The Minstrel* shows that, although Burns's final project of song revising did evoke some of his best poetry, it also corresponded to contemporary notions about all bards and how they worked their lyric magic. Beattie's injunction to other minstrels was that they should broaden and substantiate their instincts in their lyrics, and this was Burns's enterprise. Beattie assigned to minstrels the role of spokesmen for freedom and assigned them, too, an inevitable though righteous poverty. Stanza 7 is especially interesting in relationship to Burns:

> Then grieve not, thou, to whom th' indulgent Muse
> Vouchsafes a portion of celestial fire;
> Nor blame the partial Fates, if they refuse
> The imperial banquet, and the rich attire:
> Know thine own worth, and reverence the lyre.
> Wilt thou debase the heart which God refined?
> No; let thy heaven-taught soul to heaven aspire,
> To fancy, freedom, harmony, resigned;
> Ambition's grovelling crew for ever left behind.[11]

Bombast aside, Beattie's sentiments do apply to Burns as a bard. Burns reworked traditional sources precisely to expand their potential for expressing "fancy, freedom, harmony." And Burns's "reverence" for song did go along with his rejection of a grand public destiny as a poet and his "resignation" to an obscure role—often an anonymous one—as a bard. Both his "reverence" for song and his "resignation" to its transcending qualities were, as in Beattie's poem, more or less consciously undertaken as compensation for a life Burns did perceive as materially unlucky. Compensation accounts for why Burns's songs—the most serene and benign portion of his creative work— were his major interest after leaving Edinburgh, a time when his life was difficult and his mood often bitter. The dying bard who presented young Jessie Lewars with the self-effacing lyric discussed above seems a different character altogether from the embittered man who—that same month in 1796—greeted Maria Riddell at their last meeting with the guilt-inducing pleasantry, "Well, Madam, have you any messages for the other world?"[12]

Mackenzie had applied the epithet "heaven-taught" to Burns as though it simply meant unlettered. Beattie, however, intended the expression to signify the idealizing impulse of the true bard. The heaven-taught minstrel "left behind" the crass material world to seek "celestial fire." In Burns's songs, of course, the daily world was not thus rejected; but it was also not accepted without alteration. Burns simplified the circumstantial details in his folk sources and in that way amplified their significance: the effect is transcendence through description. "Oh wert thou in the cauld blast" synthesizes depressing autobiographical circumstances with mitigating fantasy; it draws on a folk text for its protective mood, yet Burns's treatment of the source has broadened the whimsy of the original into a comprehensive tenderness.

In *The Minstrel*, Beattie condemns a "witty" approach to life, which subjects everything to microscopic dissection by one critical mind:

> . . . dark, cold-hearted skeptics, creeping, pore
> Through microscope of metaphysic lore:
> And much they grope for Truth, but never hit.
> For why? Their powers, inadequate before,
> This idle art makes more and more unfit;
> Yet they deem darkness light, and their vain blunders wit.
>
> (p. 28)

Beattie's minstrel is rather a telescopic interpreter; his hero is an "enlarged" soul, whose view of life is suitably magnanimous and comprehensive: "For Nature gave him strength, and Fire, to soar / On Fancy's wing above this vale of tears." Here Beattie may be drawing on sentiments expressed by Thomas Gray in a Pindaric imitation, "The Progress of Poesy," where Gray claims total independence from circumstance:

> Oh! Lyre divine, what daring Spirit
> Wakes thee now? Tho' he inherit
> Nor the pride, nor ample pinion,
> That the Theban Eagle bear
> Sailing with supreme dominion
> Thro' the azure deep of air:
> Yet oft before his infant eyes would run
> Such forms, as glitter in the Muse's ray
> With orient hues, unborrow'd of the Sun:
> Yet shall he mount, and keep his distant way
> Beyond the limits of a vulgar fate,
> Beneath the Good how far—but far above the Great.
>
> (Gray, *Complete Poems*, pp. 16–17)

Earlier I discussed some tendencies Burns shared with other mid and late eighteenth-century poets. A distinction of Burns's songs is that, while as linked to an established convention as Gray's Pindaric odes, they do not disdain "the limits of a vulgar fate" as do so many poems of the day. In his songs Burns moves beyond the sentimental heroics of his early poems; he incorporates the magnanimous, bardic perspective on life with the detailed circumstantial spirit of his folk sources. Burns's songs demonstrate a profound respect for people as they really are; but at the same time they also manage to convey the ideal capacities of human nature and the infinite dimensions of such commonly experienced feelings as pity, rebellion, tenderness, anger, and love. In his songs, then, Burns projects a sensibility simultaneously definitive and expansive.

When Christopher Smart produced his version of Scripture, he was working—as Gray was from Pindar—from a sublime model down to his personal message. The descent is sometimes from the biblically sublime ("Blessed be the meek") down to the biographically quaint ("For I bless God for the immortal soul of Mr. Pigg of DOWNHAM in NORFOLK" [*Jubilate Agno*, p. 59]). Burns's relationship to folk song is as revisionary as Smart's to Scripture. Yet in adapting "John Anderson my Jo," Burns revised not the paradoxes of Matthew or Job but the caustic reverie of a bored farm wife. Often, his sources were just an aggregate of vivid incongruities loosely coordinated within a tune. (He very seldom tampered with already transcendent material, such as the ballads.) Such emphatic details as the sheep's head well-baked in a pie which the women in Percy's version of "John Anderson my Jo" offers as an enticement into her house are characteristic of the popular folk tradition; folk song as a model is fundamentally circumstantial. Burns, a bard trained in the eighteenth-century mode, generalizes from and in that way radically changes his sources.

Thus, Burns's revisions usually synthesize two quite different elements: the collective folk tradition and the eighteenth-century cult of heroic bards. These two elements—the one anonymous, the other conspicuously self-conscious—combine to create Burns's inimitable lyric effect: a radical, meaningful simplicity. In the best of Burns's revisions, a self-conscious artistry enlarges and intensifies the symbols implicit in the source, usually by appropriating them to the clarification of the feelings of a central speaker. At the same time, the vividly circumstantial spirit of the folk source enters into and substantiates the bard's self-conscious idealism.

My sense of Burns's transcendence of folk models is supported in an odd way by the hostility with which antiquarians have always treated his songs. From Ritson to Legman to MacDiarmid, a chorus of objection has accused Burns of unwittingly killing the Scots vernacular tradition by the very success of his own free adaptations. The folklorists understandably wish that Burns's idealization of realistic folk models were not so commonly confused with folk realism as it is expressed in the authentic (genuinely collective) folk tradition. While even the folklorists do not wish Burns's revisions away, they see him essentially as a forger—a vernacular Chatterton claiming to discover texts that were actually shaped by his own complex vision.

My aim has been to apply perspective to Burns's life and art by describing some of the ways he resembled or diverged from his contemporaries and predecessors. In concluding, I will discuss Burns's procedures as they shape his most intricately balanced work. "Tam o' Shanter," a long narrative poem written in 1790 to oblige Burns's friend the antiquary Captain Grose, is Burns's most complex synthesis of local folklore with "magnanimous" narration and emotionally charged perception. To understand "Tam o' Shanter" is to understand Burns at his best.

10

"Tam o' Shanter": The Truth of the Tale

"Tam o' Shanter" tells the story of a drunken farmer who encounters a witches' dance on his way home from a market day carousal in Ayr. The poem offers an adult's retrospective view of horror stories; there is an overtone of indulgent irony in the sections of the poem that describe the witches' dance and its gruesome concomitants. Thomas Carlyle, writing of the poem, objects to its evident detachment:

> "Tam o' Shanter" itself, which enjoys so high a favour, does not appear to us, at all decisively, to come under this last category [of Burns's melodious, aerial, poetical poems]. It is not so much a poem, as a piece of sparkling rhetoric; the heart and body of the story still lies hard and dead. He has not gone back, much less carried us back, into that dark, earnest, wondering age . . . he does not attempt, by any new-modelling of his supernatural ware, to strike anew that deep mysterious chord of human nature, which once responded to such things. (Low, *The Critical Heritage*, 367–68)

Carlyle's objection to Burns's "cold" treatment of supernatural themes is essentially that of a Romantic throwing off the traces of eighteenth-century skepticism and restraint to which Burns does hold in "Tam o' Shanter." It was not the grotesque activities of witches and Satan that piqued Burns's imagination as he wrote; it was the behavior of his protagonist, ordinary Tam, when confronted by those weird phenomena. Like Burns's songs, "Tam o' Shanter" adapts folk sources to emphasize a central character's independence and vitality; and like them it shares John Aikin's view that local tales should be integrated within an emotional perspective by the bard who works with them.

149

Perhaps no other poem by Burns illustrates so well the false conclusions to which false assumptions about the poet inevitably lead. The notion that Burns is always autobiographical, for instance, has led several critics to miss the irony of Burns's masterpiece. Thomas Crawford, whose discussion of "Tam o' Shanter" provided my own interpretation's point of departure ("pleasure" and "community" as key words in the poem, and the alternation between several narrative "voices"), nonetheless illustrates the shortcomings of an autobiographical approach in several of his generalizations:

> The strain of realism that runs through the work derives, at the level of the superficial and the merely obvious, from Burns's own quizzical recognition that he, too—emancipated man of the eighteenth century though he was—could, in the appropriate circumstances, feel some of the terrors that afflict the superstitious and the simple-minded. . . . ["Tam o' Shanter"] is typical not only of Burns, but of the Scottish mind; for it is—next to "The Vision"—the most genuinely *national* of all his poems. (pp. 221–22)

What Crawford praises as the "strain of realism" in "Tam o' Shanter" is its descriptive, autobiographical component. Burns was a riding officer for the Excise; in his later life, he spent most of his free time at taverns such as the Globe Inn at Dumfries. As a child, he had been spellbound by tales of local atrocities and supernatural visitations spun by a relative, Betty Davidson; many of her stories had focused on weird happenings at Alloway's nearby ruined kirk. Since "Tam o' Shanter" begins at a tavern, describes a wild, drunken ride, and features a witches' dance at Alloway kirk, it is clear that autobiographical material is an important factor. It is not all-important, however, because it fails to provide a means of analyzing the complex tone of the poem—the implied attitude toward the things described. Crawford's praise of a descriptive "strain of realism" had led him in the passage quoted above to see superstitious terror as part of the emotional message in "Tam o' Shanter." For all his reservations about "Tam o' Shanter," Carlyle is actually closer to the truth when he speaks of its sparkling "rhetoric," which distances readers from any naive immersion in horror. Burns's presentation of the supernatural material is mock-heroic (as was Pope's presentation of Belinda in one of Burns's favorite poems, *The Rape of the Lock*); in any mock-heroic work, the challenge to critics is determining where the irony stops.[1]

It is a challenge that critics working from the current assumptions about Burns fail even to perceive, let alone to meet. Critics whose thesis has been Burns's inability to master English diction become trapped when they turn to "Tam o' Shanter" in discussion of whether the epic digressions in the poem (brilliant examples of bravura English) disprove their position. (Kurt Wittig, wanting to praise the poem but disliking any English influence, concludes that these passages are "near English.")[2] Critics wedded to the notion of an earthy, "peasant" Burns usually prefer Burns's other, less obviously artful, masterwork, "Love and Liberty." Those who approach Burns from eighteenth-century perspectives usually do appreciate the elegance and irony of "Tam o' Shanter," yet seldom consider the relationship of tone to the folkloric subject. Others, such as Carlyle, are drawn to its subject but baffled by its tone. Indeed, while illustrating the partial truth of all the labels that have been applied to Burns—the poet of the people, the national bard, the Romantic in love with excess, the Augustan in love with form—"Tam o' Shanter" also illustrates their only partial adequacy by seeming to transcend them all.

Before coming to the particulars of the poem, I should make one point about Burns's ironic treatment of supernatural forces. The story of Tam's ride as Burns received it from local sources itself existed on different levels. The prose summary that Burns supplied to Captain Grose along with his poem relates the history of a nameless Carrick farmer who, while riding home from Ayr one night, discovers a witches' dance in progress at Alloway kirk (as mentioned above, a source for local ghost stories; incidentally, this was also the burial place of Burns's father). A humorous variant, however, was also current in Burns's day. Douglas Graham, an acquaintance of Burns and tenant of the farm "Shanter" in Carrick, once had told his superstitious wife a similar tale of interrupting a witches' dance—to account for his late return from a market-day journey to Ayr. The joke was that shrewish Helen Graham had actually believed her husband's story.[3] In short, the original for "Tam" himself used folk material ironically, to deceive a real-life "Kate." It is fitting, then, that Burns's poem demonstrates a dual perspective on its own truth, as it alternates narrative between an artful narrator and a drunken protagonist.

The first twelve lines of "Tam o' Shanter" provide, as usual in Burns, a context stanza for the poem to follow. Neither the poet-narrator nor Tam is yet in evidence. This stanza speaks of "we," meaning by that a convivial male fellowship of farmers and local tradesmen, drawn together temporarily at the close of the Ayr market day by a common disinclination to leave their tavern and return home to their wives:

> When chapman billies leave the street,
> And drouthy neebors, neebors meet,
> As market-days are wearing late,
> An' folk begin to take the gate;
> While we sit bousing at the nappy,
> And getting fou and unco happy,
> We think na on the lang Scots miles,
> The mosses, waters, slaps, and styles,
> That lie between us and our hame,
> Whare sits our sulky sullen dame,
> Gathering her brows like gathering storm,
> Nursing her wrath to keep it warm.
>
> (2:557)

From within this fellowship, Tam is then presented: "This truth fand honest *Tam o' Shanter*, / As he frae Ayr ae night did canter. . . ."

The poem has already begun to complicate its relationship to a local source. "Honest" Tam is drawn from real life liar Douglas Graham; and Graham's lie about witches is the "truth" that Tam will soon find (or that will soon find Tam—the phrasing is ambiguous). The poem then modulates to ironic praise of the percipience of Tam's "ain wife Kate," who has warned him about the danger of riding by the haunted kirk after midnight:

> O *Tam!* hadst thou but been sae wise,
> As ta'en thy ain wife *Kate*'s advice!
> She tauld thee weel thou was a skellum,
> A blethering, blustering, drunken blellum;
> That frae November till October,
> Ae market-day thou was nae sober;
> That ilka melder, wi' the miller,
> Thou sat as lang as thou had siller;
> That every naig was ca'd a shoe on,
> The smith and thee gat roaring fou on;
> That at the L——d's house, even on Sunday,
> Thou drank wi' Kirkton Jean till Monday.
> She prophesied that late or soon,

> Thou would be found deep drown'd in Doon;
> Or catch'd wi' warlocks in the mirk,
> By *Alloway*'s auld haunted kirk.
>
> (2:558)

Our first extended view of Tam is provided by a hostile witness, his wife. Even in this first glimpse of our "hero's" character, ironic distance prevails.

This is increased when Burns's narrator (until this point silent except for a passing couplet in praise of Ayr) emerges to underscore Kate's ill temper by appearing to regret Tam's disregard of her "sweet counsels":

> Ah, gentle dames! it gars me greet,
> To think how mony counsels sweet,
> How mony lengthen'd sage advices,
> The husband frae the wife despises!
>
> (2:558)

Kate's invective has stressed Tam's extremes of misconduct, but the narrator returns us to Tam as a norm: all husbands neglect the "sage" advice of their wives. This changing perspective on Tam is so far the most dynamic feature of the poem. There is no amassing of tension about Tam's imminent encounter with a witches' dance. The supernatural theme is actually deflated by the context in which it is first mentioned: the lurid and spiteful prophecy of Kate.

Then the tale itself properly begins. Lines 37 to 78 constitute the first segment of the poem after the introduction. Tam is described as "planted unco right" by the fireside, the best seat in the tavern. He is enjoying his drink ("reaming swats that drank divinely"), the "queerest stories" of his crony Souter (cobbler) Johnny, and even the "secret" favors of the landlady. All these pleasurable activities work as Burns undoubtedly intended: to create an atmosphere of total gratification for Tam. This tavern is a perfect place:

> Care, mad to see a man sae happy,
> E'en drown'd himsel amang the nappy:
> As bees flee hame wi' lades o' treasure,
> The minutes wing'd their way wi' pleasure:
> Kings may be blest, but *Tam* was glorious,
> O'er a' the ills o' life victorious!
>
> (2:559)

Here the narrator has taken over the poem to meditate on the implications of Tam's simple pleasures, and in the next fifteen lines, he warms
to his meditative theme:

> But pleasures are like poppies spread,
> You seize the flower, its bloom is shed;
> Or like the snow falls in the river,
> A moment white—then melts for ever;
> Or like the borealis race,
> That flit ere you can point their place;
> Or like the rainbow's lovely form
> Evanishing amid the storm.—
> Nae man can tether time nor tide;
> The hour approaches *Tam* maun ride;
> That hour, o' night's black arch the key-stane,
> That dreary hour he mounts his beast in;
> And sic a night he taks the road in,
> As ne'er poor sinner was abroad in.
>
>   (2:559)

In earlier chapters, I have dwelt on Burns's adaptations from sentimental literature and his similarly personal revisions from folk and bardic
materials. Passages such as the last two quoted from "Tam o' Shanter"
show an unusually condensed integration of local and literary influences. Critics have mentioned literary sources for these epic digressions in "Tam o' Shanter" from writings as diverse as *The Rape of the
Lock*, Thomson's *The Seasons* (the rainbow image), Ovid, Dr. Johnson,
and, from the vernacular poets, Allan Ramsay and Hamilton of
Gilbertfield (3:1356–57). And in telling the tale of Douglas Graham,
Burns also suggests a number of autobiographical themes. His point of
departure is Ayr—close to his birthplace at Alloway—and behind his
description of tavern life at Ayr is his own adult experience of its
pleasures at Dumfries.

Burns's letters often distinguish between his life and his art, assert-
ing his values in two modes—"as a man and as a poet." In "Tam o'
Shanter," especially in these early lines on the pleasures of sociable
carousing and the reluctance with which working men leave them for
home and renewed responsibility, Burns views the tavern culture both
descriptively (as a man) and evocatively (as a poet). Tam is his "man"
and the narrator is his "poet," and the narrative alternates between
their two levels of appreciation.

In the ensuing section—lines 74 to 104—Burns seems to remember he had promised Captain Grose a horror story, and he describes the violent storm into which Tam reluctantly emerges from the shelter and good fellowship of the tavern. It is worth mentioning, as do most commentators on this poem, that Burns rode through many night storms in the course of his work. As usual, when Burns is moved to describe natural forces in order to explicate his human theme, his description is authoritative and precise:

> The wind blew as 'twad blawn its last;
> The rattling showers rose on the blast;
> The speedy gleams the darkness swallow'd;
> Loud, deep, and lang, the thunder bellow'd:
> That night, a child might understand,
> The Deil had business on his hand.
>
>   (2:559)

Like line 13, in which Tam either finds or is himself found out by "truth," lines 77 and 78 are fundamentally equivocal. A "child might understand" that the bad weather signified Satan's presence in the countryside: how might an adult react? The narrator seems daunted, but feckless Tam mounts his old mare Meg, "despising wind, and rain and fire." The difference between Tam and the narrator is drink. Tam is just sober enough for a gesture of prudence, "glowring around . . . / Lest bogles catch him unawares" (2:560). Tam proceeds without incident until he reaches the ruined kirk, the very place mentioned in Kate's "prophecy." Before description of the witches' dance Tam discovers there, the narrator describes some grim local landmarks: the boulder where "Charlie" had broken his neck in a drunken fall, the well at which "Mungo's mither" had committed suicide, the cairn of a murdered infant. This is local color directed to Captain Grose, a collector of such stories.

Tam's ride brings him to Alloway, where he hears in the distance, through the noise of the storm, unholy sounds of "mirth and dancing." Yet the narrator interrupts, with another digression, any focusing of tension that may have been created by the description of Tam's stormy progress:

> Inspiring bold *John Barleycorn!*
> What dangers thou canst make us scorn!
> Wi' tipenny, we fear nae evil;

> Wi' usquabae, we'll face the devil!—
> The swats sae reamed in *Tammie*'s noddle,
> Fair play, he car'd na deils a boddle.
>
> (2:560)

Such passages, in which an external voice ironically discusses "Tammie," seem to disprove the notion of James Kinsley and Ian Campbell that this poem is a "dramatic monologue."[4] The digressions seem intentionally to distance us from any immediate identification with Tam; at least, his simplicity is deliberately contrasted with the more intricate consciousness of the narrator.

What Tam sees at Alloway follows his wife Kate's prediction. It is a satanic festival, with "Auld Nick" himself playing the pipes for a community of witches. In contrast to the male fellowship at Ayr, the witches' dance at Alloway is largely female. The sole woman of the prologue, a tavern landlady, is here paralleled by the "proprietor" at the dance, musician Satan. (Warlocks are mentioned, but not described.) And Kate's admonitory presence in the opening section of the poem is paralleled by Tam's appreciative presence at the witches' dance. After more scene setting (swords, scimitars, tomahawks, a knife, the enshrouded dead holding candles, the chained corpse of a hanged murderer, two more dead infants), Burns proceeds to his central interest: Tam's response to all this. Drunken Tam, "amaz'd and curious," watches the dance, while the narrator again interposes himself—he has aesthetic objections to Tam's involvement:

> Now *Tam!* O *Tam!* had thae been queans,
> A' plump and strapping in their teens,
> Their sarks, instead o' creeshie flannen,
> Been snaw-white seventeen hunder linnen!
> Thir breeks o' mine, my only pair,
> That ance were plush, o' gude blue hair,
> I wad hae gi'en off my hurdies,
> For ae blink o' the bonie burdies!
>
> But wither'd beldams, auld and droll,
> Rigwoodie hags wad spean a foal,
> Lowping and flinging on a crummock,
> I wonder didna turn thy stomach.

Tam's taste is vindicated, however; there is one young recruit at the dance. In yet another of the poem's symmetrical oppositions, the narrator's offer of his worn-out breeches is quickly followed by description of the young witch Nannie largely in terms of her scanty shift—a present received in childhood from her grandmother which she has now outgrown:

> But *Tam* kend what was what fu' brawlie,
> There was ae winsome wench and wawlie,
> That night enlisted in the core,
> (Lang after kend on *Carrick* shore;
> For mony a beast to dead she shot,
> And perish'd mony a bony boat,
> And shook baith meickle corn and bear,
> And kept the country-side in fear:)
> Her cutty sark, o' Paisley harn,
> That while a lassie she had worn,
> In longitude tho' sorely scanty,
> It was her best, and she was vauntie.—
>
> (2:562)

The poem perceives the witches' dance much as it has perceived the drunkenness of market-day tradesmen in Ayr: not as something to be censured so much as something that is a feature of local life. Incidentally, the folkloric content of the narrative has at this point become explicitly parenthetical.

The next section begins with the narrator's confession of the inadequacy of his Muse to "sing" of Nannie's dance in suitably epic terms. For the only moment in the poem, Tam takes initiative away from the narrator when, losing his "reason a' thigither," he cries out, "Weel-done, Cutty-sark!" in response to an especially bold leap of Nannie's. My earlier discussion of sentimental fiction stressed its voyeuristic overtones, and Tam's presence at the witches' dance has created some tension related to voyeurism. Will Tam just look on, or will he assert himself as a responsive presence and deal with the consequences? Made heroic by drink, pot-valiant Tam does "roar out" a reaction to what he sees. His outcry stops the dance, and the "hellish legion" "sallies" out against him.

In an earlier section of the poem, Tam's precious hours of respite at the tavern were compared to the homeward journey of bees. Here, the angry sortie of the witch community is evoked with the same simile:

As bees bizz out wi' angry fyke,
When plundering herds assail their byke;
As open pussie's mortal foes,
When, pop! she starts before their nose;
As eager runs the market-crowd,
When "Catch the thief!" resounds aloud;
So Maggie runs, the witches follow,
Wi' mony an eldritch skreech and hollow.

(2:563)

This poem began with a description of market-day crowds. Its transition to a conclusion is marked by another reference to them; in this case, to the market outcry against a petty thief. The earlier allusion stressed the common inclination of the community to relax after work; this instance stresses their common organization against an intruder.

Burns's earlier long poem, the cantata "Love and Liberty," offered a mirror image of Calvinism. The narrative in "Tam o' Shanter" also presents a series of opposing reflections on central themes. Indeed, "Tam o' Shanter" is structured by the opposition of the hedonistic community of men-drinkers at the beginning of the poem and the hedonistic community of women-dancers at its climax. The distance between the two societies is bridged in literary terms by the narrator because he applies similarly epic descriptions to both. The two cultures are bridged emotionally by Tam, with his instinctive shout of approval for Nannie. Kate stood opposed to the tavern culture in the prologue, but Tam, though an outsider, reacts to Nannie with an instinctive shout of "weel done" in the gesture that earns him the "heroic" status the narrator has applied ironically to him from the beginning. This response changes him from outsider to intruder, and another bridge becomes central to the poem: Tam must reach the keystone of the bridge of Doon to elude the witches' pursuit.

The concluding twenty-five lines, in which Tam's old mare Meg saves her master's life but loses her tail to a vindictive Nannie, account for Tam's fate after his exclamation. By now, a reader is sure that Tam is heroic enough to deserve survival, if only to prove Kate's "prophecy" ultimately false. He is not found drowned at Doon, but Meg and Tam do not come off entirely unscathed. There is a warning implicit in Maggie's lost tail:

Now, wha this tale o' truth shall read,
Ilk man and mother's son, take heed:
Whene'er to drink you are inclin'd,
Or cutty-sarks run in your mind,
Think, ye may buy the joys o'er dear,
Remember Tam o' Shanter's mare.

(2:564)

It is characteristic of the symmetrically inclined narrator that he concludes his "tale" with Maggie's loss of hers (or its homonymic coun-
terpart). However, this warning is no strong deterrent: like all the
narrator's warnings throughout the poem, it seems designed to be
disregarded.

What is the truth of the tale, then? It is not to be found in the
narrator's parodic moral. The tale, in fact, suggests exactly its opposite: don't think, don't remember. "Tam o' Shanter" celebrates the
tendency of people—for good or ill—to refuse to reckon the price of
their pleasures. The drinking at the tavern goes on each evening despite the disapproval of the farmers' wives. (The purpose of the prologue is to emphasize Tam's habitual, not just occasional, drunkenness.) The dancing in the kirkyard goes on with similar regularity,
despite societal and even divine sanctions. Indeed, the witches are a
perfect symbol for the tendency Burns saw in human nature to prefer
self-assertion to prudent abstention. Witches give up a hope for a
feeling, a concept of redemption for a sensation of present pleasure.
The narrator does not stint his description of the gruesome trappings
of the witches' dance, but it is basically hedonism, not evil, that he
perceives in their conduct. Tam himself acts from a motive similar to
Nannie's when his "roar" of approval indicates the victory of his instinct for pleasurable response over his less powerful one for self-protection and caution.

If this notion of the inexorably instinctive basis for human behavior
were the whole "truth" of "Tam o' Shanter," however, the poem
would not sound so different from "Love and Liberty," which shares
that central theme. The difference is that in "Tam o' Shanter" the
view that imprudence is a prerequisite to heroism is stated ironically:
the reader is left to puzzle out views on instinct and repression that
Burns presented unequivocally in "Love and Liberty." No character
in "Tam o' Shanter" is unequivocally perceived. (Even Kate,

spokeswoman for prudence, demonstrates in her diatribe a quality of reckless energy that is not exactly circumspect.) And in "Tam o' Shanter," Burns complicates the tone by his artist-in-residence narrator, whose high-flown digressions actually keep the poem going until Tam reaches the witches' dance. The cautious narrator's application of literary allusion to Tam's simple pleasures and temptations shows that Burns uses art itself as a kind of "prudence" in the poem: he uses it to anticipate consequences, to order and control things, and to counter Tam's policy of playing life by ear.

The poem shifts perspective between Tam and the narrator, the man and the poet—between life and literature. In a way, the truth of the tale is this very sense that human instinct and creative synthesis follow parallel if not always contiguous paths and that an affectionate irony in presenting both can be the "bridge" between them. In "Tam o' Shanter" it is a double consciousness, expressed as irony, that brings both life and art, energy and order, into the world of the poem. The tendency of the narrator to enlarge and reflect on the events in the poem is as necessary to "Tam o' Shanter" as the tendency of its "hero" to pursue immediate gratification. A special feature of the irony in Burns's poem is that, though certainly not tragic, it is not exclusively comic. In the ironic distance between Tam's and the narrator's perspectives we can see Burns's assertion of a mediating consciousness somewhere between the facts of life and the seductive lies of fancy. "Honest Tam's" heroism may be qualified by drunkenness and some other defects of character, but he is still much more than the butt of a poet's joke, as was Cowper's John Gilpin, for instance. Cowper's "diverting tale" also features the misadventures of a working man on horseback, but Cowper's mockery is directed against incompetent Gilpin, who cannot get his horse to stop. Burns's ironic view of Tam stops short of imposing haplessness on him. Tam is a good rider and his one speaking line, "Weel done," establishes him as an aggressive presence. The irony in "Tam o' Shanter" is a sympathetic and integrating force, like the stress on mutual affection that underlies Burns's love songs. In "Tam o' Shanter," an affectionate irony brings together an artful narrator and artless Tam in a world where both can operate freely. Like so much of Burns's best work, "Tam o' Shanter" chooses to perceive its world optimistically.

In "Night the Second" of *The Four Zoas* (1795–1804), William

Blake introduces to his epic some of the same themes that engaged Burns in his mock-epic:

> What is the price of Experience? do men buy it
> 　for a song?
> Or Wisdom for a dance in the street? No, it is
> 　bought with the price
> Of all that a man hath, his house, his wife, his
> 　children.
> Wisdom is sold in the desolate market where none
> 　come to buy,
> And in the wither'd field where the farmer
> 　plows for bread in vain.
> 　　　　　　　　　(*Complete Writings*, p. 290)

It is either Burns's shortcoming or his distinction—I think chiefly the latter—that perceiving as Blake did a central disjunction between joyous human instincts and the generally downhill course of life, Burns still addressed himself to issues like Blake's largely in an affirmative spirit. For Burns in his later years, whatever his personal disappointments, a song—a Scottish song—became exactly the "price of Experience." In "Tam o' Shanter" the market is far from "desolate"; and the beauty of a song—or the "wisdom" of a witches' dance— happens to be truth enough.

Notes

Introduction

1. Robert Burns, *The Poems and Songs of Robert Burns,* ed. James Kinsley (Oxford: Clarendon Press, 1968), 1:320. Subsequent quotations are from this edition unless otherwise noted.

2. Raymond Bentman, "Robert Burns's Declining Fame," *Studies in Romanticism 2,* no. 3 (Summer 1972): 207–9.

3. J. DeLancey Ferguson, *Pride and Passion: Robert Burns* (New York: Oxford University Press, 1939), p. ix.

4. Vladimir Nabokov, *Strong Opinions* (New York: McGraw-Hill, 1973), p. 103.

5. Matthew Arnold, "The Study of Poetry," in *Essays in Criticism: Second Series* (London: Macmillan, 1905), pp. 44–45.

6. Samuel Johnson, *The Lives of the English Poets,* ed. George Birkbeck Hill (Oxford: Clarendon Press, 1905), 1:45.

7. Samuel Johnson, *Johnson on Shakespeare,* ed. Arthur Sherbo (New Haven: Yale University Press, 1968), 1:62.

8. "Longinus," *The Sublime,* in *Aristotle: The Poetics, "Longinus": The Sublime, Demetrius: On Style* (Cambridge: Harvard University Press, 1960), p. 139.

9. Robert Burns, *Robert Burns: Selections,* ed. John C. Weston (Indianapolis: Bobbs-Merrill, 1967), p. xxvi.

10. Donald A. Low, *Robert Burns: The Critical Heritage* (London: Routledge and Kegan Paul, 1974), p. 132.

11. James Kinsley, *Robert Burns and the Peasantry,* Proceedings of the British Academy, vol. 9 (London: Oxford University Press, 1974), p. 6.

12. Thomas Crawford, *Burns: A Study of the Poems and Songs* (Stanford: Stanford University Press, 1960), pp. xii–xiii.

13. Maria Riddell, "Character Sketch," *Dumfries Journal* (August 1796); reprinted in Low, *The Critical Heritage,* p. 102.

14. James Anderson, unsigned review, *Monthly Review* (December 1786); reprinted in Low, *The Critical Heritage,* pp. 71–72.

15. Burns, *The Poems and Songs,* 3:1402.

16. Kinsley, *Robert Burns and the Peasantry*, p. 3.

17. David Buchan, *The Ballad and the Folk* (London: Routledge and Kegan Paul, 1972), p. 69.

18. Patricia Meyer Spacks, *The Poetry of Vision: Five Eighteenth Century Poets* (Cambridge: Harvard University Press, 1967), pp. 90–91.

19. Raymond Bentman, "Robert Burns's Use of Scottish Diction," in *From Sensibility to Romanticism: Essays Presented to Frederick A. Pottle*, ed. Frederick W. Hilles and Harold Bloom (London: Oxford University Press, 1965), pp. 239–40.

20. Sir Walter Scott, undated manuscript note; reprinted in Low, *The Critical Heritage*, p. 259.

21. Carol McGuirk, "Augustan Influences on Allan Ramsay," *Studies in Scottish Literature* 16 (1981): 97–109.

22. *Critical Essays on Robert Burns*, ed. Donald A. Low (London: Routledge and Kegan Paul, 1975), p. 4.

Chapter 1. *Sentimental Encounter*

1. Gilbert Burns to Alexander Peterkin, 29 September 1814, quoted by Low, *The Critical Heritage*, p. 271.

2. Laurence Sterne, *A Sentimental Journey*, ed. Gardner D. Stout, Jr. (Berkeley and Los Angeles: University of California Press, 1967), pp. 115–16.

3. This notion of Johnson's will be discussed at greater length in subsequent chapters.

4. Henry Mackenzie, *The Man of Feeling*, ed. Brian Vickers (London: Oxford University Press, 1967), p. 131. Italics are mine.

5. Robert Burns, *The Letters of Robert Burns*, ed. J. DeLancey Ferguson (Oxford: Clarendon Press, 1931), 1:14. Subsequent quotations are from this edition.

6. Arnold, "The Study of Poetry," p. 44.

7. David Hume, "Of the Standard of Taste," in *Of the Standard of Taste and Other Essays*, ed. John W. Lenz (Indianapolis: Bobbs-Merrill, 1965), p. 6.

8. James Boswell, *Life of Johnson*, ed. George Birkbeck Hill and L. F. Powell (Oxford: Clarendon Press, 1934), 2:453.

9. Samuel Taylor Coleridge, *Biographia Literaria*, quoted by Low, *The Critical Heritage*, p. 110.

10. Alexander Pope, *The Rape of the Lock and Other Poems*, ed. Geoffrey Tillotson (New Haven: Yale University Press, 1962), p. 368.

11. Third Earl of Shaftesbury, *Characteristics of Men, Manners, Opinions, Times*, ed. John W. Robertson (1900; reprint Gloucester, Mass.: Peter Smith, 1963), 2:144.

12. David Sillar to Robert Aiken, quoted in David Daiches, *Robert Burns* (New York: Macmillan, 1966), p. 69.

Chapter 2. *"Love and Liberty"*

1. Alexander Pope, *Minor Poems*, ed. Norman Ault (New Haven: Yale University Press, 1954), p. 96.

2. Johnson, "Life of Addison," *The Lives of the English Poets*, 2:132.

3. As R. L. Brett notes in "The Influence of Shaftesbury's Thought," Voltaire thought the *Essay on Man* a mere restatement of Shaftesbury's *Characteristics* and could not understand why Pope addressed it to Bolingbroke rather than to Shaftesbury. (Voltaire was overlooking Shaftesbury's political affiliation with the Whigs.) In *The Third Earl of Shaftesbury* (London: Hutchinson's University Library, 1951), p. 190.

4. James Kinsley's edition of Burns (Clarendon, 1968) finally overturned the common practice of referring to this poem as "The Jolly Beggars," a title applied to it by Thomas Stewart, who supervised its unauthorized publication in 1799 and 1801. Burns's title, "Love and Liberty," heads the manuscript copy at Alloway (cf. *The Poems and Songs*, 3:1151). A letter dated 17 September 1796 from Cunningham to Syme, the friends who tried to arrange financial help for Burns's widow and children, also refers to the cantata (then suppressed) as "Love and Liberty" (cf. W. E. Henley and T. F. Henderson, *The Poetry of Robert Burns* [London: Caxton, 1896], 2:305).

5. The correspondence of Burns's title with "Eloisa to Abelard" is briefly noted by Frederick L. Beaty, "Burns and the Triumph of Empathic Humor," in *Light from Heaven* (deKalb: Northern Illinois University Press, 1971), p. 18.

6. Pope, *The Rape of the Lock and Other Poems*, p. 325.

7. Section 10 of Joseph Warton's annotations of the Moral Epistles, in *Alexander Pope: A Critical Anthology*, ed. F. W. Bateson and N. A. Joukovsky (Baltimore: Penguin, 1971), p. 115.

8. Burns, *The Poems and Songs*, 1:195n. Pope prefaced "Eloisa to Abelard" with a similar distancing prose "argument" which placed her in a historical context.

9. Pope, *The Rape of the Lock and Other Poems*, p. 349. In a note to this line Tillotson mentions the line's resemblance to Addison's conclusion in *The Campaign*.

10. Joseph Addison, *Works*, ed. George W. Greene (New York: Putnam's, 1856), 1:196.

11. Burns, *The Poems and Songs*, 1:348.

12. Thomas Crawford reaches a parallel conclusion: "It would seem, then, that even when due weight is given to the native sources, the general content of *The Jolly Beggars* is affected by traditions of which all principle

records are English, not Scottish." *Society and the Lyric* (Edinburgh: Scottish Academic Press, 1979), p. 200.

13. Allan Ramsay, comp., *The Tea Table Miscellany* (Glasglow: J. Crum, 1871; reprinted from the 14th ed.), 2:148.

14. Ibid., p. 179.

15. Ibid., pp. 179–80. Kinsley (*The Poems and Songs*, 3:1149) also quotes from these stanzas in his notes to "Love and Liberty."

16. Incidentally, this stanza is one of very few in "Love and Liberty" bearing any resemblance to the old Scottish song "The Gaberlunzie Man," frequently mentioned by critics as a major source for "Love and Liberty." The old song uses the same comic mechanism as traveling salesman jokes. The guidwife on an isolated farm agrees to lodge a beggar for the night, but worries about her movables, as beggars are notorious thieves. In the morning she inspects her stockyard and is surprised to find that nothing is missing. She calls out to her daughter that their beggar has stolen nothing, but there is no answer: the beggar has persuaded the daughter to join him in his wanderings. The final stanza ("Wi' cauk and keel I'll win your bread, / And Spindles and whorles for them wha need, / Whilk is a gentle trade indeed, / To carry the gaberlunzie on") does sound like Burns's paean to free love and free movement. Otherwise, the song concentrates on the comic figure of the guidwife and does not use the beggar perspective (from *Ancient and Modern Scottish Songs, Heroic Ballads, Etc. . . .* , ed. David Herd [1776; reprint Edinburgh: William Paterson, 1870], 2:51).

17. Burns's "Extempore—To Mr. Gavin Hamilton" does similar things with the word "naething."

18. J. C. Weston, "The Text of Burns's 'The Jolly Beggars,'" *Studies in Bibliography*, 13 (1960): 239–47.

19. Arnold, *Essays in Criticism*, p. 51.

Chapter 3. *Sentimental "Election" in the Vernacular Epistles and "The Vision"*

1. For a discussion of the New Licht–Auld Licht controversy in Burns's community, see Hans Hecht, *Robert Burns*, trans. Jane Lymburn (London: William Hodge, 1936), pp. 61–77. Also of interest is Rev. David Cairns's "Robert Burns and the Religious Movement in Scotland of His Day" (Edinburgh: Carlyle Society Lecture, no. 3, 1962).

2. James Maxwell, *Animadversions . . .* (Paisley, Scotland: J. Neilson, 1788), p. 7. The first line quoted contains a reference to Burns's satire "The Holy Fair."

3. Ebenezer Picken, *Poems and Epistles, Mostly in Scottish Dialect* (Paisley, Scotland: John Neilson, 1788), p. 35.

4. David Sillar, *Poems* (Kilmarnock, Scotland: J. Wilson, 1789), p. v.

5. Burns, *The Poems and Songs*, 1:68.

6. John Lapraik, "Rhyming Epistle to Mr. R—— B——, "Ayrshire," in *Poems on Several Occasions* (Kilmarnock, Scotland: John Wilson, 1788), pp. 30–31. Lapraik here seems to emulate a stanza in John Byrom's "Careless Content" (1773): "Not that I rate myself the Rule / How all my Betters should behave; / But Fame shall find me no Man's Fool, / Nor to a Set of Men a Slave: / I love a Friendship free and frank, / And hate to hang upon a Hank" (*The Oxford Book of Eighteenth Century Verse*, ed. David Nichol Smith [Oxford: Clarendon Press, 1966], p. 229).

7. James Macauley, quoted by Low, *The Critical Heritage*, pp. 83–84.

8. Low, *The Critical Heritage*, p. 169.

9. Edward Young, "Conjectures on Original Composition," in *Edward Young: The Complete Works*, ed. James Nichols (London: William Tegg, 1854), 2:553–54.

10. William Blake, "Annotations to Reynold's *Discourses*" and "The Marriage of Heaven and Hell," in *Complete Writings*, ed. Geoffrey Keynes (Oxford: Oxford University Press, 1970), pp. 454, 149.

Chapter 4. *Laws of Sentimental Polity*

1. Sarah Fielding, *Remarks on Clarissa* (London: J. Robinson, 1749), p. 37.

2. See Richard A. Lanham's excellent study *Tristram Shandy: The Games of Pleasure* (Berkeley and Los Angeles: University of California Press, 1973).

3. Wolfgang von Goethe, *The Sorrows of Young Werther*, trans. Victor Lange (New York: Holt, Rinehart and Winston, 1960), p. ix.

4. H. H. Houben, ed., *Gespräche mit Goethe* (Wiesbaden: F. A. Brockhaus, 1959), p. 413.

5. Friedrich von Schiller, *On Naive and Sentimental Poetry*, trans. Julius A. Elias (New York: Frederick Ungar, 1966), p. 137.

6. Anna Barbauld, *Introduction to Zeluco*, vol. 34 of *British Novelists* (London, 1810), p. v.

7. Schiller, *On Naive and Sentimental Poetry*, p. 139.

8. Hannah More, quoted by Lodwick C. Hartley, *William Cowper, Humanitarian* (Chapel Hill: University of North Carolina Press, 1938), p. 14.

9. James Boswell, *The London Journal*, ed. F. Pottle (New York: McGraw Hill, 1950), p. 110. Italics are mine.

10. Ibid., p. 106.

11. Johnson, *The Lives of the English Poets*, 1:460.

12. Shaftesbury, *Characteristics*, 1:276.

13. Burns, *Letters*, 1:112.

14. As mentioned in the Introduction, I am much indebted for informa-

tion on which writers Burns read to John Robotham's compilation, "The Reading of Robert Burns," in the *Bulletin of the New York Public Library* 74 (1970): 561–76. *Rameau's Nephew* was not published until the early nineteenth century; interestingly enough, it first appeared in a German translation by Goethe.

15. William Shenstone, *Poetical Works* (Edinburgh: James Nichol, 1863), p. 18.

16. Another excerpt from Shenstone that Burns must have savored in the intervals of his harassment by factors, Jean Armour's relatives, and Auld Licht preachers: "Ah! What is native worth esteem'd of clowns? / 'Tis thy false glare, O Fortune! thine they see" (*Poetical Works*, p. 21).

17. Burns, *Letters*, 1:244; quoting Smollett.

18. Even Thomson, who was usually disastrous as a stylistic influence, contributed some fine sentiments to Burns's stock. One instance of a successful adaptation from Thomson to Burns is the transformation of an undistinguished passage from "Winter" into the nucleus of "Man Was Made to Mourn." Musing on the ills of human existence, Thomson wrote: "How many feel this very moment death, / And all the sad variety of pain, / How many sink in the devouring flood, / Or more devouring flame. How many bleed / By shameful variance twixt man and man" (*The Complete Poetical Works of James Thomson*, ed. J. Logie Robertson [Oxford: Oxford University Press, 1908], p. 126). Burns's adaptation of these lines did not produce a great poem, but it did bring forth a justly famous phrase: "Many and sharp the num'rous Ills / Inwoven with our frame! / More pointed still we make ourselves / Regret, Remorse and Shame! / And Man, whose heav'n-erected face, / The smiles of love adorn, / Man's inhumanity to Man / Makes countless thousands mourn!" (1:118).

19. Hugh Blair, "Lectures on Rhetoric and *Belles Lettres*," ms. 850, National Library of Scotland, p. 152. The criticism of Johnson, which was deleted in the published lectures, calls Johnson's style derivative of Isocrates and too monotonous. Blair's papers (mss. 850 and 3408) are used with permission of the Trustees, National Library of Scotland.

20. Mackenzie gave as his reason for the inclusion of "To a Mountain Daisy" the suitability of its length to the bounds of his essay, but many of the poems in the Kilmarnock edition are of similar length.

Chapter 5. *The Sentimental Critics*

1. Henry Mackenzie, et al., *The Lounger*, vol. 37 of *British Essayists* (London, 1817), p. 300.

2. Harold Thompson discusses the *Mirror* essay on Michael Bruce and its influence on Mackenzie's subsequent praise of Burns in *A Scottish Man of Feeling* . . . (London: Oxford University Press, 1931), p. 215.

3. When Sir Walter Scott dedicated *Waverley* to Henry Mackenzie, he called him "the Scottish Addison."

4. Mackenzie, *British Essayists*, 34:188. In his biography of Mackenzie, cited in note 2 above, Thompson suggests that Mackenzie himself wrote the paragraph "describing the poet's cot" for inclusion in Craig's review. *A Scottish Man of Feeling*, p. 216.

5. Adam Smith, *The Theory of Moral Sentiments* (1853; reprint New York: Augustus M. Kelley, 1966), pp. 22–23.

6. Robert Burns changed the spelling of his surname: he was born either Robert Burness (as he signed several early letters), or Robert Burnes. Hans Hecht notes that the poet's father, born in Kincardineshire—where a two-syllable pronunciation was customary—moved to southwest Scotland, which favored a one-syllable pronunciation of the name (*Robert Burns*, p. 3n).

7. Henry Mackenzie to Elizabeth Rose, 1779, quoted by Thompson, *A Scottish Man of Feeling*, p. 215.

8. Boswell, *The London Journal*, p. 96.

9. One anonymous reviewer of the Kilmarnock edition asked this question in so many words: "Who are you, Mr. Burns?" (Low, *The Critical Heritage*, p. 63).

Chapter 6. *Sentimental Civilization and Its Discontents*

1. Alison Cockburn to a friend, December 1786, quoted by Franklyn Bliss Snyder, *The life of Robert Burns* (New York: Macmillan, 1932), p. 197.

2. Robert Couper to James Currie, 23 November 1798, Cowie Collection, Mitchell Library, Glasgow. The papers of Couper and Currie are used with permission of the Mitchell Library.

3. Robert Burns, *The Life and Works of Robert Burns*, ed. Robert Chambers; rev. William Wallace (Edinburgh: W. and R. Chambers, 1896), 2:98. Blair's original letter is included in manuscript 3408 in the National Library of Scotland.

4. Robert Burns, "Second Commonplace Book," ed. W. Jack, *Macmillan's Magazine* 39 (November 1878–April 1879), p. 455.

5. Burns, *The Poems and Songs*, 2:720, 731.

6. Unsigned review, *Gentleman's Magazine*, 57 (July 1787): 617.

7. The rents for farms in the process of being "improved" were set more in view of eventual yield than current capacity, a practice which ruined many tenant farmers of the day, including the poet's father. See Thomas Crawford, "Burns and the New Farming," *Geographical Magazine* 32 (1959): 186–90.

8. Jane Austen, *Emma*, vol. 4 of *The Novels of Jane Austen*, ed. R. W. Chapman (London: Oxford University Press, 1933), p. 29.

9. Henry Dundas, Lord Melville, was in charge of Civil Service appointments in Scotland. Among other things, Couper's rage is that of a Tory against the patronage decisions of a Whig administration. Of course, the Excise itself was a "Whig" tax.

Chapter 7. *Naive and Sentimental Burns*

1. R. S. Crane, "Suggestions Towards a Genealogy of 'The Man of Feeling'" (1934); Donald Greene, "Latitudinarianism and Sensibility: The Genealogy of the 'Man of Feeling' Reconsidered" (1977; a rebuttal of Crane that traces back even further the roots of the movement); G. S. Rousseau, "Nerves, Spirits and Fibres: Towards Defining the Origins of Sensibility" (1973; offering a background for the development of the sentimental in terms of contemporary science and physiology); and George A. Starr, "Only a Boy: Notes on Sentimental Novels" (1977; an excellent essay on sentimental characters and their relationship to language). See bibliography for full references.

2. James Beattie, *The Letters of James Beattie, LL.D., Chronologically Arranged from Sir William Forbes's Collection* (London: J. Sharpe, 1820), p. 133.

3. James Beattie, *Essays* (Edinburgh: William Creech, 1776), pp. 11–12.

4. Low, *The Critical Heritage*, p. 306. The "God's spies" figure is from *King Lear* and occurs in the last scene between Lear and Cordelia.

5. Franz Kafka, *Miscellany*, trans. Sophie Prombaum (New York: Twice a Year Press, 1946), p. 51.

6. All are identified in DeLancey Ferguson's notes to *The Letters of Robert Burns*.

7. James Beattie, a sweet-tempered and accommodating man, still could not countenance Goldsmith's lack of social address, dismissing him as a "poor fretful creature": "He envied even the dead; he could not bear that Shakespeare should be so much admired" (Beattie, *Letters*, p. 168).

8. This is suggested in Goldsmith's "The Deserted Village," where the narrator speaks of poetry as "my shame in crowds, my solitary pride."

9. Friedrich von Schiller, *Sammtliche Werke* (Munich: Carl Hanser, 1962), 5:764.

10. In the source for "Cumberland Lass" the girl cuts up her mother's shroud to make the shirts for her lover. This grotesque touch is typical of the sort Burns softened or edited when he revised (a major reason antiquarians and folklorists often dislike his songs). The original is included in Thomas D'Urfey, comp., *Wit and Mirth; or, Pills to Purge Melancholy* (London; J. Tonson, 1719–20), 4:133–35.

11. "Ossian," named in chapter 4 as a model Burns imitated in his weaker work, also transferred feelings from the finite opinions of a speaker into his

subject. The difference is that "Ossian" worked with archaic, exotic subjects, aiming at effects of sublime nostalgia. Burns's song revisions deliberately align his feelings with the nonexotic, the universal. The importance of recognizable human types—not ideal archaic ghosts—is his subject.

Chapter 8. *Paradoxes of Self-Expression and Tradition after 1740*

1. Burns's quotation ("reverence thyself") echoes stanza 7 of Beattie's *The Minstrel* ("Know thine own worth, and reverence the lyre"). Other correspondences between Beattie's poem and Burns's career will be discussed in chapter 9.

2. Burns, *Letters*, 2:356.

3. Ferguson, *Pride and Passion*, p. 217.

4. John Dryden, preface to *Fables*, in *Essays*, ed. W. P. Ker (Oxford: Clarendon Press, 1900), 2:255.

5. The imitation of Dryden occurs in "Ode on the Death of a Favorite Cat." See Thomas Gray, *The Complete Poems of Thomas Gray: English, Latin and Greek*, ed. Herbert W. Starr and J. Raymond Hendrickson (Oxford: Clarendon Press, 1966), p. 203.

6. Northrop Frye, *Fables of Identity: Studies in Poetic Mythology* (New York: Harcourt, Brace and World, 1963), p. 133.

7. William Cowper, *The Poetical Works of William Cowper*, ed. H. S. Milford (London: Oxford University Press, 1967), 166. Subsequent quotations are from this edition.

8. Spack's *The Poetry of Vision* contains an extensive discussion of traditional images in *The Olney Hymns* and *The Task*. There is a list of images characteristic of Cowper on page 172.

9. Samuel Johnson, *Samuel Johnson: Poems*, ed. E. L. McAdam, Jr., and George Milne (New Haven: Yale University Press, 1964), pp. 343–44.

10. See Walter Jackson Bate, *The Burden of the Past and the English Poet* (Cambridge: Harvard University Press, Belknap Press, 1970), and Harold Bloom, *The Anxiety of Influence: A Theory of Poetry* (New York: Oxford University Press, 1973).

11. Hester Thrale reports that the Service for the Dead invariably caused "a flood of tears" when Johnson tried to read it. *Anecdotes of Samuel Johnson* (London: T. and J. Allman, 1822), pp. 160–61.

12. *The Poems of Gray, Collins, and Goldsmith*, ed. Roger Lonsdale (London: Longmans, 1969), p. 435.

13. Christopher Smart, *A Song to David*, in *Poems by Christopher Smart*, ed. Robert Brittain (Princeton: Princeton University Press, 1950), p. 211.

14. Christopher Smart, *Jubilate Agno*, ed. W. H. Bond (Cambridge: Harvard University Press, 1954), p. 55.

15. George Eliot, "Worldliness and Otherworldliness: The Poet Young," in *Essays*, ed. Thomas Pinney (New York: Columbia University Press, 1963), p. 381.

16. Wallace Stevens, "Notes Toward a Supreme Fiction," in *Collected Poems* (New York: Knopf, 1955), p. 381.

17. Christopher Grieve [pseud. Hugh MacDiarmid], *Selected Essays* (London: Jonathan Cape, 1969), p. 140.

18. Robert Burns, *The Songs of Robert Burns* with *Notes on Scottish Songs by Robert Burns*, ed. J. C. Dick (1903, 1908; reprinted together, Hatboro, Pa.: Folklore Associates, 1962), pp. ix, xviii.

19. James Johnson et al., eds., *"The Scots Musical Museum"* . . . *with "Illustrations of the Lyric Poetry and Music of Scotland"* by *William Stenhouse* (1879; reprint Hatboro, Pa.: Folklore Associates, 1962). The Stenhouse commentary on Johnson comprises the second volume.

20. Robert Burns, *The Merry Muses of Caledonia*, ed. G. Legman (New Hyde Park, N.Y.: University Books, 1965), p. xxxvi.

21. Robert Burns, quoted by Dick in *The Songs of Robert Burns*, p. 26.

22. Robert Burns, *The Glenriddle Manuscripts of Robert Burns*, ed. Desmond Donaldson (Hamden, Conn.: Archon Books, 1973), 2:41–42. Burns had transcribed this sentiment earlier in life, in his *First Commonplace Book, 1783–85*, ed. J. C. Ewing and Davidson Cook (Glasgow: Gowans and Gray, 1938), pp. 38–39.

Chapter 9. *The Songs*

1. In Dick's edition of *Notes on Scottish Songs by Robert Burns*, "Preen up her apron Johnie" is given as the last line. This is corrected by Davidson Cook in *Annotations of Scottish Songs* (reprinted 1962 with Dick's two books). Kinsley's note to "Corn rigs" uses Cook (Burns, *The Poems and Songs*, 3:1010).

2. Allan Ramsay, quoted by Stenhouse, in Johnson, *The Scots Musical Museum*, 2:94.

3. [John Aikin], *Essays on Song-Writing, with a Collection of such English Songs as are Most Eminent for Poetical Merit, to which are Added, Some Original Pieces* (London: Joseph Johnson, n.d.), pp. 22–23.

4. Joseph Ritson, "A Historical Essay," in *Scotish Songs* (London: J. Johnson, 1794), 1:lxii–lxiii, lxx.

5. Ritson's name was supplied in a note to this letter in volume 4 of Chambers and Wallace's edition of *The Life and Works of Robert Burns*. Incidentally, Ritson did include musical notation in his later miscellany *Scotish Songs*, saying "the words and melody of a Scotish song should be ever insep-

arable" (p. i). And in *Joseph Ritson, Scholar at Arms* (Berkeley and Los Angeles: University of California Press, 1938), 1:90, Bertrand Bronson identifies Ritson's English collection, criticized by Burns in the letter quoted above, as the same "Select Collection" of English songs heartily praised by Burns in his earlier autobiographical letter to Dr. John Moore. The inference is that Burns was offended by Ritson's remarks on his lyric-writing ability.

6. W. B. Yeats, *Ideas of Good and Evil* (London: Macmillan, 1903), pp. 241–43.

7. Crawford, *Burns: A Study of the Poems and Songs*, p. 305. Legman, too, praises the psychological accuracy of Burns's female characters in his bawdry.

8. Grieve [pseud. MacDiarmid], *Selected Essays*, p. 142.

9. Herd, *Ancient and Modern Scottish Songs, Heroic Ballads, Etc.*, 1:vii.

10. Allan Cunningham, ed., *The Songs of Scotland . . .* (London: J. Taylor, 1825), 2:349–50.

11. James Beattie, *Poetical Works of James Beattie* (1854; reprint Freeport, N.Y.: Books for Libraries Press, 1972), pp. 9–10.

12. Ferguson, *Pride and Passion*, p. 184.

Chapter 10. *"Tam o' Shanter"*: The Truth of the Tale

1. For an excellent essay on mock-heroic and epic elements in "Tam o' Shanter," see M. L. Mackenzie, "A New Dimension for 'Tam o' Shanter,' " *Studies in Scottish Literature*, 1, no. 2 (1963): 87–92.

2. Kurt Wittig, *The Scottish Tradition in Literature* (Edinburgh: Oliver and Boyd, 1958), p. 202.

3. Burns, *The Poems and Songs*, 3:1354–55, citing notes to the Chambers-Wallace and Henley-Henderson editions of Burns's poems.

4. Ian Campbell, "Burns's Poems and Their Audience," in Low's *Critical Essays on Robert Burns*, p. 43; and Burns, *The Poems and Songs*, 3:1352: "The poem is not a duologue woven about—and justifying—a folk-tale; it is a narrative, like many of Burns's poems, in dramatic monologue." Though Kinsley is keenly attuned to the irony of the poem, he agrees with Kurt Wittig that the evident "narrator" is a consciousness "flitting in and out of Tam's own mind."

Bibliography

Editions and Reference Works

Burns, Robert. *The Glenriddle Manuscripts of Robert Burns*. Ed. Desmond Donaldson. Hamden, Conn.: Archon Books, 1973.

——. *The Letters of Robert Burns*. Ed. J. DeLancey Ferguson. 2 vols. Oxford: Clarendon Press, 1931.

——. *The Life and Works of Robert Burns*. Ed. Robert Chambers; rev. William Wallace. 4 vols. Edinburgh: W. and R. Chambers, 1896.

——. *The Merry Muses of Caledonia*. Ed. G. Legman. New Hyde Park, N.Y.: University Books, 1965.

——. *The Poems and Songs of Robert Burns*. Ed. James Kinsley. 3 vols. Oxford: Clarendon Press, 1968.

——. *Poems: 1786 and 1787*. Menston, England: Scolar Press Facsimile, 1971.

——. *The Poetry of Robert Burns*. Ed. W. E. Henley and T. F. Henderson. 4 vols. London: Caxton, 1896.

——. *Robert Burns's Commonplace Book, 1783–85. Reproduced in Facsimile from the Poet's Manuscript in the Possession of Sir Alfred Joseph Law, M.P.; with Transcript, Introduction and Notes by James Cameron Ewing and Davidson Cook*. Glasgow: Gowans and Gray, 1938.

——. *Robert Burns: Selections*. Ed. John C. Weston. Indianapolis: Bobbs-Merrill, 1967.

——. "The Second Commonplace Book." Ed. W. Jack. *Macmillan's Magazine* 39 (March–November 1879): 448–60, 560–72; 40:32–43, 124–32, 250–59.

——. *The Songs of Robert Burns* and *Notes on Scottish Songs by Robert Burns* ed. J. C. Dick with *Annotation of Scottish Songs by Burns* by Davidson Cook. Foreword by Henry George Farmer. Hatboro, Pa.: Folklore Associates, 1962.

Johnson, James, et al., eds. *"The Scots Musical Museum" originally published by James Johnson with "Illustrations of the Lyric Poetry and Music of Scotland" by William Stenhouse*. 2 vols. 1879. Reprint. Hatboro, Pa.: Folklore Associates, 1962.

Roy, G. Ross. *Robert Burns*. University of South Carolina Press: Department of English Bibliographical Series, no. 1, 1966.

Criticism and Biography

Angellier, Auguste. *Etude sur la vie et les oeuvres de Robert Burns*. 2 vols. Paris: Hachette et Cie., 1893.

Angus-Butterworth, Lionel. *Robert Burns and the Eighteenth Century Revival in Scottish Vernacular Literature*. Aberdeen: Aberdeen University Press, 1969.

Arnold, Matthew. *Essays in Criticism: Second Series*. London: Macmillan, 1905.

Bentman, Raymond. "Robert Burns's Declining Fame." *Studies in Romanticism* 2, no. 3 (Summer 1972): 207–24.

———. "Robert Burns's Use of Scottish Diction." *From Sensibility to Romanticism: Essays Presented to Frederick A. Pottle*. Ed. Frederick W. Hilles and Harold Bloom. London: Oxford University Press, 1965.

Carlyle, Thomas. *On Heroes, Hero Worship and the Heroic in History*. Lincoln: University of Nebraska Press, 1966.

Collins, Frederick Boyd. "The Neoclassical Elements in the Mind and Art of Robert Burns." Ph.D. diss., University of North Carolina, 1958.

The Contemporaries of Burns. Edinburgh: Hugh Paton, 1840.

Crawford, Thomas. "Burns and the New Farming." *Geographical Magazine* 32 (1959): 186–90.

———. *Burns: A Study of the Poems and Songs*. Stanford: Stanford University Press, 1960.

Currie, James. Transcript of a letter to Cadell and Davies, n.d. Cowie Collection. Mitchell Library, Glasgow.

Daiches, David. *Robert Burns*. New York: Macmillan, 1966.

Ferguson, J. DeLancey. *Pride and Passion: Robert Burns*. New York: Oxford University Press, 1939.

Fitzhugh, Robert. *Robert Burns, the Man and the Poet: A Round, Unvarnished Account*. Boston: Houghton Mifflin, 1970.

Hadden, J. Cuthbert. *George Thomson, the Friend of Burns*. London: John C. Nimmo, 1898.

Hecht, Hans. *Robert Burns*. Trans. Jane Lymburn. London: William Hodge, 1936.

———. *Songs from David Herd's Manuscripts*. Edinburgh: William J. Hay, 1904.

Keith, Christina. *The Russet Coat: A Critical Study of Burns's Poetry and of Its Background*. London: Robert Hale, 1956.

Kinsley, James. *Robert Burns and the Peasantry*. Proceedings of the British Academy, vol. 9. London: Oxford University Press, 1974.

Low, Donald A., ed. *Robert Burns: The Critical Heritage*. London: Routledge and Kegan Paul, 1974.

———, ed. *Critical Essays on Robert Burns*. London: Routledge and Kegan Paul, 1975.

Maxwell, James. *Animadversions on some Poets and Poetasters of the present Age especially R——t B——s, and J——n L——k. With a Contrast of some of the former Age.* Paisley, Scotland: J. Neilson, 1788.

"Notice" of *Poems, Chiefly in the Scottish Dialect. Gentleman's Magazine* 57, p. 2 (July 1787): 615–18.

Robotham, John. "The Reading of Robert Burns." *Bulletin of the New York Public Library* 74 (1970): 561–76.

Snyder, Franklyn Bliss. *The Life of Robert Burns.* New York: Macmillan, 1932.

Stevenson, Robert Louis. "Some Aspects of Robert Burns." In *Familiar Studies of Men and Books.* New York: Scribner's, 1891.

Strawhorn, John. *Ayrshire at the Time of Burns.* Ayr, Scotland: Archaeological and Natural History Society, 1959.

Thompson, Harold. *A Scottish Man of Feeling: Some Account of Henry Mackenzie, Esq., of Edinburgh and of the Golden Age of Burns and Scott.* London: Oxford University Press, 1931.

Thornton, Robert Donald. *James Currie, the Entire Stranger, and Robert Burns.* Edinburgh: Oliver and Boyd, 1963.

Weston, John C. "The Narrator of 'Tam o' Shanter.'" *Studies in English Literature* 8 (1968): 537–50.

_____. "Robert Burns's Use of the Scots Verse Epistle Form." *Philological Quarterly* 48 (April 1970): 188–210.

_____. "The Text of Burns' 'The Jolly Beggars.'" *Studies in Bibliography* (Va.) 13 (1960); 239–47.

Whitman, Walt. "Robert Burns as Poet and Person." In *Complete Prose Works.* Philadelphia: David McKay, 1897.

Witte, W. *Schiller and Burns.* Oxford: Blackwell, 1950.

Eighteenth-Century Writings

Addison, Joseph. *Works.* Ed. George W. Greene. 6 vols. New York: Putnam's, 1854–56.

[Aikin, John.] *Essays on Song-Writing, with a Collection of such English Songs as are Most Eminent for Poetical Merit, to which are Added, Some Original Pieces.* London: Joseph Johnson, n.d.

Audrea, E. and Aubrey Williams, eds., *Alexander Pope: Pastoral Poetry and "An Essay on Criticism."* New Haven: Yale University Press, 1969.

Austen, Jane. *Emma.* Vol. 4 of *The Novels of Jane Austen,* ed. R. W. Chapman. London: Oxford University Press, 1933.

Barbauld, Anna Aikin. "An Inquiry Into Those Kinds of Distress Which Excite Agreeable Sensations." In *Works.* 2 vols. London: Longmans, 1825.

Beattie, James. *Essays.* Edinburgh: William Creech, 1776.

_____. *The Letters of James Beattie, LL.D., Chronologically Arranged from Sir William Forbes's Collection.* London: J. Sharpe, 1820.

————. *Poetical Works of James Beattie.* 1854. Reprint. Freeport, N.Y.: Books for Libraries Press, 1972.

Blair, Hugh. "Lectures on Rhetoric and *Belles Lettres.*" Ms. 850, National Library of Scotland.

————. Papers. Ms. 3408, 4 May 1787. National Library of Scotland.

Blake, William. *Complete Writings.* Ed. Geoffrey Keynes. Oxford: Oxford University Press, 1970.

Boswell, James. *Life of Johnson.* Ed. George Birkbeck Hill and L. F. Powell. 6 vols. Oxford: Clarendon Press, 1934–1950.

————. *The London Journal.* Ed. F. Pottle. New York: McGraw Hill, 1950.

Brescher, Horst W., ed. *Henry Mackenzie: Letters to Elizabeth Rose of Kilravock.* Edinburgh: Oliver and Boyd, 1967.

Carlyle, Alexander (of Inveresk). *Autobiography.* 2 vols. Edinburgh: William Blackwood, 1860.

Collins, William. *Drafts and Fragments of Verse.* Ed. J. S. Cunningham. Oxford: Clarendon Press, 1956.

Couper, Robert. Letter to James Currie, 23 November 1798. Cowie Collection. Mitchell Library, Glasgow.

Cowper, William. *The Poetical Works of William Cowper.* Ed. H. S. Milford. London: Oxford University Press, 1967.

Cunningham, Allan, ed. *The Songs of Scotland, Ancient and Modern; with an Introduction and Notes, Historical and Critical, and Characters of the Lyric Poets.* 4 vols. London: J. Taylor, 1825.

Dryden, John. *Essays.* Ed. W. P. Ker. 2 vols. Oxford: Clarendon Press, 1900.

D'Urfey, Thomas, comp. *Wit and Mirth; or, Pills to Purge Melancholy.* 6 vols. London: J. Tonson, 1719–20.

Fielding, Sarah. *Remarks on Clarissa.* London: J. Robinson, 1749.

Goethe, Wolfgang von. *The Sorrows of Young Werther.* Trans. Victor Lange. New York: Holt, Rinehart and Winston, 1960.

Gray, Thomas. *The Complete Poems: English, Latin and Greek.* Ed. Herbert W. Starr and J. Raymond Hendrickson. Oxford: Clarendon Press, 1966.

Herd, David, ed. *Ancient and Modern Scottish Songs, Heroic Ballads, Etc.* 2 vols. 1776. Reprint. Edinburgh: William Paterson, 1870.

Houben, H. H., ed. *Gespräche mit Goethe.* Wiesbaden: F. A. Brockhaus, 1959.

Hume, David. *Of the Standard of Taste and Other Essays.* Ed. John W. Lenz. Indianapolis: Bobbs-Merrill, 1965.

————. *Johnson on Shakespeare.* Ed. Arthur Sherbo. 2 vols. New Haven: Yale University Press, 1968.

————. *The Lives of the English Poets.* Ed. George Birkbeck Hill. 3 vols. Oxford: Clarendon Press, 1905.

————. *Samuel Johnson: Poems.* Ed. E. L. McAdam, Jr. and George Milne. New Haven: Yale University Press, 1964.

Lapraik, John. *Poems on Several Occasions.* Kilmarnock, Scotland: John Wilson, 1788.

Lonsdale, Roger, ed. *The Poems of Gray, Collins, and Goldsmith.* London: Longmans, 1969.

Macauley, James. *Poems on Various Subjects: Mostly in Scots and English.* Edinburgh: Printed for the author, 1788.

Mackenzie, Henry. *The Lounger.* Vols. 37–38 of *British Essayists.* London, 1817.

_____. *The Man of Feeling.* Ed. Brian Vickers. London: Oxford University Press, 1967.

_____. *The Mirror.* Vols. 34–35 of *British Essayists.* London, 1817.

Mackenzie, M. L. "A New Dimension for 'Tam o' Shanter.'" *Studies in Scottish Literature* 1, no. 2 (1963): 87–92.

Moore, John. *Zeluco.* Ed. Anna Aikin Barbauld. Vols. 34–35 of *British Novelists.* London, 1810.

Picken, Ebenezer. *Poems and Epistles, Mostly in Scottish Dialect.* Paisley, Scotland: J. Neilson, 1788.

Piozzi, Hester Lynch Thrale. *Anecdotes of Samuel Johnson, LL.D, During the Last Twenty Years of his Life.* London: T. and J. Allman, 1822.

Pope, Alexander. *Minor Poems.* Ed. Norman Ault. New Haven: Yale University Press, 1954.

_____. *The Rape of the Lock and Other Poems.* Ed. Geoffrey Tillotson. New Haven: Yale University Press, 1962.

Ramsay, Allan, comp. *The Tea Table Miscellany.* 2 vols. Glasgow: J. Crum, 1871, reprinted from the 14th ed.

Ritson, Joseph. *Scotish Songs.* 2 vols. London: J. Johnson, 1794.

Schiller, Friedrich von. *On Naive and Sentimental Poetry.* Trans. Julius A. Elias. New York: Frederick Ungar, 1966.

_____. *Sammtliche Werke.* 5 vols. Munich: Carl Hanser, 1962–65.

Shaftesbury, Third Earl of (Anthony Ashley Cooper). *Characteristics of Men, Manners, Opinions, Times.* 2 vols. 1900. Reprint. Gloucester, Mass.: Peter Smith, 1963.

Shenstone, William. *Poetical Works.* Edinburgh: James Nichol, 1863.

Shirrefs, Andrew. *Poems Chiefly in the Scottish Dialect.* Paisley, Scotland: J. Neilson, 1790.

Sillar, David. *Poems.* Kilmarnock, Scotland: J. Wilson, 1789.

Skinner, John. *Amusements of Leisure Hours; or, Poetical Pieces, Chiefly in the Scottish Dialect.* Edinburgh: Stuart Cheyne, 1809.

Smart, Christopher. *Jubilate Agno.* Ed. W. H. Bond. Cambridge: Harvard University Press, 1954.

_____. *Poems by Christopher Smart.* Ed. Robert Brittain. Princeton: Princeton University Press, 1950.

Smith, Adam. *The Theory of Moral Sentiments*. 1853. Reprint. New York: Augustus M. Kelley, 1966.

Sterne, Laurence. *A Sentimental Journey*. Ed. Gardner D. Stout, Jr. Berkeley and Los Angeles: University of California Press, 1967.

Tannahill, Robert. *Poems and Songs Chiefly in the Scottish Dialect*. Paisley, Scotland: J. Neilson, 1815.

Thomson, James. *The Complete Poetical Works*. Ed. J. Logie Robertson. Oxford: Oxford University Press, 1908.

Wilson, Alexander. *Poems*. Paisley, Scotland: J. Neilson, 1790.

Young, Edward. *Edward Young: The Complete Works*. Ed. James Nichols. 2 vols. London: William Tegg, 1854.

Scottish Literary History

Allardyce, Alexander. *Scotland and Scotsmen in the Eighteenth Century from the Mss. of John Ramsay, Esq. of Ochtertyre*. 2 vols. Edinburgh: William Blackwood, 1888.

Buchan, David. *The Ballad and the Folk*. London: Routledge and Kegan Paul, 1972.

Cairns, David. *Robert Burns and the Religious Movements in Scotland of His Day*. Edinburgh: Carlyle Society Lecture no. 3, 1962.

Craig, David. *Scottish Literature and the Scottish People, 1680–1830*. London: Chatto and Windus, 1961.

Crawford, Thomas. *Society and the Lyric: A Study of the Song Culture of Eighteenth-Century Scotland*. Edinburgh: Scottish Academic Press, 1979.

Daiches, David. *The Paradox of Scottish Culture: The Eighteenth Century Experience*. London: Oxford University Press, 1964.

Forbes, Margaret. *Beattie and His Friends*. Westminster: Constable and Co., 1904.

Grieve, Christopher [Hugh MacDiarmid]. *Selected Essays*. London: Jonathan Cape, 1969.

Henderson, T. F. *Scottish Vernacular Literature: A Succinct History*. Edinburgh: John Grant, 1910.

Jack, R. D. S. *The Italian Influence on Scottish Literature*. Edinburgh: Edinburgh University Press, 1972.

Kinsley, James, ed. *Scottish Poetry: A Critical Study*. London: Cassell and Co., 1955.

Law, Alexander. *Robert Fergusson and the Edinburgh of His Time*. Edinburgh: City Libraries, 1974.

McElroy, David D. *Scotland's Age of Improvement: A Survey of Eighteenth Century Literary Clubs and Societies*. Washington: Washington State University Press, 1969.

McGuirk, Carol. "Augustan Influences on Allan Ramsay." *Studies in Scottish Literature* 16 (1981): 97–109.

Martin, Burns, *Allan Ramsay: A Study of His Life and Works.* Cambridge: Harvard University Press, 1931.

Phillipson, N. T., and Rosalind Mitcheson, eds. *Scotland in the Age of Improvement: Essays in Scottish History in the Eighteenth Century.* Edinburgh: Edinburgh University Press, 1970.

Speirs, John. *The Scots Literary Tradition.* London: Chatto and Windus, 1940.

Wittig, Kurt. *The Scottish Tradition in Literature.* Edinburgh: Oliver and Boyd, 1958.

Other Related Works

Aldridge, A. O. "The Pleasures of Pity." *ELH* 16 (1949): 76–87.

Bate, Walter Jackson. *The Achievement of Samuel Johnson.* New York: Oxford University Press, 1955.

———. *The Burden of the Past and the English Poet.* Cambridge: Harvard University Press, Belknap Press, 1970.

———. *From Classic to Romantic.* New York: Harper and Row, 1961.

Bateson, F. W., and N. A. Joukovsky. *Alexander Pope: A Critical Anthology.* Baltimore: Penguin, 1971.

Beaty, Frederick L. *Light From Heaven: Love in British Romantic Literature.* DeKalb: Northern Illinois University Press, 1971.

Beers, Henry A. *A History of English Romanticism in the Eighteenth Century.* 1899. Reprint. New York: Gordian Press, 1966.

Bloom, Harold. *The Anxiety of Influence: A Theory of Poetry.* New York: Oxford University Press, 1973.

Braudy, Leo. "The Form of the Sentimental Novel." *Novel* 7, no. 1 (Fall 1973): 5–13.

Bredvold, Louis I. *The Natural History of Sensibility.* Detroit: Wayne State University Press, 1962.

Brett, R. L. *The Third Earl of Shaftesbury: A Study in Eighteenth Century Literary Theory.* London: Hutchinson's University Library, 1951.

Brissenden, R. F. *Virtue in Distress: Studies in the Novel of Sentiment from Richardson to Sade.* New York: Barnes and Noble, 1974.

Bronson, Bertrand. *Joseph Ritson, Scholar at Arms.* 2 vols. Berkeley and Los Angeles: University of California Press, 1938.

Cohen, Ralph. *The Art of Discrimination: Thomson's "The Seasons" and the Language of Criticism.* London: Routledge and Kegan Paul, 1964.

———. *The Unfolding of "The Seasons."* London: Routledge and Kegan Paul, 1970.

Crane, R. S. "Suggestions Towards a Genealogy of 'The Man of Feeling.'"

Studies in the Literature of the Augustan Age: Essays Collected in Honor of Arthur Ellicott Case. Ed. Richard C. Boys. New York: Gordian Press, 1966.

Eliot, George. "Worldliness and Otherworldliness: The Poet Young." *Essays*, Ed. Thomas Pinney. New York: Columbia University Press, 1963.

Erametsa, Erik. *A Study of the Word "Sentimental" and of Other Linguistic Characteristics of Eighteenth Century Sentimentalism in England*. Helsinki: Helsingin Liikikirjapaino Oy., 1951.

Essays on the Eighteenth Century Presented to D. Nichol Smith. 1945. Reprint. New York: Russell and Russell, 1963.

Frye, Northrop. *Fables of Identity: Studies in Poetic Mythology*. New York: Harcourt, Brace and World, 1963.

Golden, Morris. *The Self Observed: Swift, Johnson, Wordsworth*. Baltimore: Johns Hopkins University Press, 1972.

Greene, Donald. "Latitudinarianism and Sensibility: The Genealogy of the 'Man of Feeling' Reconsidered." *Modern Philology* 75 (1977): 159–83.

Hagstrum, Jean. *Sex and Sensibility: Ideal and Romantic Love from Milton to Mozart*. Chicago: University of Chicago Press, 1980.

Harder, Johannes Hendrick. *Observations on Some Tendencies of Sentiment and Ethics Chiefly in Minor Poetry and Essay in the Eighteenth Century*. Amsterdam: M. J. Portielje, 1933.

Hartley, Lodwick C. *William Cowper, Humanitarian*. Chapel Hill: University of North Carolina Press, 1938.

Hartman, Geoffrey. *Beyond Formalism*. New Haven: Yale University Press, 1970.

———. "Christopher Smart's 'Magnificat': Toward a Theory of Representation." *The Fate of Reading and Other Essays*. Chicago: University of Chicago Press, 1975.

Humphries, A. R. "The Friend of Mankind (1700–1768): An Aspect of Eighteenth Century Sensibility." *Review of English Studies* 24 (1948): 203–18.

Kafka, Franz. *Miscellany*. Trans. Sophie Prombaum. New York: Twice a Year Press, 1946.

Kroeber, Karl. *Romantic Narrative Art*. Madison: University of Wisconsin Press, 1960.

Lanham, Richard A. *Tristram Shandy: The Games of Pleasure*. Berkeley and Los Angeles: University of California Press, 1973.

Longinus. *On the Sublime*. In *Aristotle: The Poetics; "Longinus": On the Sublime; Demetrius: On Style*. Cambridge: Harvard University Press, 1960.

Nabokov, Vladimir. *Strong Opinions*. New York: McGraw-Hill, 1973.

Pittock, Joan. *The Ascendency of Taste: The Achievement of Joseph and Thomas Warton*. London: Routledge and Kegan Paul, 1973.

Price, Martin. *To the Palace of Wisdom: Studies in Order and Energy from Dryden to Blake.* Garden City, N.Y.: Doubleday, 1964.

Rousseau, G. S. "Nerves, Spirits and Fibres: Towards Defining the Origins of Sensibility." *Studies in the Eighteenth Century,* III. In *Papers Presented at the Third David Nichol Smith Memorial Seminar, Canberra, 1973.* Ed. R. F. Brissenden and J. C. Eade. Toronto: University of Toronto Press, 1976.

Smith, D. Nichol. *Some Observations on Eighteenth Century Poetry.* London: Humphrey Milford, 1937.

Spacks, Patricia Meyer. *The Poetry of Vision: Five Eighteenth Century Poets.* Cambridge: Harvard University Press, 1967.

Starr, George A. "Only a Boy: Notes on Sentimental Novels." *Genre* 10 (1977): 501–27.

Stevens, Wallace. *Collected Poems.* New York: Knopf, 1955.

Tinker, Chauncey Brewster. *Nature's Simple Plan.* 1922. Reprint. New York: Gordian Press, 1964.

Watkins, W. B. C. *Perilous Balance: The Tragic Genius of Swift, Johnson, and Sterne.* Princeton: Princeton University Press, 1939.

Wright, Walter Francis. "Sensibility in English Prose Fiction 1760–1814: A Reinterpretation." *Illinois Studies in Language and Literature* 22, nos. 3–4 (1937).

Yeats, W. B. *Ideas of Good and Evil.* London: Macmillan, 1903.

Index